Quantitative
Research in
Communication

Quantitative Research in Communication

Mike Allen
University of Wisconsin, Milwaukee

Scott Titsworth
Ohio University

Stephen K. Hunt
Illinois State University

Los Angeles • London • New Delhi • Singapore • Washington DC

For information:

SAGE Publications, Inc.
2455 Teller Road
Thousand Oaks,
  California 91320
E-mail: order@sagepub.com

SAGE Publications India Pvt. Ltd.
B 1/I 1 Mohan Cooperative Industrial Area
Mathura Road, New Delhi 110 044
India

SAGE Publications Ltd.
1 Oliver's Yard
55 City Road
London EC1Y 1SP
United Kingdom

SAGE Publications Asia-Pacific Pte. Ltd.
33 Pekin Street #02-01
Far East Square
Singapore 048763

Printed in the United States of America

Library of Congress Cataloging-in-Publication Data

Allen, Mike, 1959–
Quantitative research in communication/Mike Allen, Scott Titsworth, Stephen K. Hunt
    p. cm.
Includes bibliographical references and index.
ISBN 978-1-4129-5695-6 (cloth)
ISBN 978-1-4129-5696-3 (pbk.)
    1. Communication—Statistical methods. 2. Communication—Data processing.
I. Titsworth, Scott. II. Hunt, Stephen K. III. Title.

P93.7.A44 2009
302.2072'7—dc22   2008017666

This book is printed on acid-free paper.

08   09   10   11   12   10   9   8   7   6   5   4   3   2

Acquisitions Editor:	Todd R. Armstrong
Editorial Assistant:	Aja Baker
Production Editor:	Astrid Virding
Copy Editor:	Gillian Dickens
Typesetter:	C&M Digitals (P) Ltd.
Proofreader:	Dennis W. Webb
Marketing Manager:	Carmel Schrire

CONTENTS

PREFACE

The three of us each have different stories to tell about how we became interested in using statistics to study communication. The differences in our stories are important; for instance, some of us had excellent math backgrounds, whereas others did not. Yet, differences in our stories are probably less salient than similarities. All three of us share similar experiences in terms of being part of successful high school and collegiate debate teams. As is often the case for debaters, our experiences in the activity continue to shape our viewpoints on topics ranging from politics to research. For instance, we learned through debate the value of being able to develop strong arguments using a variety of types of evidence. As such, we approach research as the development of claims based on strong evidence, clear reasoning, and careful explanation.

Although the three of us likely hold different views on particular epistemological and ontological positions, we share a common conviction that important knowledge can be gained from well-conceived quantitative studies of communication. To the extent that communication researchers want to have an opportunity to recommend improvements in communication practice, to prevent communication problems, and to effectively use research to develop, test, and refine theory, quantitative research is very valuable. In essence, quantitative studies provide a type of evidence that allows for certain types of claims to be advanced.

Like all good debaters, we are more than capable of arguing both sides. Although quantitative research offers many advantages, such approaches are certainly not the only or best way to ask and answer important theoretical and applied questions. Indeed, just as good debaters learn to use a variety of types of evidence, communication researchers are increasingly aware of the need to triangulate approaches. That said, we also feel that it is important to have strong knowledge of a particular method. All too often, we see students' desires to "be mixed methods" as a way of sidestepping highly advanced training in any particular method. This should not be the case—in-depth knowledge of a particular method should serve as a springboard for any "multiperspectival" orientation.

Thus, our intent in writing this book is to provide communication students with a practical resource for undertaking advanced study of quantitative methods in the discipline. Our aim is to provide a strong conceptual orientation to a litany of techniques and procedures that range from the "moderately basic" to "highly advanced." In essence, this book is meant to bridge the gap between basic and very advanced statistics texts while also providing practical tips and suggestions for quantitative communication scholars of all experience levels. For example, most chapters contain example templates for writing statistical results in APA style and also provide examples of how procedures are used in communication research articles. Our hope is that both instructors and students will appreciate the flexible nature of this text as well as its practical utility.

We should mention that part of our intent in writing this book was to humbly pay tribute to those who have influenced our views on scholarship in general and quantitative methods in particular. Although there are numerous teachers who deserve thanks here, for undoubtedly the voices of people like John Bourhis, Char Berquist, Gloria Galanes, John Lehman, Ray Preiss, Steven B. Hunt, John Hunter, Frank Boster, and others are, in some way, part of this book, we want to especially highlight two scholars who have shaped and continue to shape the social scientific study of communication: Gustav Friedrich and Pamela Cooper. Through their scholarship, teaching, and service to the discipline, Gus and Pam have touched many of us. It is for that reason that we are pleased to donate all author royalties from this book to the Central States Communication Association to support the awards named in honor of Pam and Gus.

Finally, we are very thankful to several reviewers who generously provided feedback to improve the book. Their valuable insights resulted in very substantial changes to the first version of the manuscript, and those changes will surely result in benefits for teachers and students. The following individuals provided reviews: Kelli L. Fellows (Appalachian State University), Mark A. Hamilton (University of Connecticut), Erika L. Kirby (Creighton University), Andrew M. Leadbetter (Ohio University), Brian L. Quick

(University of Illinois at Urbana-Champaign), and Jordan Soliz (University of Nebraska–Lincoln).

Mike Allen, Milwaukee, WI

Scott Titsworth, Athens, OH

Stephen Hunt, Normal, IL

⊰ ONE ⊱

INTRODUCTION TO
QUANTITATIVE RESEARCH

———•◦•———

Suppose that three communication scholars interested in organizational communication were sitting around a conference table with the intent to plan and execute a research project. As the conversation ensued, the following dialogue took place:

Adonis: *I think an interesting thing to study would be organizational culture. We know from our own backgrounds that culture has a big impact on people's experiences in the organization.*

Katherine: *Sure, culture is critical, but how should we study it?*

Adonis: *I know some scales that exist, which can be used to assess people's perceptions of culture—we could use those.*

Kirby: *But, those scales only assess people's perceptions. Can we get at something that recognizes the co-created meanings that create culture? Why can't we do observations and interviews? Wouldn't that be more consistent with theory?*

Adonis: *Sure, but if our goal is to generalize and build theory, shouldn't we try to get a broad and generalizable sample?*

Kirby: *Maybe we should build theory from our observations of some unique organizations—sort of a theory about the process of culture rather than the product or effects?*

Katherine: *We are also forgetting about how culture is officially enacted by organizations. What about analyzing the public discourse stemming from organizations to see what type of culture they aspire to? News releases, talks by the CEO, even quarterly reports would be great sources to analyze.*

Adonis: *Great, we have three great ideas. How should we decide?*

Kirby: *Simple. Don't decide, do all three and we can sell it as a mixed-methods piece.*

This dialogue is not all that farfetched from the discussions we have with colleagues on a daily basis. Because we study interesting, real-world phenomena in the discipline of communication, the ways we choose to enact studies vary widely. Although there is increasing interest in and use of mixed-methods designs—those that enact multiple ways of conducting research—this textbook is intended to help you make well-reasoned decisions with respect to one type of research method—namely, quantitative research.

The communication discipline is on one hand blessed and on the other cursed by the rich variety of epistemological perspectives used to study communication phenomena. Our discipline's approach to asking and answering questions defies monolithic approaches or, some would even say, unified understandings about what constitutes communication. Nonetheless, one might presume that the study of communication falls into one of three overlapping traditions: rhetorical, quantitative, and qualitative. Although unifying threads tie these epistemological traditions together, each is conceptually and pragmatically distinct from the other and has relative advantages and disadvantages when compared.

The first of these traditions, rhetorical, has its roots in antiquity. Aristotle and the sophists heightened our awareness of communication as an aesthetic while at the same time laying the groundwork for the scientific study of persuasion and other forms of communication. Although the nature of rhetoric is vastly different today, some of the fundamental issues raised by the Greeks and Romans remain relevant in contemporary society: How do audience members/listeners assign meaning to messages? How do speakers/rhetors create messages and with what effect? How can evidence be effectively used in persuasion? Of course, the list could be limitless. When viewed as a whole, the rhetorical tradition is very well suited to holistically understanding the interrelationships between people, situations, and messages, especially from a more philosophical and/or artistic point of view.

Qualitative research is similar to rhetoric in that a sense of the whole typically guides the research process. Qualitative researchers, whether they employ interviews, ethnography, participant observation, or some combination thereof, are interested in asking "how questions." How do doctors provide emotional support to patients? How do teachers communicate motivational messages to students? How do romantic couples negotiate conflict? These are all examples of questions that qualitative researchers might seek to answer. Like rhetorical scholars, qualitative researchers are interested in an understanding of the whole. Whereas a rhetorical scholar might seek a prime example of communication to analyze (perhaps similar to studying fine art), a qualitative researcher might be much more interested in studying the more typical and common day-to-day communicative behaviors of people.

Quantitative researchers are similar to their rhetorical and qualitative peers in the sense that the whole is important; however, quantitative researchers might define what is meant by the whole differently. Quantitative researchers are often interested in how an understanding of a particular communication phenomenon might be generalized to a larger population. What effect do punitive behavioral control statements have on a classroom? What communicative behaviors are associated with different stages in a romantic relationship? What communicative behaviors are used to respond to coworkers displaying emotional stress? As you can see, quantitative researchers tend to ask and answer "what questions" in an attempt to generalize about a certain type of communication behavior. A synthesis of the three research traditions is presented in Table 1.1.

The preceding paragraphs highlight differences (and some similarities) among methods. Worth noting are the similarities (though sometimes hidden) between the three. First, all three methods attempt to raise knowledge about communication practice. In fact, most methods aim to improve practice. Second, each method is designed to promote the generation of theory. Whether you are analyzing a speech apologizing for some mistake, a persuasive message for its effect on behavior, or a conversation to understand how people talk about themselves, you are trying to make some theoretical statement about communication as a result of the study. Although not every method strives to generalize, all try to promote general theorizing (Preiss & Allen, 2007). Finally, the use of any method is discursive in nature. The decision to collect discourse, to engage in ethnography, or to analyze survey results is partly a

Table 1.1   Three Research Traditions in Communication

	Rhetorical	*Qualitative*	*Quantitative*
Primary objective	Create, expand, and refine theory through critical analyses of public discourses guided by particular theoretical stances and perspectives	Create, expand, and refine theory by observing and interacting with people in their natural environment to discover rich explanations and unique instances	Create, expand, and refine theory through systematic observation of hypothesized connections among variables
Data used	Public discourses, including speeches, documents, and other publicly available statements	Interviews, observations, and other techniques that allow the researcher access to individuals' accounts and stories	Operational variables created through surveys and/or intentional manipulation (i.e., an experiment)
Role of researcher	To be a thoughtful and informed critic	To be a careful and reflective observer	To be a precise analyst of data
Standard of rigor	Conclusions that are well reasoned and grounded in a theoretically driven reading of discourses	Conclusions that are reflective and deeply grounded in the words and behaviors of participants	Conclusions based on observed connections that are unlikely due to chance or errors on the part of the researcher
Example question	How do organizations use metaphors to describe ideal organizational cultures?	What types of messages do people enact and receive to maintain and resist the enactment of organizational culture?	What is the relationship between the amount of time someone works for an organization and his or her perceptions of that organization's culture?

question of what type of evidence you want to use in support of your claim(s). Quantitative evidence allows you to make a different type of claim than does qualitative evidence. From this perspective, all three methods share a common bond in that they are different methods of invention for a very specific form of discourse—academic writing. Notice along the bottom of Table 1.1 how each tradition seeks to draw conclusions. Those conclusions are rhetorical arguments suggesting a plausible interpretation of a particular type of data. As noted by Tracey and Glidden-Tracey (1999), the validity of the conclusions drawn is directly dependent on how well the theory, method, and analysis was enacted by the researcher.

Because many researchers tend to specialize in one particular method (though multimethod training is becoming somewhat common), people often orient themselves toward a favorite approach or one more consistent with their background and training. Such specialization is beneficial because scholars can better focus their efforts and develop a strong depth of understanding. However, such specialization should not lead to assumptions of superiority. We hope you will join us in concluding that the communication discipline profits from multiple approaches and multiple types of questions. Moreover, as scholars, we benefit substantially from understanding other methods—if for no other reason than to intelligently react to studies that take approaches different from our own.

The focus of this book, obviously, is on helping you understand more advanced approaches to quantitative methods. While some review of basic statistics is necessary (e.g., measures of central tendency and dispersion, the correlation coefficient, the *t* test), our aim is to go beyond a simple introduction and to provide foundational knowledge for several advanced quantitative approaches. Before moving to the specific procedures covered in the book, we begin with introductory material that should (re)familiarize you with the rationale and procedures for quantitative methods. Additional description of basic introductory statistics is provided in Chapter 2.

AN OVERVIEW OF QUANTITATIVE
RESEARCH IN COMMUNICATION

Quantitative methods in the social sciences can be traced back to the time of Aristotle. We might think of treatises such as *The Rhetoric* as an early version of a scientifically driven quantitative study (though don't mention that claim to the rhetoricians in your department). After all, Aristotle's work attempted to influence the practice of speaking by systematically observing and drawing generalized conclusions about the effectiveness of certain practices. As such, we might define *quantitative methods* as any approach that uses systematic observations to account for and generalize about human behavior. By systematic observation, we mean that which is (a) intentional, (b) replicable, and (c) valid. You must have intent because without it you would not know how to focus your observations. Suppose we gave you an assignment to quantify everything communicative about each person you see over the course of one day. How would you start? What would you do to ensure consistency and validity? Answers to those questions are nearly impossible because you don't know what the intent of the "study" actually is. Intent provides focus, which serves as a foundation for systematic observation.

In addition to being intentional, systematic observation must be replicable. If you are making claims using quantitative data, you must be able to replicate your findings to help rule out the potential of chance causing the results in question—this issue of replication is an important and unique aspect of arguments advanced by quantitative researchers. In fact, a conservative view of quantitative research is that no conclusion is warranted before several replications have been conducted and similar results observed. Replication simply means that another researcher should be able to employ similar (if not identical) methods and observe similar (if not identical) results. Through replication, the possibility of chance findings are reduced; as a consequence, more credibility can be attached to the conclusions drawn.

Finally, your observation must be valid. If you want to systematically observe expressions of emotion, for example, you must devise an appropriate way of observing emotion. For instance, if you analyze statements that people make during conversation, how do you know that you are learning about emotion rather than verbal ability? If you use a survey, how can you separate their emotions from what they think they should have indicated about the emotion to reflect social desirability? In both situations, you may want to study one thing but, through imprecision, may end up studying something entirely different and not even know the mistake has occurred. A systematic and valid observation would ensure that you are observing what you intend to observe rather than some other phenomenon.

Besides systematic observation, our definition of quantitative research also requires the researcher to account for human behavior. By this we mean that you are able to count and quantify the behaviors. You might make a tally mark, you might average responses to questions on a survey, or you might assign an arbitrary number representing membership in a certain group; regardless, you are quantifying behavior. Finally, quantitative methods tend to generalize about human behavior. Although some types of quantitative studies do not attempt to generalize (a census, for example), such approaches are rare. *Most quantitative studies use a sample of individuals and behaviors to draw generalized inferences about those same behaviors in larger groups or populations.* To the extent that the sample used in the quantitative study is both typical and representative, results observed for the sample are generalizable to the larger population. Of course, no such generalization is exactly perfect, and consequently, there is always some error associated with the inferential leap from the sample to the population. The job of the researcher, as suggested by Table 1.1, is to minimize the influence of such error.

With this general understanding of quantitative methods, we explore several specific issues that elaborate on the purposes and approaches of quantitative scholars ranging from why you might opt to do quantitative research to how you might design a study.

THE PURPOSE OF QUANTITATIVE RESEARCH

As mentioned previously, quantitative methods generally try to answer "what questions" by making generalizations about communicative behavior. One purpose of quantitative communication research is to try and apply principles of the scientific method to human action. For this approach, the researcher is trying to observe, explain, predict, and perhaps control specific phenomena. For example, a researcher may try to find a particular type of campaign message that tends to always be effective at mobilizing voters. In that example, the researcher uses observations of previous campaign messages to devise an explanation of what messages work. On the basis of that explanation, or what we might label as a "theory," the researcher might recommend that a campaign manager emphasize messages similar to the effective ones observed so that voters will be mobilized to support their candidate.

A key component of the scientific method is verification and absolutism—that through replication, theories become "verified" and accepted as universally true. Although application of the scientific method to the study of communication and other social sciences was very popular at one time, more contemporary theory embraces a postpositivist approach that does not rely on absolute truth. From the postpositivist perspective, theories are assumed to be good descriptions of human behavior, but exceptions are expected because of unique circumstances and the tendency for some unpredictability to be present in any situation.

Contemporary quantitative scholars assume that there are patterns of communicative behaviors within the population. Most typically, researchers are interested in one of two types of questions: questions of relationships and questions of differences. Relationship questions tend to explore how one behavior exhibited by people is related to other types of behaviors. For instance, are verbally aggressive behaviors related to physical aggression—that is, when a person has high levels of verbally aggressive behaviors, does he or she also tend to be physically aggressive? Are students' communication skills related to classroom performance? Are certain supervisor communication skills related to the emotional experiences of employees? All of these are examples of relationship-oriented questions.

Questions of difference explore how patterns of behavior or perceptions might differ from one group or type of person to another. For example, do people with disabilities experience emotional labor differently from those without disabilities? Do women perceive talkativeness (or lack thereof) differently than men? Do communication styles differ from one culture to the next? In reality, questions of difference are simply a particular type of relationship question—that is, the "difference" between men and women could just as easily (and accurately) be described as a "relationship" between gender and communication. But until you fully understand why the two are really asking the same question, it might be helpful for you to think about questions of relationships and questions of difference as two distinct things.

When researchers explore questions of difference or questions of relationships, they do so in an attempt to uncover certain patterns of behavior. If the researcher discovers that a certain relationship exists in a sample that she or he has drawn from the population, that person is then in a position to draw generalizations about patterns expected in human behavior. A common misconception is that statements about patterns are assumed to be universally true.

Patterns are just that, patterns. Any statement about the pattern does not imply that all people act in a certain way or perceive certain phenomena similarly. There are patterns that sports fans share, yet supporters of the Indianapolis Colts act and behave very differently than those of the New England Patriots. Similarly, just because women tend to be more empathetic than men (a pattern), this does not imply that any particular man that you know would be less empathetic than a particular female friend.

THE NATURE OF VARIABLES AND DATA

As mentioned previously, quantitative researchers try to count human behavior. Actually, most researchers attempt to count multiple variables at the same time to determine various relationships or differences. Generally speaking, variables are classified as one of four types (for additional discussion, see Kerlinger, 1964):

- **Nominal variables** represent *categories that cannot be ordered in any particular way.* Examples of nominal variables include biological sex (e.g., males vs. females), political affiliation (Democrat, Republican, or independent), football fan affiliation, and whether or not someone is in a certain type of randomly assigned experimental group (e.g., a group viewing a speech using statistical evidence vs. a group viewing a speech using narrative evidence).

- **Ordinal variables** represent *categories that can be ordered from greatest to smallest.* Examples of ordinal variables include education level (e.g., freshman, sophomore); income brackets (e.g., annual income between $25,000 and $30,000); those with low, moderate, or high communication apprehension (e.g., using a scale for communication apprehension to classify people into one of the three groups); and certain types of groups created in a randomized experiment (e.g., groups of students viewing lectures with high, medium, and low immediacy).

- **Interval variables** have *values that lie along an evenly dispersed range of numbers.* Examples of interval data include the temperature, a person's net worth (how much money you have when you subtract your debt from your assets), and values stemming from certain scales where numbers can range from the negative (e.g., a negative value representing nonimmediate communication behaviors) to the positive (e.g., a positive value representing an immediate communication behavior).

• **Ratio variables** have *values that lie along an evenly dispersed range of numbers where there is an absolute zero.* As opposed to net worth, which can have a negative debt-to-income ratio, income itself is a ratio-level variable. That is, you cannot have a negative income—you either have no income or some positive amount of income. Similarly, education, nonverbal behaviors, and the amount of time spent listening are all ratio-level variables. For example, you cannot have negative education—at some very early age, you have "no education," and once you begin school, you always have some positive amount of educational experience. Most scores stemming from responses to survey items are ratio-level values because they typically cannot go below zero.

The differences between these types of variables are important because they have implications for what types of statistical procedures can be run with a given combination of variables. You will also notice that there are similarities among the types of variables. Nominal and ordinal variables are often described as *categorical,* whereas interval and ratio are often described as *continuous.* We will use these terms when describing situations in which you should use certain types of statistical procedures. For now, data sets including only continuous variables will typically use tests of association such as correlations and regressions, data sets with only categorical variables will typically use nonparametric tests such as the chi-square, and data sets with both categorical and continuous variables will often use tests of mean difference between groups such as the *t* test and ANOVA.

TYPES OF QUANTITATIVE RESEARCH DESIGNS

Before creating a set of variables for your data set, you must first plan an appropriate design for your study. As you previously read, two broad approaches underlie most statistical procedures: tests of association and tests of mean difference. These procedures are related to but do not perfectly correspond to the two predominant research designs: experiments and surveys. Most typically, survey designs use tests of association such as correlation and regression, whereas experiments typically rely on tests of mean difference such as *t* tests and ANOVA.

Survey designs are similar in nature to opinion polls. That is, a series of questions are generated, and after collecting responses to those questions, conclusions can be drawn. A typical "survey" used in one of these designs is more accurately several surveys put together into a survey packet. For instance, if you were conducting a study to determine the relationships between communication apprehension, size of class, and the number of times a person speaks during class, you would need to create a packet with three surveys: the Personal Report of Communication Apprehension (PRCA)–24 to measure communication apprehension, a set of questions to find out about the class (including the size of the class), and a space to tally how many times the student spoke during class. In more complex survey designs, participants might respond to seven or more surveys that comprise the actual survey packet. Once participants complete the surveys, responses to individual items on each survey may be analyzed using factor analysis (you will learn more about factor analysis in Chapter 11) to create variables; those variables are then analyzed using statistical procedures such as correlation and regression.

The advantages of using survey designs are numerous. Surveys can be obtained from large random samples of people, thus allowing for more robust conclusions. Moreover, surveys typically take place in naturalistic settings and can therefore have strong generalizability. The disadvantage of a survey design is that such approaches can typically not provide compelling evidence of causation. That is, although survey designs can help identify relationships between variables, they are not well suited to identifying cause-effect relationships among variables. For instance, a survey design might show a statistical relationship between communication ability and school achievement; however, such a design cannot show whether communication ability causes students to get better grades or vice versa.

The second general type of quantitative design involves experiments. In an experiment, the research manipulates one variable—the independent variable—to see how that manipulation affects another variable—the dependent variable. The key to successful experimental designs is effective planning. In particular, the researcher must carefully plan how to manipulate the independent variable to test predictions guiding the study. For example, take a moment to think about how you would design a study to test the effects of teacher immediacy (being warm and open to students) on student note taking. How would you manipulate the variable of teacher immediacy? What would the "high-immediacy" teacher do differently from the "low-immediacy" teacher?

Would you have the same teacher or different teachers enact both roles? These are the types of questions that must be carefully thought out when planning an experiment. In addition, the researcher must find a way of observing or measuring the dependent variable. Common approaches might involve participants completing a survey or the researcher directly observing and counting some behavior (e.g., "grading" the notes taken by participants in a lecture) to measure the dependent variable.

In some ways, the advantages and disadvantages of survey and experimental designs are complementary. Whereas surveys cannot typically provide evidence of causation, experiments can. Because of the careful planning involved in an experiment, the researcher is in a better position to conclude that changes in one variable (the independent variable) result in a certain type of change in the dependent variable. However, unlike surveys, most experiments must take place in ideal "laboratory" conditions. So, rather than learning about the effects of teacher immediacy over the course of an entire semester, an experiment is limited to a few hours. In essence, experiments require so much planning and control that they oftentimes represent ideal conditions that do not necessarily approximate well to the messiness of the "real world" (or what researchers tend to call "the field"). Surveys, on the other hand, typically assess variables in more natural settings and provide more breadth and possibly greater generalizability than experiments.

To help plan different types of research designs, Campbell and Stanley (1963) created a simple notation system that can be used to represent various types of quantitative design options. Although the potential number of options is beyond the scope of this chapter, several common designs are depicted in Figure 1.1. The notation system used by Campbell and Stanley involves observations or measures (O), programs or treatments (X), and groups or individuals (R = randomized group, N = nonrandomized group, for instance). Each line in the various designs typically represents a different group of people. The designs presented in Figure 1.1 build on one another such that the first design involves one observation consisting of two measures that are correlated with one another. The second involves a simple causal relationship tested with one group; the third adds the element of a control group. More complex designs such as the fourth and fifth use multiple measurements and multiple groups. All of the examples depicted in Figure 1.1 use random assignment (the "R" preceding each group) because random assignment is most common. As noted by Campbell and Stanley, the design selected should match the claims that you

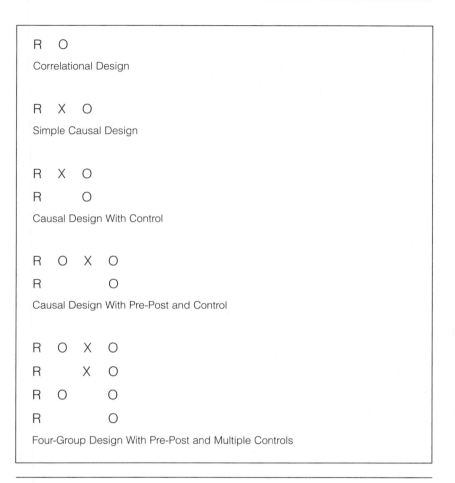

R   O

Correlational Design

R   X   O

Simple Causal Design

R   X   O
R   O

Causal Design With Control

R   O   X   O
R   O

Causal Design With Pre-Post and Control

R   O   X   O
R   X   O
R   O   O
R   O

Four-Group Design With Pre-Post and Multiple Controls

Figure 1.1   Example Research Designs Using Campbell and Stanley's Notation

want to make. For instance, if you want strong evidence for causation, more complex designs using multiple groups and pre-post tests might be necessary.

We should note here that some people identify another general type of research design in quantitative research—content analysis. Content analysis is where (oftentimes) qualitative data are collected and then categorized into discrete categories. For instance, suppose you tape-record several supervisors as they interact with employees to learn whether sex of the supervisor is related to the types of messages they tend to provide. After collecting the recordings, your next task in a content analysis is to separate the transcription into distinct statements and then categorize those statements into a category system, such as (a) positive with explanation, (b) positive without explanation, (c) negative with explanation, and (d) negative without explanation. After categorizing the results, you can then see if there are differences between men and women with regard to the types of statements used with employees.

Because content analysis is a somewhat specialized form of design and is often used to operationalize variables integrated into other statistical analyses, we will not address content analysis in detail. For additional information on this approach, you should consult Weber's (1990) text.

STEPS IN QUANTITATIVE RESEARCH

Quantitative research can seem daunting if you think only about the end product. However, like any problem, quantitative research is fairly straightforward if you break it down into sequential parts. Although each project varies slightly, the process of quantitative research generally follows the following seven steps.

1. Isolate a problem. Using previous research as well as your own instincts as a researcher, you must use theory to predict relationships among or differences between variables. By selecting appropriate variables and providing a theoretical explanation of how they are related, you have isolated a particular research problem and can then identify appropriate hypotheses to be tested.

2. Select a design. Once you have identified appropriate variables relevant to your theory, you must select a design. As mentioned previously, you have two general design options: experimental designs and survey designs. Your decision should be guided based on the variables in question as well as your need to make causal inferences—experiments are typically best suited to making causal claims (however, as you will learn in Chapter 11, survey designs coupled with strong theoretical explanations might be used to advance causal claims).

3. Operationalize variables. Once you have identified your variables and selected a design, you must determine how you will operationalize variables in your study. Operationalization is simply the act of taking a conceptual definition and determining exactly how you can observe or manipulate that variable. For example, you might operationalize communication apprehension as a person's score from McCroskey's (1970) PRCA scale; for an experiment, you might operationalize fear appeal as pictures of severe automobile accidents involving drunk drivers. Taking care to find valid and reliable scales and/or to carefully manipulate variables will determine the eventual effectiveness of your study.

4. Generate a sample. You must select an appropriate number of people from the population that you want to study to comprise your sample. Besides having a sufficient number, you must also take care to randomly select participants in order to make reasonable generalizations to the population in question. Moreover, if you are conducting an experiment, you should randomly assign participants to the various groups in your experiment.

5. Collect data. Collecting data might seem like a straightforward issue. However, you must make several decisions about collecting data that could affect the results of your study. For instance, if you use a survey design, should you use Web-based forms? The advantage of Web forms over paper-and-pencil surveys is that Web forms eliminate the need for you to manually enter the data into SPSS or some other program; the disadvantage is that some people may not be able to access the form, and you cannot observe people while they complete the survey to ensure that they do it correctly. If you are conducting an experiment, consider what location should you use, what time of day should people come, and so on. All of these decisions about data collection are potentially important.

6. Analyze data. Once you have collected data, your next step is to analyze the results. The class you are currently taking and other advanced statistics courses teach you how to analyze the data.

7. Write results. Once all results have been analyzed, you are then left with the task of writing up results. Besides completing a paper for your class, you might consider submitting your final manuscript for presentation at a communication research conference or for publication in a journal.

AN OVERVIEW OF THE BOOK

This book is designed to help you develop a more advanced understanding of quantitative research. Many quantitative methods textbooks tend to be math driven and highly technical. Although we do discuss some math behind various procedures, our primary objective is to help you understand various statistical procedures available to you as you conduct quantitative research. Each chapter covers a different advanced statistic (e.g., correlations, *t* tests, ANOVA, and regression); in some cases, you will learn the math behind the statistic, and in others, you will learn only about the concepts associated with the procedure. In each chapter, we provide a checklist for using the procedure, a thorough explanation of the procedure, an "engaged research" box that asks you to think about how you might use the procedure, and several examples illustrating concepts associated with the procedure. In addition, a distinctive feature of this book is that we provide an in-depth example of how the procedure has been used in actual communication research. Through the examples and other features of the chapters, you should be able to interpret the meaning behind statistics reported in articles written by other researchers and, with some coaching from your instructor, be able to use the statistics in your own research.

Chapter 2 provides additional introductory information about quantitative methods, and remaining chapters are organized into three sections: tests of difference, tests of association, and advanced procedures. Although we intend to provide a usable and clear explanation of each statistic covered, you should understand that a little knowledge makes people dangerous. Effective use of these and other procedures takes experience and good mentoring. We sincerely hope that this course excites you to continue studying quantitative methods and to learn one or more of these methods in even greater depth.

REFERENCES

Campbell, D. T., & Stanley, J. C. (1963). *Experimental and quasi-experimental designs for research.* Chicago: Rand McNally.

Kerlinger, F. N. (1964). *Foundations of behavioral research.* New York: Holt, Rinehart & Winston.

McCroskey, J. C. (1970). Measures of communication-bound anxiety. *Speech Monographs, 37,* 269–277.

Preiss, R., & Allen, M. (2007). Understanding and using meta-analysis. In R. Preiss, B. Gayle, N. Burrell, M. Allen, & J. Bryant, J. (Eds.), *Mass media effects research: Advances through meta-analysis* (pp. 15–30). Mahwah, NJ: Lawrence Erlbaum.

Tracey, T. G., & Glidden-Tracey, C. E. (1999). Integration of theory, research, design, measurement, and analysis: Toward a reasoned argument. *The Counseling Psychologist, 27,* 299–324.

Weber, R. P. (1990). *Basic content analysis.* Newbury Park, CA: Sage.

TWO

USING STATISTICS IN QUANTITATIVE RESEARCH

P lease take a moment to read and interpret the following statement:

> Results of the regression analysis showed that a significant amount of variance was accounted for ($R^2_{ADJ} = .67$, $F(2, 57) = 34.56$, $p < .05$) by trait willingness to communicate ($\beta = .18$, $t(57) = 2.14$, $p < .05$) and the categorical independent variable ($\beta = .51$, $t(57) = 5.67$, $p < .05$). Males in the study ($M = 12.4$, $SD = 1.2$) had higher levels of communication apprehension than did females ($M = 9.4$, $SD = .87$). The null hypothesis was rejected for both predictor variables.

When you are able to accurately interpret and summarize everything in the statement, stand and shout in joy.

If you found interpreting the statement challenging, don't feel bad. Quantitative research essentially requires you to learn a different language. For instance, you will notice that in addition to the various symbols (e.g., $M = 9.4$ and $\beta = .51$), there were also several technical terms such as *null hypothesis* and *significant* that have specific and important meanings. If you have had only limited exposure to statistics, the statement in question would very likely be meaningless.

Indeed, a principal aim of ours is to help you decipher some of the language surrounding statistics. While some knowledge of computation and computer software is essential to your growth as a quantitative researcher, any such knowledge must begin with a basic understanding of concepts and terms. Consequently, this chapter focuses mainly on the language of statistics.

In fact, Chapter 1 started your new language training by introducing the notion of "design." You learned, for instance, that there are different ways to sequence observations and manipulations to achieve research designs with varying levels of sophistication. In this chapter, we begin with a "nuts-and-bolts" discussion of various types of statistics—many of which you may already be familiar with. Second, we discuss how statistics are used to engage in hypothesis testing. We conclude with a discussion of how statistical shorthand (i.e., various symbols and other notations) are used when writing the results of statistical analyses.

TYPES OF STATISTICS

Any initial understanding of statistics should be grounded in an understanding of how we can use numbers to describe a sample. Typically, descriptive statistics help us understand how to describe the frequency of values, the central tendency of values, and/or the dispersion of values. Using these basic descriptors, you can move on to calculate more advanced statistics and diagnose potential problems with your data set. This section reviews those basic statistics.

Frequency Distributions

When you have a range of values, it is often valuable to determine how frequently each value is represented. For example, if you selected a sample of college students, you might want to know the frequency with which men and women were randomly selected or the frequency with which freshmen, sophomores, juniors, or seniors are represented. By calculating a frequency distribution, you can determine just that—the number of people within each category as well as the percentage of the whole represented by that number. So, for instance, you might observe that out of a random sample of 100 college students, there are 42 men (42%) and 58 women (58%).

Although frequency distributions are commonly used to analyze categorical variables (e.g., the sex or year in school examples), they can also be used to analyze continuous variables. Just as you can count how many men are represented, you can also count how many times people had the same total for a set of survey questions or the same number of vocal pauses during a speech—both of these would be examples of continuous variables. Because continuous variables have many more possible values than categorical variables, frequency distributions potentially overwhelm you with details (e.g., the number of people with a value of 11 vs. 12 vs. 34 vs. 67, etc.) while at the same time not giving you a parsimonious sense of the big picture. For that, measures of central tendency might be more appropriate.

Measures of Central Tendency

Nearly every statistical procedure begins with a basic description of a set of values (i.e., cases or observations) that comprise a variable. For instance, if you wanted to explore the relationship between sex (i.e., males vs. females) and self-disclosure, you would first need to determine the average amount of self-disclosure for both sexes; later you could determine the average for men and the average for women. In essence, you want to know the central tendency for the overall group as well as subsets. Although the average, or mean, is most common, there are actually three measures of central tendency found in research:

- *Mean:* The average of a set of values obtained by adding all values and dividing by the number of values in the set.
- *Median:* The midpoint of a set of values when arranged from least to greatest.
- *Mode:* The most commonly occurring value in the set.

Depending on what you are using the data for, some measures of central tendency are more meaningful than others. For instance, the mean is sensitive to outliers (e.g., very extreme cases) and therefore could skew the "central tendency" of the variable in question. The mode, on the other hand, could be influenced by a small number of equivalent values that are not close at all to the mean or median. The median, while an accurate midpoint, could conceal that there is a large range on one side of the median but not the other. So, each measure has benefits and drawbacks. That said, the mean is the most commonly used measure of central tendency and, as you will learn in subsequent chapters, is the foundation for most advanced procedures.

Measures of Dispersion

In addition to understanding the central tendency of a data set, you should also obtain information on its dispersion or variance. Basically you want to know how consistent the values are in the data set you are working with. To answer this question, you should examine various measures of dispersion.

- *Range:* This statistic is obtained by subtracting the smallest value in the data set from the largest. Though intuitively simple, the range does not provide a highly useful estimate of variation because it conceals how well values in the data set tend to clump together.

- *Variance:* Each value departs in some way from the mean. If you take each value (X) and subtract the mean (M), you are left with a deviation score. Squaring and then summing those deviation scores for each value provides the variance for that data set. Larger variances indicate that the values in the data set depart substantially from the mean.

- *Standard deviation:* The standard deviation is simply the square root of the variance. Standard deviations are often used because they are smaller than the variance estimate and provide a meaningful understanding of how far the sampling distribution is expected to depart from the mean.

Tying It All Together in the Normal Distribution

Based on a frequency of values, the mean, and the standard deviation, you can create a histogram (a visual representation of the frequency distribution) that shows how your data conform to a normal distribution. Assume that we wanted to collect data to determine whether students elect speech topics that they are interested in. After having 50 students complete a few survey questions, we are then confronted with 50 different values and need some way of making a decision about students' interest. As seen in Figure 2.1, the histogram is useful for visually seeing both the central tendency and level of dispersion associated with a set of values.

Of course, distributions rarely fit along a normal curve perfectly. As you see in the figure, there is sort of a "dip" in values right around where the mean should be (the apex of the normal distribution line). And, as a result of that dip, the distribution appears to have two "humps" rather than the single hump we would expect in a normal distribution. Moreover, you can see that there are a

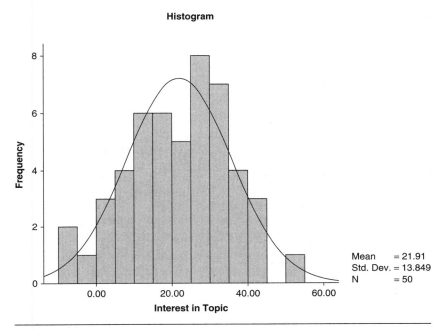

Figure 2.1   Histogram

few cases in the high end of the set of values (the right side of the distribution) that stand apart from the others—these cases could be skewing the distribution somewhat.

So, just looking at Figure 2.1, we start to see some evidence that our distribution of values might depart from normality. Not to worry—we expect some nonnormality in any sample. The question, though, is whether any abnormality present is enough to cause misinterpretation. Fortunately, there are tests to answer that question. In addition to the mean and standard deviation, you can ask the computer to calculate *skewness* and *kurtosis,* both of which help you determine whether your sample is close enough to being normal. Refer to the values in Table 2.1 as skewness and kurtosis are defined.

- *Skewness* indicates the degree to which the sample distribution is being "pulled" by outliers. In the interest data set, we might, for instance, want to know if the outliers on the positive end of the distribution are negatively affecting the accuracy of the mean. The skewness statistic should be less than 2 or less than twice the standard error of skewness. As seen in Table 2.1,

Table 2.1   Descriptive Statistics for Interest

Statistic	Value
Valid	50
Missing	0
Mean	21.9124
Median	21.5300
Mode	−7.13[a]
Standard deviation	13.84904
Skewness	−.075
Standard error of skewness	.337
Kurtosis	−.389
Standard error of kurtosis	.662
Range	60.61

a. Multiple modes exist. The smallest value is shown.

skewness is not a problem here. If it were, we might need to consider deleting the extreme cases.

- *Kurtosis* helps you assess the shape of the distribution—is it tall and narrow, short and spread out, and so on? Visually, the interest data do not look abnormal. Using the same rules of thumb (the value should be less than 2 or less than twice the standard error), we can see that the distribution appears normal. Increasing your sample size is an effective way to combat kurtosis.

- A *bimodal distribution* has a "dip" like the one we see near the midpoint in Figure 2.1. Visual inspection is the only way to assess bimodality—if you have bimodality, there could be some variable "causing" an abnormal distribution. Trying to uncover and then account for that variable is your only real recourse of action. In fact, that is exactly what we would be doing if we suspected that female students generally selected topics of more interest to them than men do—the difference in interest causing the bimodal distribution could be related to a person's sex.

Looking Ahead to Test Statistics and Effect Sizes

So far, this section has described various descriptive statistics that help you understand the general properties of a variable. As you might guess, such basic statistics are rarely the sole focus of a quantitative study. Instead, we use those statistics to calculate more advanced statistics such as correlations, *t* tests, and ANOVAs. These advanced statistics are typically referred to as *test statistics*. So, if we were comparing men and women on interest in speech topics, we could compute a *t* test, where the *t* value would serve as our test statistic.

Test statistics are like any other statistic; they fall along a normal distribution and have a predictable percentage of values that fall within two standard deviations of the mean. In fact, the tables in the back of this book are created to tell you the cutoff value where a test statistic falls outside 95% of the other *t* values in that distribution. In fact, take a second to look at the critical values for *t* statistics in Appendix A. If you are calculating a two-tailed test with 5 degrees of freedom, the critical value for *t* is 2.571. This means that for all *t* tests at 5 degrees of freedom, 95% of them would be less than 2.571. Thus, if your *t* value meets or exceeds 2.571, you can conclude that you would have been unlikely to have observed that value by chance. With this ability to rule out the likelihood of chance occurrence, you can infer that there is probably a difference between men and women. Meeting or beating the critical value is important because it underpins nearly every statistic you will learn about in this book.

Whereas test statistics are useful for determining if chance is likely to have caused some effect to be observed, they do not tell us much about the size of an effect. For instance, if we learn that men and women are significantly different from one another, the natural follow-up question is, "By how much?" Effect size is a measure of "practical significance" (Vogt, 1999, p. 94) and tells us by how much groups differ or by how much two variables are related. Two of the simplest effect size statistics are Pearson's *r* (the correlation coefficient) and Cohen's *d* (for additional discussion, see Cohen, 1988). The *r* value ranges from 0 to –1 or 1; the further the value is away from 0, the stronger the effect. Large correlations are any above .35, medium correlations are between .25 and .35, and small correlations are anything up to .25, approximately. Cohen's *d* is a bit different because it assesses difference. If you took the mean for women, subtracted the mean for men, and then divided by the standard deviation of the sample, you would have Cohen's *d*. Rather than telling us about a relationship between two variables, Cohen's *d* tells us how many standard deviations apart the two groups are. Cohen loosely defines a large effect as anything greater than .8, a medium effect as anything between .5 and .8, and a small effect as anything up to .5. These benchmarks are only general rules of thumb and could vary depending on the context.

Although not an effect size per se, confidence intervals are also used to show the degree of certainty surrounding a particular statistic. When reviewing results of an opinion or political poll, you have probably heard about the margin of error. Thus, if one presidential candidate has 43% of the voters in favor of his or her candidacy and another 48%, if the margin of error for that poll is more than 3%, then the two candidates could be in a statistical dead heat (one could be 3% higher and the other 3% lower). That same principle can be applied to any statistic. An average, for example, is simply an estimated average for a population based on a particular sample. Depending on how large the sample is, the degree of confidence around that mean will be greater or smaller. In very large samples, there may be a high degree of confidence in the mean, and the 95% confidence interval would be relatively small; this implies that the observed mean is likely very close to the actual mean. In smaller samples, the degree of confidence might be much larger; consequently, the actual mean might be very different from the observed mean. Many procedures in SPSS provide a 95% confidence interval showing the possible lowest and highest estimates of the actual statistic. Smaller confidence intervals provide more precision and therefore result in more credible conclusions.

THE LOGIC OF HYPOTHESIS TESTING

As explained in Chapter 1, experiments and survey designs are well suited to making particular types of arguments. In an experiment, the observation of a significant *t* statistic can potentially suggest a significant difference between two groups—one potentially caused by the manipulation of an independent variable. In a survey design, a significant correlation can potentially indicate that two variables are related to one another. In both cases, conclusions are reached because a significant test statistic was observed (i.e., a significant *t* test or a significant correlation). In this section, you will learn a bit more about what test statistics are and how they allow certain types of conclusions to be drawn; in addition, you will learn about the most common threats to quantitative reasoning. For purposes of this chapter, we will use the correlation as a common point of explanation; what you will learn about the correlation generally applies to all test statistics.

A correlation procedure results in a test statistic called "Pearson's *r*" (this statistic is discussed at length in Chapter 9). The *r* value can range from -1 to 1, where values closer to $|1|$ indicate a nearly perfect correlation (or relationship) and values closer to 0 indicate no correlation or relationship. The sign simply indicates whether the relationship is positive or negative. For positive relationships, increases in one variable correspond to increases in another; for negative relationships, a rise in one variable corresponds to a decrease in the other. Whereas education level and reading ability are positively related, education level and the preference for using crayons are probably negatively related (though some would argue it *should* be negative, but that's for critical education scholars to debate).

Along with the *r* value, you will have a significance test indicating the probability of observing a value that large by random chance. If the observed *r* value was $r = .38$ with a probability of $p < .05$, then you would not expect to see an *r* value that large by random chance occurrence more than 5% of the time; if the probability value was $p < .001$, then you would not expect to see a correlation coefficient (i.e., *r* value) that high from random chance more than once out of a thousand times. Generally speaking, lower probability values give the researcher confidence that some systematic effect, rather than random chance, has been observed. By convention in the social sciences, any probability value of less than or equal to $p < .05$ is considered significant, which just means that random chance is unlikely to have resulted in the observed test statistic. We should note that other fields such as medicine, engineering, or physics might use a more stringent significance test because of the impact that such research could have on the health and safety of others. Would you really want your physician to accept a 5% chance that a particular medicine would not work to cure a life-threatening illness?

The combination of the test statistic and the probability value is critical to the traditional form of reasoning employed by quantitative researchers. Basically, the logic of quantitative reasoning rests with your ability to (a) observe a test statistic that is (b) likely not caused by chance occurrence. If you are able to do those two things, statistically justifiable conclusions can be drawn about the correlation, *t* test, or other observed statistic. Generally speaking, this process is called *hypothesis testing* in the social sciences.

When calculating a test statistic, you are actually testing the veracity of the null hypothesis. The null hypothesis simply states that there is no correlation between variables—in an experiment, the null hypothesis might state that there is no difference between the experimental and control groups. Figure 2.2 illustrates what researchers are attempting to do in any research project—to test an observed set of data against reality. As can be seen in the figure, the researcher may observe or not observe an effect; for instance, an observed effect might be a significant correlation coefficient, whereas a nonobserved effect would be a nonsignificant correlation coefficient between two variables. The "real" state of affairs might correspond or not correspond with what the researcher observed. That is, in reality, there may or may not be an actual relationship between the variables. Your objective, then, is to craft a study where the observation corresponds with reality. More specifically, you want to hypothesize, test, and observe relationships that are present in the real world.

If the observed test statistic shows a relationship and the associated probability value indicates that the likelihood of random chance causing the results is small, you can conclude that the null hypothesis is not a reasonable explanation for what was observed. Importantly, a significant finding does not provide support for the research hypothesis (i.e., that a relationship does exist); rather, the significant finding only shows that the null hypothesis is unlikely.

	No Effect in Reality (Null Is "True")	Actual Effect in Reality (Null Is "False")
No Effect Observed ("Failed to Reject" the Null)	Correct Acceptance No difference in groups	Type II Error Alpha too stringent High error variance Small effect size Too few participants
Effect Observed (Null Is "Rejected")	Type I Error Alpha set inappropriately low Random chance	Correct Rejection There is a difference between the groups because: The research hypothesis is correct Other factors cause the difference

Figure 2.2   Quantitative Reasoning

Of course, the ability to "reject the null" coupled with a strong theoretical explanation might make the research hypothesis the most likely explanation of a given set of data.

As you can see from Figure 2.2, reasoning behind quantitative research generally rests with your ability to use observed statistics to reject or fail to reject the null hypothesis. When drawing conclusions from test statistics about the null hypothesis, you can make one of two types of errors: Type I and Type II errors (for additional discussion of this, see Hunter & Schmidt, 1990). Type I error occurs when you reject the null hypothesis when, in fact, the null hypothesis is actually correct. For example, suppose that you tested the relationship between communication skill and liking ice cream—for whatever reason, the correlation is significant and positive. Because there was a 5% chance of making an error to begin with, you might incorrectly conclude that an increase in communication majors on campus would correspond with increased ice cream sales—this error in judgment could make investing in ice cream stands around communication buildings unwise. The best way to protect against Type I error is to maintain alpha at .05 or less, recognizing still that there is a small chance that you will make an error.

Type II error occurs because you fail to reject the null when, in fact, the null should have been rejected. Stated differently, in the real world, there is actually some effect present, but you were unable to observe that effect because the probability value associated with the relevant test statistic could not rule out random chance. For instance, theory and experience tell us that employees should like their jobs more if they have a supportive supervisor. But, because you only sampled 10 people, you were unable to observe the effect that must be there in reality. Failing to observe the effect that you know is there is Type II error. In this case, you would incorrectly conclude that the supervisor does not matter in terms of employee happiness.

Type II error is influenced by four things: the actual size of the effect, the probability level set by the researcher to determine whether something is significant (i.e., using $p < .05$ vs. using $p < .001$—the latter is more stringent), errors associated with measurement, and sample size. When trying to reduce the risk of Type II error, the most effective strategies are (a) finding measurement tools that are valid and reliable and (b) having a sufficient sample size. Recognizing that we always try to find valid and reliable measurement tools, much of our attention toward Type II error is focused on sample size. Generally speaking, your objective is to have an adequate sample size to have the "power" to detect significant effects. The size of the sample might be thought of as the power of a microscope such that larger samples make the magnifying power greater. In fact, researchers use the term *power* in just that way—you need to have enough "power" to detect meaningful results as significant. In subsequent chapters, you will learn about rules of thumb for determining adequate power based on the number of variables, effect size, and other situational factors. For now, suffice it to say that larger sample sizes (say, greater than 250 people) dramatically reduce the chance of committing Type II error under many circumstances.

WRITING RESULTS

As you saw in the opening example for this chapter, statistical results are presented using a particular (or some might say peculiar) statistical shorthand—the sentences use symbols and numbers to represent words. Although it may take you some practice getting used to writing this way, this approach ultimately makes your data reporting clearer for others. Consider the following sentence, written without using any symbols:

> The two hundred six *Baywatch* television viewers have a mean intelligence score of one hundred seven and standard deviation of fifteen. This score is significantly larger according to the *t* test of four point twenty four and three hundred four degrees of freedom at a two-tailed probability of less than five percent random chance alpha error than one hundred *Jerry Springer* viewers' average intelligence score of one hundred with a standard deviation of ten.

Although this sentence contains the relevant statistical information, you probably found it dreadful and cumbersome. Now consider the same results using standard writing conventions:

> A significant difference in intelligence was observed, $t(304) = 4.24$, $p < .05$, when comparing *Baywatch* television viewers ($n = 206$, $M = 107$, $SD = 15$) to *Jerry Springer* viewers ($n = 100$, $M = 100$, $SD = 10$).

As you can see, the second sentence is actually easier to read because it condenses information and uses words to express one type of meaning (mainly conceptual) and symbols/numbers to represent another type (mainly technical).

An important element to remember in using statistical information and symbols is that those terms are used to create a precise shorthand for an expression that has a verbal equivalent. Rather than using normal verbal expressions, you use a convention for expressing those words by replacing them with mathematical symbols, essentially creating another sentence, only using symbols instead of words. Table 2.2 provides a list of commonly used statistical notations following the American Psychological Association (APA) format. You should consult the APA manual for additional guidance on how to incorporate statistics into text, tables, and figures.

When using statistical notation, the APA manual recommends that you place spaces in between symbols because it is easier to read. So, rather than discussing a 2×3 interaction it should be a 2×3 interaction (notice the spaces as indicated by "carets": 2^×^3). Also, symbols involving Greek characters (β, Δ, η^2, Λ, Σ, χ^2, ω^2) are not italicized; other symbols are. For additional information, you should consult the fifth edition of the *Publication Manual of the American Psychological Association* (American Psychological Association, 2001, Section 3.58).

REFERENCES

American Psychological Association. (2001). *Publication manual of the American Psychological Association* (5th ed.). Washington, DC: Author.

Cohen, J. (1988). *Statistical power analysis for the social sciences* (2nd ed.). Hillsdale, NJ: Lawrence Erlbaum.

Hunter, J., & Schmidt, F. (1990). *Methods of meta-analysis: Correcting error and bias in research findings.* Newbury Park, CA: Sage.

Vogt, W. P. (1999). *Dictionary of statistics & methodology.* Thousand Oaks, CA: Sage.

Table 2.2   Statistical Notation in APA Style

Symbol	Use
d	Cohen's measure of effect size, which is commonly used in conjunction with *t* tests and other tests of mean difference
df	Degrees of freedom. However, degrees of freedom are typically reported in parentheses alongside test statistics, and in such cases, this abbreviation is not used: for example, $F = 88.88$ (1, 8), $p < .05$, $\eta^2 = .75$.
f	Frequency
F	*F* ratio typically reported for ANOVA and regression
M	The mean or average in a set of values
Mdn	Median for a set of values
n	Used to indicate the number of people/cases in a subsample. For instance, if reporting the number of men ($n = 20$) and women ($n = 23$) in a study, you would use the lowercase *n*.
N	Used to report the size of the overall sample
ns	Used to indicate that a test statistic is not significant
p	The alpha level, or risk of Type I error, accepted. Typically, this is set to $p < .05$.
r	Pearson's correlation coefficient
r^2	Coefficient of determination, or variance accounted for in a model
R	Multiple correlation typically reported from a regression analysis
R^2	Squared multiple correlation from multiple regression
SD	Standard deviation
t	The *t* statistic reported as part of a *t* test or planned comparison in ANOVA
z	A standardized score obtained by subtracting the mean from a specific value and dividing by the standard deviation
β	Beta, the standardized regression coefficient
Δ	Delta is used to indicate an increment of change, often used in a hierarchical regression analysis to show changes for each step of the model.
η^2	Eta squared, an estimate of effect size in ANOVA
Λ	Wilks' lambda used in multivariate procedures such as MANOVA
Σ	Sigma is commonly used in formulas to indicate the sum of something.
χ^2	Chi-square
ω^2	Omega squared, an estimate of effect size in ANOVA

❧ Sample SPSS Printouts ❧

The sample printout that follows shows statistics for two variables. The first variable, CONSWEEK, is the number of times that college freshmen in the study consult others in their social network for reasons related to social support. The other variable, SSEFFECT, is the effectiveness of social support offered by each person's network. In both cases, higher numbers represent greater amounts for that variable (i.e., more consults per week and greater effectiveness). In addition, the sex of participants is reported. The descriptive routine was used to create the descriptive statistics table for CONSWEEK and SSEFFECT, and the frequencies routine was used to obtain the frequency distribution and histogram for SEX. You will notice that the histogram is somewhat meaningless for a categorical variable such as sex. However, you could use the frequencies command to obtain a histogram for continuous variables such as CONSWEEK and SSEFFECT—those histograms are included for comparison purposes. Notice the positive skew of CONSWEEK and the negative skew of SSEFFECT.

Descriptive Statistics

| | N | Range | Minimum | Maximum | Mean | Std. Deviation | Variance | Skewness | | Kurtosis | |
	Statistic	Statistic	Statistic	Statistic	Statistic	Statistic	Statistic	Statistic	Std. Error	Statistic	Std. Error
consweek	167	64.40	.60	65.00	5.2371	6.41563	41.160	6.318	.188	50.640	.374
sseffect	232	9.80	.20	10.00	6.9440	2.17227	4.719	-.996	.160	.431	.318
Valid N (listwise)	167										

SEX

		Frequency	Percent	Valid Percent	Cumulative Percent
Valid	.00	1	.4	.4	.4
	Female	173	74.6	74.6	75.0
	Male	58	25.0	25.0	100.0
	Total	232	100.0	100.0	

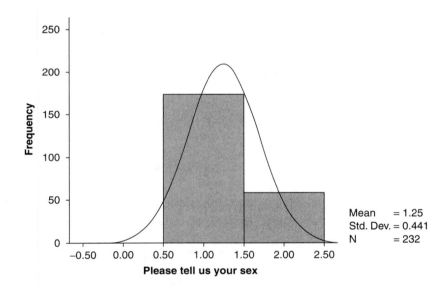

Mean = 1.25
Std. Dev. = 0.441
N = 232

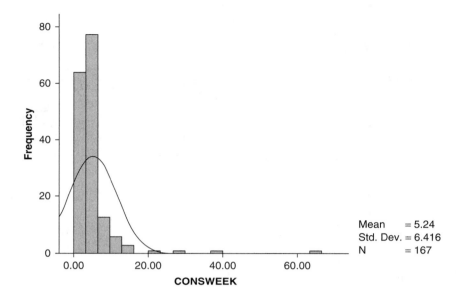

Mean   = 5.24
Std. Dev. = 6.416
N   = 167

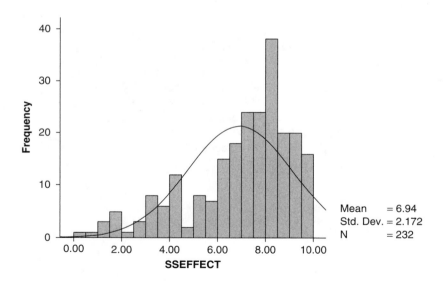

Mean   = 6.94
Std. Dev. = 2.172
N   = 232

THREE

INDEPENDENT SAMPLES OR STUDENT'S *t* TEST

Sarah and Scott are communication students interested in the role newspaper readership plays in students' political knowledge. As part of a class research project, they administered a measure of political knowledge to students in one of two groups of an introductory public speaking course. One of the groups of students experienced the standard course without a newspaper readership program. The other group of students experienced the same public speaking instruction but also received copies of a national newspaper throughout the semester. Using the independent samples t test procedure, Sarah and Scott were able to determine that students in the readership sections of the public speaking course ended the semester with significantly higher scores on the measure of political knowledge compared with their counterparts in traditional sections of the course.

UNDERSTANDING THE INDEPENDENT SAMPLES *t* TEST

An independent samples or Student's *t* test examines the mean difference between two groups. In Sarah and Scott's example, students were enrolled in one of two sections of the introductory public speaking course—sections that used a newspaper readership program or traditional sections of the course without such a program. Statistical tests are often named after the person who invented or published them. Interestingly, Fisher (who also invented the *F* test) wrote about the *t* statistic under the pseudonym "Student," and the test has been referred to as the Student's *t* test ever since. There are several different versions of the *t* test, and you will need to be aware of those differences when you are working with a computer program because choosing the correct test is essential to ensuring proper interpretation of the results. The independent samples test is one version of the *t* test; the other option is the "paired sample" test. The example of Sarah and Scott uses an independent samples test because the participants were divided into separate groups.

Another version of the *t* test is used when you want to compare two values for the same person. This version is called a paired samples *t* test because it matches to scores for each person and then determines, overall, whether there is a significant difference between the two scores. For example, a common reason for using a paired samples *t* test is when you have a pretest, some sort of manipulation or intervention, and a posttest. As a researcher, you are interested in learning whether the intervention caused a significant change from the pre- to the posttest. Whereas a significant *t* value in an independent samples test tells you that the two groups have significantly different means, a significant *t* value in a paired samples test tells you that the mean for the pretest is significantly different from the mean for the posttest.

Like all sample statistics, the question of whether two means are "significantly" different is answerable by estimating the mean difference and comparing that score to amount of overall variability expected in the sample, factoring in sample size. In other words, for a given sample, we would expect that there is a certain amount of natural variability stemming from random error and chance. The *t* test determines whether the variability between the two groups (or between the two observations) is larger than the expected natural variability present—if so, you have found a mean difference that is not likely to be the result of chance. The larger the sample, the more likely or probable that any observed difference between means is statistically significant, assuming that the level of variability is unrelated to the size of the sample.

If you recall from Chapter 2, all sample statistics are calculated with knowledge of the sample size; furthermore, the confidence interval around those sample statistics is influenced by the size of the sample. So, for instance, a mean calculated for a sample of people will have a corresponding confidence interval—the larger the sample, the smaller the confidence interval. Thus, when calculating the *t* test, a large sample will have a small confidence interval (thus, a small amount of error variance), and it will be easier for mean differences between groups to be significant. That is why virtually any methodology book advises those conducting an investigation to increase the size of the sample. The larger the sample, the more accurate the estimation of any statistical parameter as an increase in sample size diminishes the size of sampling error associated with the estimation of that statistic.

CALCULATING THE INDEPENDENT SAMPLES *t* TEST

Recall that Sarah and Scott were interested in whether students participating in a newspaper readership program as a part of their public speaking course would finish the semester with higher levels of political knowledge than their peers in traditional sections of the course. Political knowledge could be assessed using a simple recall test asking students to answer factual questions about current political events and political figures. They found that the end-of-semester mean on the political knowledge test was 7.33 for those in the readership sections and 5.17 for those in regular sections of the course. The fact that the samples have means that are not exactly the same suggests a difference; however, it does not tell us whether the difference is due to random chance. A *t* test examines the difference between two means and evaluates whether that difference is statistically significant. The computational formula for the independent samples *t* test is shown in Formula 3.1 (for additional discussion of the formula, see Williams, 1995):

$$t = \frac{\bar{X}_1 - \bar{X}_2}{\sqrt{\left[\frac{(n_1 - 1)s_1^2 + (n_2 - 1)s_2^2}{n_1 + n_2 - 2}\right]\left[\frac{n_1 + n_2}{n_1 n_2}\right]}}. \tag{3.1}$$

The numerator of the formula is simply the mean of Group 1 minus the mean of Group 2—it does not matter which group is designated Group 1 or Group 2. The denominator is simply a way of estimating total variance (the *n* represents the number of people in each group, and the *s* represents the estimate of variance). As you can see, this formula is the difference between the two means divided by the square root of the two terms in the denominator. The first term is a weighted average standard deviation, and the second term is called the sample correction. The steps for computing the independent samples *t* test are summarized in Figure 3.1.

Table 3.1 presents the data Sarah and Scott collected regarding students' political knowledge.

1. Enter data so that each participant is coded for the condition he or she was in followed by his or her score on the dependent variable.

2. Determine the number of participants in each group.

3. Calculate the means for the dependent variable for each group.

4. Calculate the standard deviations for each group.

5. Calculate the degrees of freedom.

6. Determine the *t* value using Formula 3.1.

7. Test the significance of the *t* value by examining the critical value.

8. Write up results.

Figure 3.1   Steps in Calculating the Independent Samples *t* Test

Table 3.1   Political Knowledge Scores by Section of Public Speaking Course

Readership Group			Nonreadership Group		
8	8	8	6	5	6
8	9	9	6	4	4
9	7	7	7	4	9
7	5	4	4	4	5
6	7	7	5	6	6
7	7	6	4	5	6
8	9	8	5	5	5
7	7	7	9	4	4
6	8	8	3	2	5
8	8	7	6	7	5

NOTE: The columns above are simply used to conserve space. There are 30 values under "readership group" and 30 under "nonreadership group." The values are presented in random order.

Applying the formula for a *t* test based on the sample data above reveals the following:

$$t = \frac{7.33 - 5.17}{\sqrt{\left[\dfrac{(30-1)1.15^2 + (30-1)1.51^2}{30+30-2}\right]\left[\dfrac{30+30}{30 \times 30}\right]}},$$

$$t = \frac{2.16}{\sqrt{\left[\dfrac{(29)(1.32) + (29)(2.28)}{58}\right]\left[\dfrac{60}{900}\right]}},$$

$$t = \frac{2.16}{\sqrt{(1.8)(.07)}},$$

$$t = \frac{2.16}{.35},$$

$$t = 6.17.$$

To determine whether this *t* value is significant, consult Appendix A, which lists critical values for *t* tests. However, before you examine the critical values, you need to determine your degrees of freedom (*df*). Using Sarah and Scott's example, the degrees of freedom are $n_1 + n_2 - 2$, or 58. Using the degrees of freedom (58), the level of risk you are willing to take (Sarah and Scott selected the .05 level), and a two-tailed test (a two-tailed test means that they did not specify in advance which mean would be larger than the other), look up the critical value in Table 3.2.

As you have likely noticed, this table does not include a listing for 58 degrees of freedom. In this case, Sarah and Scott selected the degrees of freedom closest to their sample size (recall that their actual sample size was 60). As a result, the value Sarah and Scott need to reject the null hypothesis with 58 degrees of freedom at the .05 level is 2.001. Alternatively, most statistical programs (such as SPSS) will provide an actual measure of significance. If the *p* value (significance) is estimated to be less than .05, then the difference between the two values is statistically significant. An example of how to write up the results for a *t* test can be found in Figure 3.2.

It is important that you use a lowercase *t* when reporting this statistic because another statistic uses an uppercase or capital *T* (usually called Hotelling's *T*). Hotelling's *T* is used in multivariate analysis (usually as part of

Table 3.2   Critical Values for *t*

	One-Tailed Test			Two-Tailed Test	
df	.05	.01	*df*	**.05**	.10
40	1.684	2.424	40	2.021	2.705
45	1.68	2.412	45	2.014	2.69
50	1.676	2.404	50	2.009	2.678
55	1.673	2.396	55	2.004	2.668
60	1.671	2.39	**60**	**2.001**	2.661
65	1.669	2.385	65	1.997	2.654

NOTE: The bolded values in the fifth row show the critical value (2.001) for a two-tailed test at $p < .05$ and 60 degrees of freedom.

"Students enrolled in sections of the public speaking course with a newspaper readership program reported significantly higher levels of political knowledge at the end of the semester compared to their counterparts in regular sections of the course, $t(58) = 6.17$, $p < .05$."	
$t = 6.17$	This represents the actual value of the *t* test that Sarah and Scott calculated using the formula presented in this chapter.
(58)	This is the number of degrees of freedom, which they obtained by subtracting 2 from the total number of participants in the sample.
$p < .05$	As noted previously, the significance or probability level is governed by convention in the social sciences. In this case, the *t* test is statistically significant.

Figure 3.2   Deciphering the Write-Up of *t* Tests

MANOVA) and should not be confused with the application to a comparison of two group means. Also, remember to put spaces before and after the "=" signs as well as before and after the "<" sign. Doing so makes it much easier for the reader to decipher your results.

ASSUMPTIONS OF THE *t* TEST

As with other tests discussed throughout this text, the independent samples *t* test assumes that your dependent variable is measured on either an interval or ratio scale. If you perform an experiment, the independent samples *t* test also assumes that you employed randomization in sampling and assignment of participants to experimental and control conditions. If you are using the *t* test to examine whether two naturally occurring groups (e.g., men vs. women) are significantly different, the test assumes that you randomly selected people. Again, you should be confident that if you collect data from the entire population, the results will be normally distributed. Finally, the independent samples *t* test assumes equal variances of the dependent variable in the population.

Engaged Research

Many departments of communication have developed speech laboratories for their introductory public speaking courses to provide students with expanded opportunities to develop their communication skills. However, some question whether visiting the lab actually translates to important course outcomes such as reduced fear of speaking during classroom presentations. For your project, develop a simple survey categorizing students into groups of those that do and do not attend the speech lab prior to a classroom speech (if you do not have a speech lab, simply use a different grouping variable such as whether students practiced their speech before giving it in the classroom). Your survey should also include a measure of public speaking anxiety. Administer this survey to at least 30 people and use the independent samples *t* test to determine if there is a difference between the groups on your measure of public speaking anxiety.

USING COMPUTER PROGRAMS TO CALCULATE *t* TESTS

We expect that you will be using software such as SPSS to generate the actual statistic in most situations. As you familiarize yourself with the tests available in the software you are using, pay particular attention to the options for comparing means. In this section, we cover several options and features that you need to examine in order to successfully execute an independent samples *t* test.

The problem with most statistical packages (such as SPSS) is that you will get far more statistical information than you ever want. Fortunately, as your research skills develop, you will learn to focus on what you need and ignore that which you do not need.

Independent Samples/Groups. Select this option for the independent samples *t* test. Other choices likely include "within-person" or "paired" tests; however, select the groups test when conducting the independent samples analysis.

Significance Levels. Typically, most social scientists use a .05 significance level. Some researchers report the actual *p* value (e.g., *p* = .013) rather than indicating that the value was greater or less than .05. Doing so provides the actual level of probability that the results were due to random chance. As we have noted, if you are use a .05 level of probability, the *t* test must produce a *p* value less than .05 to be significant. This test indicates that for the observed difference between the two means, the probability that such a level would occur due to random chance is estimated at "X" percent. For example, if you found an actual *p* value of .99, the differences you observed could have occurred 99% of the time randomly. Essentially, one would say that the confidence is low in assuming a significant difference between the two means. However, suppose the significance value is .001. In this case, the probability that the observed difference is due to random chance is about 1 in 1,000. To put it another way, one could assume that the difference was unlikely due to random chance.

Equal or Weighted Variance. It is possible to calculate a *t* test using a weighted variance. Generally, most researchers assume equal variance. The biggest difference between equal and weighted variance is found in the calculation of the degrees of freedom (*df*). For equal variance, the *df* is a whole number (e.g., 25, 33, 102); however, for weighted variance, the *df* is often not a whole number (e.g., 25.67, 33.99, 111.92). The difference between these two estimates is that the weighted version is slightly more conservative in determining the critical value for *t*. The more conservative estimate would be used to reduce (slightly) the risk of Type I error that could result from unequal variance among the groups. If the two groups have unequal variance, as indicated by a significant Levine test, you should use the more conservative estimate based on weighted degrees of freedom (the ones with decimals); if the Levine test is not significant, you are safe in using the unweighted estimates. Practically speaking, however, we have rarely seen instances where the unweighted *t* test is significant and the weighted *t* test is not—when both result in significant tests, you may want to report the unweighted *df* to avoid confusion on the part of readers.

Means, Standard Deviations, and Sample Size. You will usually be required to report these in the text of your manuscript unless the information is incorporated in a table. So make sure that you select an option that provides these parameters for each group. In many statistical packages, this will be the default and automatically provided but not always.

INTERPRETING RESULTS
OF AN INDEPENDENT SAMPLES *t* TEST

One important item to remember when interpreting your results is that a *t* test can be positive or negative. Whether the *t* test is positive or negative is simply a function of which group was designated as group "one" and which group was designated as group "two" in the numerator of the formula. For example, if you were examining sex differences (biological male and biological female), you could code males as "1" and females as "2." If males were to score more on the variable of interest (e.g., verbal aggressiveness), the *t* test would be positive $(\bar{X}_1 - \bar{X}_2)$. However, suppose you decided to code males as "2" and females as "1". The same *t* test would be negative $(\bar{X}_1 - \bar{X}_2)$—although the size of the *t* test would be identical, the direction would be reversed. Thus, the sign of the *t* value is arbitrary and unimportant. In fact, when reporting the *t* value, you are safe in reporting the absolute value of *t*, which, of course, would always be positive.

There is a distinction between research questions and directional hypotheses. A research question simply asks if the two means differ. This constitutes what is known as a two-tailed test. With a two-tailed test, you set the alpha level (usually 5%) and then divide the area under the curve into an upper and a lower region. In this case, the researcher states that the two means will differ but makes no argument about which mean will be larger or smaller. Therefore, the test of significance examines whether the *t* is greater than a particular critical value (1.96, for example). If *t* is greater than that value, mean one is greater than mean two (mean one minus mean two is positive). If *t* is less than the value (–1.96; the curve is symmetrical), mean two is smaller than mean one (mean one minus mean two is negative). A one-tailed t test is usually associated with a hypothesis that stipulates that the researcher believes one mean is greater than the other. If you hypothesize that mean one is greater than mean two, you are using a one-tailed test. However, the value of t must be positive; a large negative value of t (–4.22, for example) would not be considered significant. The reason for this is that the hypothesis was not supported—the hypothesis stated mean one would be greater than mean two. In other words, the hypothesis posited does not permit mean one to be significantly less than mean two, even if it is true. For a more detailed discussion of the implications for this kind of treatment of both positive and negative t values, see O'Keefe (2003).

This discussion suggests that it is very important that you remember which group was coded as one and which group was coded as two. You cannot simply look at the t test by itself and interpret the results. Instead, you need to interpret the results in the context of how the group designations correspond to the mean scores. This also makes it important that you report means, standard deviations, and the sample size of each group in your manuscript. Such information permits the reader to understand what you did and why the conclusion you are drawing is related to the particular values observed in your analysis. You should also check to ensure that the values expressed in the results section are defined in the methods section of your manuscript. In the methods section, you need to define what the quantities indicate. For example, if you are using a Likert statement, does a 1 indicate agreement or disagreement with the particular item? Since a scale can run in either direction, reporting the polarity of the items is a necessity in the methods section. By providing that information, you can be assured that readers will know what the results indicate about the comparison you are making.

THE INDEPENDENT SAMPLES t TEST IN COMMUNICATION RESEARCH

Dutta, M. J. (2007). Health information processing from television: The role of health orientation. *Health Communication, 2,* 1–9.

Because television has become commonplace in American culture, a variety of social scientific theories have emerged that attempt to account for and explain potential negative effects of television viewing habits. Recently, those theories have been applied to explicit and implicit health messages on television. For example, Gerbner's cultivation theory suggests that television would create a distorted view of health issues, while Bandura's social cognitive theory would explain how viewers learn health behaviors from watching television. Using these theories as a foundation, Mohan Dutta explored the effects of entertainment education health messages on how television viewers learn from those messages.

The topic of how viewers learn from television has received moderate attention with respect to news programming. That research has identified three variables important to learning effects: exposure, attention, and motivation. Small effect sizes have been observed between exposure to television messages and learning; however, the theoretical explanation for this link has not been fully elaborated. Attention is the degree to which audience members allocate cognitive attention to messages. While attention predicts more variance in learning than simple exposure, researchers emphasizing this explanation go beyond simple attention to also include other aspects of information processing such as assimilation of new information with existing knowledge. Finally, a variety of studies have linked audience members' motivations with how they learn from television messages. For example, audience members with particular motivations will use the media in particular ways that are different from viewers with other motivations.

Dutta posits that viewers who learn from health messages on television will differ in their health orientation—those who learn from the messages will be high in health orientation, and those who do not learn from the messages will be low in health orientation. Dutta advances six hypotheses suggesting this same pattern of difference across these types of television shows: television news or magazine shows (Hypothesis 1a), television talk shows (Hypothesis 1b), soap operas (Hypothesis 1c), prime-time programs (Hypothesis 1d), documentaries (Hypothesis 1e), and medical or health shows (Hypothesis 1f). Dutta obtained data from a national survey and was able to analyze information from just over 2,500 respondents. Each respondent was asked to respond using a yes/no answer to indicate whether he or she had learned from each type of television source (e.g., news programs, documentaries, soap operas). These questions created a dichotomous (did learn vs. did not learn) independent variable for each television source. Respondents were also asked to provide information about their health orientation by answering questions on a survey that produced four health orientation variables: health consciousness, health information orientation, health beliefs, and healthy activities.

To conserve space, Table 3.3 provides results for health information orientation and healthy activities (two of the four dependent variables). Because of the number of tests performed, Dutta used a Bonferroni adjustment to protect against overall alpha inflation. With four different dependent variables (and these four tests) for each television source, the conventional $p < .05$ was reduced to .0125 (.05/4 = .0125) to identify significant effects. Those t values with probabilities less than .0125 have an asterisk as well as the actual significance level reported. As you can see from the table, Dutta was able to reject the null hypothesis for Hypotheses 1a, 1b, 1c, and 1e but not for Hypotheses 1d and 1f. Moreover, the pattern of means showed that his initial supposition was correct—those who reported learning from television had more healthy orientations than did those who did not report learning from various television sources.

REFERENCES

Barbee, A. P., & Cunningham, M. R. (1995). An experimental approach to social support communications: Interactive coping in close relationships. In B. R. Burleson (Ed.), *Communication yearbook 18* (pp. 381–413). Thousand Oaks, CA: Sage.

O'Keefe, D. J. (2003). Colloquy: Should familywise alpha be adjusted? Against familywise alpha adjustment. *Human Communication Research, 29,* 431–447.

Williams, F. (1995). *Reasoning with statistics* (4th ed.). New York: Holt, Rinehart & Winston.

Table 3.3   Differences in Health Orientation for Learners and Nonlearners
Across Television Sources

	Learners		*Nonlearners*			
Variable	M	SD	M	SD	t	p
TV news magazine (Hypothesis 1a)						
Health information orientation	3.73	.72	3.53	.75	6.11*	.00
Healthy activities	3.98	2.43	3.46	2.49	4.67*	.00
TV talk shows (Hypothesis 1b)						
Health information orientation	3.84	.64	3.63	.75	6.49*	.00
Healthy activities	4.05	2.46	3.79	2.45	2.38	.02
TV soap operas (Hypothesis 1c)						
Health information orientation	3.91	.69	3.65	.73	5.87*	.00
Healthy activities	3.61	2.43	3.89	2.46	1.80	.07
TV prime-time shows (Hypothesis 1d)						
Health information orientation	3.71	.71	3.67	.73	1.21	.23
Healthy activities	3.84	2.39	3.86	2.48	.15	.88
TV documentaries (Hypothesis 1e)						
Health information orientation	3.81	.69	3.58	.74	8.16*	.00
Healthy activities	4.06	2.42	3.69	2.47	3.94*	.00
TV medical shows (Hypothesis 1f)						
Health information orientation	3.97	.67	3.94	.65	1.38	.017
Healthy activities	3.95	2.44	3.81	2.46	1.38	.17

NOTE: Values marked with a "*" have probability values of $p < .0125$. That value was used to flag
significant t values because of a Bonferroni adjustment.

✒ Sample SPSS Printouts ✒

Output shown in the following example provides an independent samples *t* test comparing women to men in terms of the amount of immediacy they show during a conversation. As you will notice, the output first provides a table showing descriptive statistics for both groups. The *t* test table provides a test to determine if the variance is equal and then the actual *t* test, degrees of freedom, and two-tailed significance level. Printouts for a paired samples *t* test follow the same basic pattern.

Group Statistics

	sex	N	Mean	Std. Deviation	Std. Error Mean
immediac	Females	6	2.1667	1.16905	.47726
	Males	5	4.8000	.83666	.37417

Independent Samples Test

		Levene's Test for Equality of Variances		t test for Equality of Means					95% Confidence Interval of the Difference	
		F	Sig.	t	df	Sig. (2-tailed)	Mean Difference	Std. Error Difference	Upper	Lower
immediac	Equal variances assumed	.535	.483	-4.203	9	.002	-2.63333	.62647	-4.05052	-1.21615
	Equal variances not assumed			-4.342	8.854	.002	-2.63333	.60645	-4.00866	-1.25800

49

ONEWAY ANALYSIS OF VARIANCE

To test the effects of using different types of evidence in a persuasive health message, Kim created four messages urging people to eat more vegetables and fruits: one containing no evidence, one containing statistical evidence, one containing narrative evidence, and one containing celebrity testimony. After creating the messages and randomly assigning participants to view the messages, Kim used data from a survey completed immediately after viewing the messages as well as a 1-week eating diary to determine what, if any, effects the different types of evidence had on intended and actual eating behaviors. She used the ONEWAY ANOVA to compare the scores on the two dependent variables (intended and actual behaviors) between the four groups in the experiment.

Researchers who study communication by conducting various types of experiments often must analyze differences in a dependent variable between two or more groups in the experiment. Similarly, those studying naturally occurring variables, such as year in school (e.g., freshman, sophomore) and political affiliation (e.g., Democrat, Republican, and independent), may want to compare groups within those variables on some continuous dependent measure. As you will learn, various types of analysis of variance (ANOVA) procedures allow such comparisons. In this chapter, you will learn about the simplest of the ANOVA procedures, the ONEWAY ANOVA, which involves one continuous dependent variable and one categorical independent variable with at least three groups.

UNDERSTANDING THE ONEWAY ANOVA

Recall from Chapter 3 that a t test compares the means of two groups. For example, you might wish to compare levels of empathy among men and women. A ONEWAY ANOVA, or F test, extends the t test by comparing more than two means; that is, you can use any number of means so long as they are all part of the same variable. ONEWAY ANOVA tests nearly always involve a categorical independent variable (IV) with three or more groups and a continuous dependent variable (DV). The objective of using the test is to determine whether there are significant differences in the DV among the groups of the IV.

Results of the F test tell you whether the group means are significantly different and, specifically, which of the means are significantly different from one another. The test requires a two-step process. First, the omnibus F test must be run; if the F test is significant ($p < .05$), then a follow-up test is recommended to examine whether any of the group means are significantly different. A significant F value does not indicate which means are different; it only indicates a potential difference between at least two of the means. This is unlike a t test, where a significant result indicates the two means are different. If a t test is significant, you simply examine the value of the means to determine which one is greater; that is not the case for the F test.

The omnibus F test is a test that determines whether differences between the overall mean and the means for each group are significant compared with the variability of individual scores. The F test is often called the F ratio because the F test is calculated by creating a ratio of the impact of group difference compared with the impact of individual differences (often called the "error" term). The ratio provides evidence about whether you need to examine the multiple means to determine which, if any, are different from each other.

The analysis of variance term comes from the fact that the statistic estimates the total amount of variability in the data (often called the total sum of squares or SS_T) and then determines what contributes to that variability. In the ONEWAY ANOVA, there are two sources of variability: (a) the variable of interest (the assignment to a group, often called the sum of squares for the effect or SS_A) or (b) the individual differences between participants in the investigation (sometimes called the error term or often called the sum of squares for error or SS_E). A significant F test indicates that there exists at least two means that are significantly different from each other.

A nonsignificant F test indicates that no evidence exists for significant difference between means. If the omnibus F test is significant, the researcher will likely use a follow-up or post hoc test to determine which group means are significantly different from one another. There are many different kinds of post hoc tests (e.g., student-Newman-Kuels or SNK, Tukey, LSD, etc.). All of the tests involve taking the available means and then comparing them in pairs. With three means, there will be three comparisons; with four means, there will be six comparisons; and so on. The different derivations and applications of the tests are predicated on different assumptions about the nature of calculating variances and/or assumptions about how to correct for familywise error, as well as other mathematical features of interest.

If you are testing a more developed theory, you have the option of using effect coding, sometimes also referred to as planned comparisons, to test a theoretical model. For example, suppose there are four groups (A, B, C, D) and you predict that the value of the means increase as one goes from A to B to C to D. Another example would be a theory predicting that A, B, and C are not different from each other, but D should be significantly higher. Basically, this set of comparisons might reflect a set of theoretical expectations that can be directly tested. The ONEWAY procedure allows you to use simple commands to directly test such custom hypotheses. The advantage of specific, planned tests is that the level of Type I and Type II error is diminished because you are able to use one-tailed tests and have strong theoretical support for your findings. The disadvantage is that the tests are sensitive to deviations from the relationships specified in the planned comparisons. Moreover, employing only planned comparisons without examining an omnibus test could miss serendipitous findings and opportunities for drawing new conclusions. Strangely enough, Fisher, the creator of the F test, had intended the examination to be theoretical and effects-coded models to dominate the use of this statistic. The omnibus test was simply a means of examining whether the research had missed anything in the effects model.

CALCULATING A ONEWAY ANOVA

Although computers are commonly used to calculate ONEWAY ANOVAs, knowledge of how they are calculated can assist in developing a strong conceptual understanding of what the statistics tell you. In the following data set, we are exploring relationship satisfaction, a variable with a mean of 100, among people who are dating, engaged, or married. The independent variable is the type of relationship—dating, engaged, or married. The dependent variable is the relational satisfaction level of each group—higher values indicate higher levels of relational satisfaction. These data are shown, divided by group, in Table 4.1.

We are going to take this information and perform a ONEWAY ANOVA. An ANOVA procedure eventually requires the generation of an ANOVA summary table. The basic information contained in an ANOVA summary table as well as the basic source of such information is shown in Table 4.2.

Calculating an ANOVA is essentially a step-by-step process (see Figure 4.1) of performing various calculations to complete the table. What you should look for on a computer printout is the ANOVA table, which will provide you with all values reported in the summary table. Each step of this process is defined here. In a general sense, the ANOVA provides an F ratio that tells you whether the between-group difference significantly "outweighs" the within-group difference. The F statistic itself is analogous to a scale weighing each type of

Table 4.1   Relational Satisfaction Data by Group

Dating	Engaged	Married
89	99	109
90	100	110
91	101	111

NOTE: The values under each heading represent individual relational satisfaction scores.

Table 4.2   ANOVA Summary Table Template

Source	Sum of Squares	df	MS	F	η^2
Group	SS_A	$c - 1$	$SS_A/c - 1$	MS_A/MS_E	SS_A/SS_T
Individual	SS_E	$n - c - 1$	$SS_E/n - c - 1$		
Total	SS_T	$n - 1$			

variance—between and within group. If the associated significance level is less than the standard .05, you conclude that the between-group variance out-weighed the within-group variance.

The first step is calculating the overall or grand mean; this is done by taking all the scores, adding them, and dividing by the number of scores. The overall mean, 100 (900/9) or (M_G), is usually referred to as the grand mean.

The next step is finding the mean for each level of the group variable—in this case, the type of relationship.

Mean for group (M_A)   90 (270/3) (Dating)

100 (300/3) (Engaged)

110 (330/3) (Married)

The next step is to calculate the total sums of squares (SS_T). This provides the total amount of variability in the scores:

$$SS_T = \Sigma \ (X - M_G)^2.$$

1. Identify one categorical independent variable with at least three levels (or groups) and one continuous dependent variable.

2. Calculate the means for each group as well as the overall/grand mean.

3. Calculate the total sums of squares to determine overall variability.

4. Calculate between-group variability and within-group variability.

5. Calculate the overall degrees of freedom, within-group degrees of freedom, and error degrees of freedom.

6. Divide the sums of squares for each row by the corresponding degrees of freedom to arrive at the mean squares.

7. Divide the mean squares error into the mean squares effect to determine the *F* ratio.

8. If the *F* ratio meets or exceeds the critical value for *F* where $p < .05$, there are significant differences between the groups.

9. Perform planned comparison or post hoc tests as necessary to determine which groups are different from one another.

Figure 4.1   Steps in Calculating a ONEWAY ANOVA

What this formula means is that you take each raw score (X) and subtract the grand mean ($X - M$) and then square that quantity, noted below as $(X - M)^2$. The summation symbol at the beginning of the above formula (Σ) means that you add that column to get the answer. Assuming that the grand mean is 100, the following calculations would be performed:

X	X – M	$(X - M)^2$
89	−11	*121*
90	−10	*100*
91	−9	*81*
99	−1	*1*
100	0	*0*
101	1	*1*
109	9	*81*
110	10	*100*
11	11	*121*
SUM	**0**	**606**

The italicized numbers indicate the column of interest, and the 606 represents the total sum of squares or SS_T. Think of SS_T as the total amount of variability—according to this, we have 606 units. In a ONEWAY analysis of variance, there are two sources of variability, group membership and individual variability. What we are going to do is figure out for the 606 units of variability how much of that variability is attributable to the difference on the basis of group membership (SS_A) or simply on the basis of individual differences (SS_E).

To calculate this, we start by taking the mean for each group and subtracting the grand mean, squaring, but we weight or multiply that figure by the size of the particular group. The weighting in the formula permits you to analyze data where each group is not identical in size (i.e., the number of people or observations in each group). Group membership is designated at variable A, so SS_A represents the variability due to group membership. That variability is defined as

$$SS_A = \Sigma (M_A - M_G)^2 * N_A.$$

Essentially, you take the mean for each group, subtract the grand mean, square that, and then multiply by the size of the sample.

$$SS_A = (90 - 100)^2 * 3 + (100 - 100)^2 * 3 + (110 - 100)^2 * 3.$$

The term $(90 - 100)$ is the mean for dating. By subtracting the overall mean, you obtain a value of -10. Similarly, the subtraction for engaged respondents $(100 - 100)$ gives a score of zero, and for married respondents, the subtraction $(110 - 100)$ provides a score of 10.

$$(-10)^2 * 3 + (0 * 3) + (10)^2 * 3.$$

Now each term is squared $(-10, 0, 10)$ and then multiplied by the number of persons in the group (in this case, three are in each group).

$$300 + 0 + 300$$

$$600$$

This indicates that you can now go back to the ANOVA table and substitute 600 for SS_A.

The other sum of squares is for individuals (SS_E); this is often called the error term. The error term simply accounts for variability not attributable to group membership—sometimes this is also referred to as *within-group variance*. The error term is defined by the following formula:

$$SS_E = \Sigma \Sigma (X - M_A)^2.$$

This formula asks you to take the raw score for each person and subtract the mean for the group that person (or observation) belongs to. So for dating respondents, you subtract the dating mean, for engaged respondents the engaged mean, and for married respondents the married mean. This is considered a double sum because you apply the formula within each group (dating, engaged, and married), and then you add the scores for each group.

$$\text{Dating } (89 - 90)^2 + (90 - 90)^2 + (91 - 90)^2 = 1 + 0 + 1 = 2$$

$$\text{Engaged } (99 - 100)^2 + (100 - 100)^2 + (101 - 100)^2 = 1 + 0 + 1 = 2$$

$$\text{Married } (109 - 110)^2 + (110 - 110)^2 + (111 - 110)^2 = 1 + 0 + 1 = 2$$

Notice how this is done for each group individually; you simply take each value for the groups and add them again (this is the second summation).

So that means $2 + 2 + 2 = 6$ (SS_E).

You can now substitute the value 6 in the table for the SS_E.

The df is degrees of freedom (you learned about degrees of freedom in Chapter 2). The total df is for the grand mean and is determined by taking the number of scores and subtracting 1 (or, $N - 1$). There are nine scores, so the df for the grand mean and the sum of squares total (SS_T) is 8 ($9 - 1$).

For A, the first group variable, the df should be the number of groups or levels minus 1 ($c - 1$). In this case, there are three different groups so the df for A is 2 ($3 - 1$). The error for individuals is a combination of $N - (k - 1) - 1$. You take the number of scores and subtract the df for A and then 1; in this case, that is 6 ($9 - 2 - 1$). The df for individuals and for groups should be equivalent to the total df.

The third column is the mean square; the mean square is the SS for the row divided by the corresponding df. What this means for the example is that for the row labeled A or type of relationship, you take 600 and divide by 2 to obtain 300. The mean square for individuals is 6 divided by 6 or 1.

The F is obtained by dividing the MS for error by the MS for A, or 300/1 or 300. That is why you will often hear persons refer to an F ratio. A significant F ratio means that group membership contributes to predictability in an important manner and is more important, on average, than differences between individuals. When using a computer program such as SPSS, the program will tell you whether the F ratio is significant; if you are calculating the test by hand, you will need to use the degrees of freedom and desired significance level (typically .05) to look up the critical value for F on an F table. If your obtained F meets or exceeds that critical value, your F ratio is significant.

Finally, eta is a measure of effect size. Recall from Chapter 2 that effect sizes are estimates of size; in the case of η^2, you are estimating the percent of variance being accounted for in the dependent variable by group membership (i.e., the independent variable). The calculation of η^2 is easy once you have the ANOVA summary table completed: You take the SS for effect/SS for total, 600/606—or this case, about .99. Using the calculations from the above explanation results in the ANOVA summary table presented in Table 4.3. There are other potential estimates of effect sizes used in ANOVA (partial η^2 and ω^2); however, η^2 is appropriate in most circumstances (see Levine & Hullett, 2002).

Table 4.3   The ANOVA Summary Table for Relationship Type

Source	SS	df	MS	F	η^2
A (Type of Rel)	600	2	300	300	.99
Error (Indiv)	6	6	1		
Total	606	8			

ASSUMPTIONS OF THE ONEWAY ANOVA

The ONEWAY ANOVA procedure is commonly used to test for significant differences between groups of randomly selected participants. Results of the ANOVA can provide meaningful evidence to make causal claims provided that certain assumptions are met. All ANOVA procedures (the ONEWAY ANOVA discussed here, the more advanced factorial design discussed in the next chapter, and multivariate designs discussed later) meet the "big three" assumptions to allow credible conclusions.

First, groups associated with one or more categorical independent variables must have *independence*. Independence is simply the condition where participants' scores are influenced only by the treatment involved in the manipulation of variables and any individual differences that participants had before the experiment began. Violations of this assumption often occur because participants were not randomly assigned to groups. For instance, suppose you wanted to conduct an experiment exploring differences between the use of peer narratives and expert narratives in messages trying to get college students to exercise. Rather than randomly assigning people to groups, suppose that you assigned participants for the two narrative groups from the university swim team. When answering questions about their propensity to exercise, they would be influenced by a shared but concealed variable: They are all athletes who would be predisposed to exercise. Given this violation, it would be impossible to discern whether participants' responses were due to your experimental conditions or to the hidden variable of participation in competitive athletics. Fortunately, this assumption can easily be met by not using intact groups for conditions in a study and, more directly, by using random assignment of participants to groups.

The second assumption of ANOVA is *normality*. Normality means that the scores of the dependent variable for each group are normally distributed. If, for example, the bell curve for the dependent variable was highly positively or negatively skewed, this means that there are outliers that could theoretically influence the results of the analysis. As noted in Chapter 2, you can easily check the normality of your variables through simple descriptive statistics. There are several techniques for normalizing variables, the most common of which is to convert raw values to z scores and performing the analysis on the standardized values rather than the actual values. More important, test studies show that the F value is not overly affected by small or moderate violations of normality.

The final of the "big three" assumptions for ANOVA is *homogeneity of variance*. This assumption is simply that the population variance for each sample/group in your study is relatively equal. In other words, the standard deviation for each group should be approximately the same. Of course, one issue confounds this statement: Your treatment could very well influence the standard deviation through its effect on participants. Suppose that you conducted a two-group experiment testing two teaching approaches, the first of which was a normal lecture and the second of which was a new approach that somehow made it impossible to NOT learn: in short, the perfect teaching approach. Average scores on quizzes in the new teaching method group would be perfect (say, 10 out of 10), and the standard deviation would be zero. The lecture group would have a lower average and a larger standard deviation. In this example, homogeneity of variance is violated because the treatment was so effective that it caused all students to have perfect scores.

All is not lost when homogeneity of variance is violated because after all, we expect some violation to potentially occur because of the treatment. Rather than viewing this assumption as a "meet or not meet" criterion, we should try to determine whether the degree of violation would decrease that credibility of our results. As with the normality assumption, the F ratio holds up well to even moderate violations of homogeneity of variance. There is one type of problematic condition to watch for, however. If the group sizes are unequal and the smaller of the groups has a dramatically larger standard deviation, the Type I error rate can dramatically increase. Your safest approach to preventing violations of homogeneity of variance from adversely affecting your results is to have roughly equal sample sizes across cells in your design. Many of the problems of this kind can be statistically assessed and the impact corrected.

Advanced books, particularly those dealing with meta-analysis, provide various formulas to assess and correct a number of these artifacts.

USING A COMPUTER TO CALCULATE ONEWAY ANOVA

Statistical programs such as SPSS make calculating ONEWAY ANOVAs easy. You must identify at least one dependent variable as well as an independent variable (also referred to as a *factor*). The interface in SPSS allows you to select more than one dependent variable. This should not be confused with MANOVA—the topic of another chapter. In the ONEWAY procedure, the use of multiple dependent variables results in multiple but separate tests—the MANOVA procedure you will learn about later provides you with a simultaneous test of multiple dependent variables.

After you have identified the independent and dependent variables, you should select the Post Hoc button (if you intend to use planned comparisons, consult Chapter 4 of Keppel and Wickens, 2004, or Rosenthal, Rosnow, and Rubin, 2000). When using post hoc tests in SPSS, the program automatically adjusts the significance level for each test to account for an overall alpha level of .05. You will notice that there are tests for "Equal Variance Assumed" and tests for "Equal Variance Not Assumed." You should initially run the tests assuming equal variance (e.g., Scheffé or Tukey); if after observing the output, you notice that the Levine statistic is significant, you should use one of the "Equal Variance Not Assumed" comparisons (e.g., Dunnet's *C*). When you return to the main box for ONEWAY, select the Options button and select the boxes for Descriptives, Homogeneity test, and means plot. The descriptive box will print a table of descriptive statistics divided by group, the homogeneity test will calculate a Levine statistic to determine if variance is homogeneous between groups, and the plot box will provide a graph of results. Click Continue and then OK to perform the analysis.

The results will provide you with four tables of primary interest: the table of descriptive statistics, the Levine test, the ANOVA summary table, and the Tukey multiple comparisons table. Notice that the ANOVA summary table provides you with an actual significance level. Although other ANOVA procedures in SPSS allow you to have an estimate of effect size calculated (partial η^2), the ONEWAY procedure does not—you will need to calculate the η^2 value by hand. The multiple comparisons table places an asterisk by any pairwise combination of means that are significantly different at the .01 level—you will need to use the descriptive statistics table to determine which mean is higher or lower.

INTERPRETING THE RESULTS
OF A SIGNIFICANT ONEWAY

Recall that a significant F ratio only tells you that there are significant differences among the means, not whether particular means are significantly higher or lower than other means. To find out such information, you would need to calculate a planned comparison or conduct a post hoc analysis. Planned comparisons, also called *effects comparisons* or *analytical comparisons,* use theory to generate a model of how particular group means should differ from one another. Though it is possible to calculate such comparisons by hand, we recommend that you use SPSS or some other statistical package to perform such tests.

Although still perhaps informed by theory, post hoc analyses provide a more inductive method of exploring differences among means associated with groups in the independent variable. It is entirely possible that with three means, you will conduct three tests, and only one or two of them will be significant. Or, one group might be different from the other two, and those two are not significantly different from each other. Typically, you would conduct a post hoc comparison for each unique combination of means represented in your independent variable.

Post hoc tests generally take the form of one mean subtracted from another; that difference is then divided by some estimation of the variability. Because there are various assumptions guiding how post hoc tests are used, several different options exist (see Keppel & Wickens, 2004). In most circumstances, the tests converge or reach very similar results, and the choice will not change the outcome. However, you are urged to read and consider various choices because when some conditions are present, the choice does make an enormous difference. For instance, Keppel and Wickens (2004) state, "Tukey's procedure is the simplest way to test the pairwise differences and is the one that is most applicable to any pattern of effects" (p. 124). On the other hand, the Scheffé procedure provides a more conservative adjustment for familywise alpha and therefore provides more protection against Type I error. Our suggestion is that the Tukey test should be used unless there are compelling reasons to need greater Type I protection, in which case the Scheffé procedure should be considered.

Here you will learn about the most commonly used post hoc test, the Tukey test (see Scheffé, 1959). The formula for the Tukey test is

$$\frac{M_1 - M_2}{\sqrt{MS_E \left(\frac{1}{n}\right)}}.$$

In the relationship satisfaction example, you would calculate the Tukey test for the dating and married groups as follows:

$$\frac{90 - 110}{\sqrt{1\left(\frac{1}{3}\right)}} = \frac{-20}{.57} = -35.09.$$

Similar to the omnibus F test, you would need to use a table of critical values for Tukey to determine whether the absolute value of 35.09 is significant—that is, whether the value "beats" the critical value of Tukey at the $p < .05$ level. You can use the absolute value because the ordering of the two groups in the numerator of the formula is arbitrary; thus, the obtained negative value occurred simply because the married group was subtracted from the dating group—the two values could have been reversed, and the same result would be observed. Once you obtain the Tukey value, you should compare it with the critical value—if your observed value meets or exceeds the critical value, the two means are significantly different. In this case, the observed value of 35.09 far exceeds the critical value (the Tukey tables typically do not provide values where the number of people per group is less than five, but we could interpolate that the critical value would be near 5.2 or so). Thus, we could conclude that the married group is significantly higher in relational satisfaction than is the dating group. If you perform the same calculations for the other two possible combinations, you will find that the mean for the dating group is significantly lower than the engaged group and that the married group mean is significantly higher than the engaged group mean (both comparisons involved mean differences of 10 and subsequent Tukey values of 17.42).

One word of caution is warranted regarding post hoc tests. Post hoc tests can be something of a "fishing expedition" and can therefore result in increased risk of Type I error if you have several groups. One approach for solving this inflation of Type I error is to perform a Bonferroni adjustment.

To perform the adjustment, you should divide your desired familywise alpha level (typically .05) by the number of tests that you need to perform. So, if you perform three tests, as is the case in our relationship satisfaction study, you would divide .05 by 3 and assume that your alpha level for each post hoc comparison should be .01 or less to be considered significant. Computer programs such as SPSS allow you to set the alpha level for individual tests—the default is .05. Although some scholars view Bonferroni adjustments as an overly conservative correction (see O'Keefe, 2003), many reviewers require that the adjustments be made to protect against familywise alpha inflation. A nonsignificant F value generally is not subjected to a follow-up test. The assumption of a nonsignificant F value is that no difference exists among the means. Of course, if you have strong theoretical reasons to suspect mean differences, you may want to consider using planned comparisons rather than the omnibus F followed by post hoc tests. A sample write-up for the ONEWAY ANOVA is provided in Figure 4.1.

THE ONEWAY ANOVA IN COMMUNICATION RESEARCH

Kellas, J. K. (2005). Family ties: Communicating identity through jointly told family stories. *Communication Monographs, 72,* 365–389.

Stories are key aspects of family communication because they teach individuals about their identity in a family while also helping to establish and maintain family culture. Stories reflect the norms, values, and goals of a family; as such, they are both reflective and generative. Despite the importance of stories in family communication, little research has explored the act of storytelling in a family. More specifically, little research has examined how joint stories are told by family members and with what effects. Kellas addressed this gap in the research by examining the themes found in storytelling episodes by family members and the ways that families integrate or fragment their identity within the storytelling process.

To specifically illustrate use of the ONEWAY ANOVA, we focus this summary exclusively on Kellas's fourth hypothesis. Previous research has found that storytelling is important for sensemaking, socialization, healing, and identity building. As such, Kellas hypothesized that the content and process of storytelling would be related to various facets of family functioning and overall family satisfaction. And, she is interested in joint storytelling, or times when family members construct stories in a collaborative fashion. As family members add plot elements, elaborate on characters, and generally co-create stories, they provide important insights on the nature of the family relational qualities. The specific hypotheses were as follows:

> Hypothesis 4a: The themes expressed during the joint storytelling of a family story will predict differences in family satisfaction.

> Hypothesis 4b: The themes expressed during the joint storytelling of [a] family identity story will predict differences in (a) family cohesion, (b) family adaptability, and (c) overall family functioning.

Data were obtained from 60 family triads (a college student with two parents or a parent and a sibling); two families were removed from the study because of problems with video recording. Prior to coming to the study site, each participant completed a version of the family relationship questionnaire that included demographic questions and several scales assessing family functioning, cohesion, adaptability, and family satisfaction. After arriving at the research site, family members were asked to tell a family story that others who knew them would have heard before; the stories were recorded. After data were collected, two coders watched the stories and generated seven themes that characterized the content of the stories: accomplishment, fun, tradition/culture, separateness, togetherness, stress, and child mischief.

To test Hypothesis 4, each family's story was coded to represent one of the seven themes identified through open coding. Using the theme type as an independent variable, ONEWAY ANOVAs were run for the following dependent variables: family satisfaction, $F(6, 51) = 2.79$, $p < .05$, $\eta^2 = .25$; family cohesion, $F(6, 51) = 2.35$, $p < .05$, $\eta^2 = .22$; overall family functioning, $F(6, 51) = 2.46$, $p < .05$, $\eta^2 = .22$; and family adaptability, $F(6, 51) = 2.20$, $p = .058$, $\eta^2 = .21$. Because Hypothesis 4 was embedded within a much larger study, a complete listing of means and standard deviations across each theme was not provided. Tukey post hoc test showed significant differences in family satisfaction between families that told stories of accomplishment ($M = 66.88$, $SD = 3.57$) as compared with those telling family stories of stress ($M = 54.85$, $SD = 9.31$, $p < .05$). That same pattern emerged for each of the other dependent variables: family functioning (accomplishment $M = 6.29$, $SD = .70$; stress $M = 4.19$, $SD = 1.59$, $p < .05$), family cohesion functioning (accomplishment $M = 6.43$, $SD = .79$; stress $M = 4.08$, $SD = 1.55$, $p < .05$), and family adaptability functioning (accomplishment $M = 6.14$, $SD = .69$; stress $M = 4.31$, $SD = 1.80$, $p = .07$). The fourth hypothesis was supported.

REFERENCES

Keppel, G., & Wickens, T. D. (2004). *Design and analysis: A researcher's handbook.* Upper Saddle River, NJ: Pearson.

Levine, T. R., & Hullett, C. R. (2002). Eta squared, partial squared, and misreporting of effect size in communication research. *Human Communication Research, 28,* 612–625.

O'Keefe, D. J. (2003). Colloquy: Should familywise alpha be adjusted? *Human Communication Research, 29,* 431–448.

Rosenthal, R., Rosnow, R., & Rubin, D. (2000). *Contrasts in effect sizes in behavioral research.* Cambridge, MA: Harvard University Press.

Scheffé, H. (1959). *The analysis of variance.* New York: John Wiley.

✧ Sample SPSS Printouts ✧

The ONEWAY output is for a test comparing three teaching techniques: reading a chapter, hearing a lecture, and watching a video. The ONEWAY output provides several tables. Although they are presented in the order found in the output, you typically first examine the ANOVA table to determine if significant differences are present. Next, look at the post hoc tests to see which groups differ significantly. The descriptive statistics table tells you the exact means and standard deviations for each group.

Descriptives

value

	N	Mean	Std. Deviation	Std. Error	95% Confidence Interval for Mean		Minimum	Maximum
					Lower Bound	Upper Bound		
Read	5	2.0000	.70711	.31623	1.1220	2.8780	1.00	3.00
Lecture	5	4.0000	1.00000	.44721	2.7583	5.2417	3.00	5.00
Video	5	6.0000	2.23607	1.00000	3.2236	8.7764	3.00	9.00
Total	15	4.0000	2.17124	.56061	2.7976	5.2024	1.00	9.00

Test of Homogeneity of Variances

value

Levene Statistic	df1	df2	Sig.
2.435	2	12	.130

ANOVA

value

	Sum of Squares	df	Mean Square	F	Sig.
Between Groups	40.000	2	20.000	9.231	.004
Within Groups	26.000	12	2.167		
Total	66.000	14			

Multiple Comparisons

Dependent Variable: value

Tukey HSD

(I) group	(J) group	Mean Difference (I-J)	Std. Error	Sig.	95% Confidence Interval	
					Lower Bound	Upper Bound
Read	Lecture	−2.00000	.93095	.122	−4.4836	.4836
	Video	−4.00000*	.93095	.003	−6.4836	−1.5164
Lecture	Read	2.00000	.93095	.122	−.4836	4.4836
	Video	−2.00000	.93095	.122	−4.4836	.4836
Video	Read	4.00000*	.93095	.003	1.5164	6.4836
	Lecture	2.00000	.93095	.122	−.4836	4.4836

*The mean difference is significant at the .05 level.

value

Tukey HSD[a]

group	N	Subset for alpha = .05	
		1	2
Read	5	2.0000	
Lecture	5	4.0000	4.0000
Video	5		6.0000
Sig.		.122	.122

Means for groups in homogeneous subsets are displayed.
a. Uses Harmonic Mean Sample Size = 5.000.

⋈ FIVE ⋈

FACTORIAL ANOVA

Health communication scholars are often interested in promoting healthy behaviors through effective communication campaigns. To determine what campaign messages are most likely to promote healthy behaviors, researchers often create and test the effectiveness of messages before implementing a campaign. In one such instance, Jennifer explored how two variables, message source (peer vs. expert) and message form (factual evidence vs. narratives), influenced college-age students' decisions to engage in daily exercise. Jennifer created four test messages: (a) the expert presenting factual information, (b) the expert presenting narratives, (c) the peer presenting factual information, and (d) the peer presenting narratives. After randomly assigning participants to four groups, each group heard one of the messages. Using the ANOVA procedure, Jennifer was able to determine that there were significant differences between the groups in how likely the participants were to engage in exercise.

In the previous chapter, you learned how the ONEWAY ANOVA could be used to explore differences in a dependent variable between any number of groups associated with one independent variable. Although the ONEWAY is relatively easy to use and interpret, researchers are typically interested in designs involving more than one independent variable. The factorial ANOVA extends the ONEWAY by allowing more than one independent variable to be included.

UNDERSTANDING THE FACTORIAL ANOVA

Factorial analysis of variance, which we will refer to as ANOVA, is a technique that compares values of a continuous dependent variable across various groups associated with two or more independent variables. This procedure is frequently used as part of an experimental design, though it can also be used to analyze differences in groups created by naturally occurring categorical variables. The particular focus of this chapter is on designs with only one dependent variable, usually a posttest only or quasi-experimental/survey design. An investigation using measures at multiple times is considered a repeated-measures design and will be considered in the multivariate chapter.

There are several advantages to using the ANOVA procedure coupled with rigorous experimental designs. In the case of experiments, the ANOVA procedure allows you to examine the effects of different exposure conditions on a particular dependent variable for different samples of individuals. One criterion for good internal validity for experimental design is the initial equivalency of individuals across all experimental conditions (see McNemar, 1960). Random assignment makes it more likely that each group (or sample) exposed to the stimulus is essentially equivalent. Meeting this assumption means that any difference observed is the result of different conditions controlled by the experimenter. Because each group/sample started as essentially the same, any observed difference between the groups is most likely the result of the experimental manipulation. Because controlled experiments coupled with the ANOVA procedure allow you to isolate the effects of independent variables, this technique is particularly effective when causal conclusions are desired.

In addition to allowing for causal reasoning, the ANOVA design permits very detailed analysis of both individual independent variables as well as interactions among independent variables. In the opening example for this chapter, Jennifer would be able to determine the unique effects of both independent variables—source and message form. In addition, she would be able to determine how, if at all, message source and message form interact to influence students' decisions to exercise. These same effects can also be explored for situations in which causal reasoning is not the objective. For example, you could use the factorial ANOVA to determine the main and interaction effects of sex (i.e., male vs. female) and year in school (i.e., freshman, sophomore, etc.) on individuals' time spent text messaging. The steps in calculating an ANOVA are summarized in Figure 5.1.

1. Enter data so that each participant is coded for the condition he or she was in for each categorical independent variable followed with his or her score on the dependent variable.

2. Calculate the overall mean, the mean associated with each level of each independent variable, and means associated with each combination of independent variables in your design.

3. Calculate the sums of squares using Formulas 5.1, 5.2, and 5.3.

4. Calculate the degrees of freedom using Formula 5.4.

5. Calculate mean squares by dividing the sums of squares by the associated degrees of freedom.

6. Calculate the F ratio by dividing the MS of the effect by the MS of the error.

7. Compare the resulting F value to a table of critical F values to determine if it is significant.

8. Calculate the effect size for each effect using Formula 5.5.

9. Perform post hoc tests or planned comparisons as necessary and write up results.

Figure 5.1   Steps in the Factorial Analysis of Variance

Consider the various combinations of possible outcomes from the exercise message design experiment. This design should permit the comparison of experts and peers; in ANOVA, this would be called Factor A. The second variable, factual versus narrative messages, would be called Factor B. The term *factor* in this instance is synonymous with *independent variable,* and the designation of Factor A or Factor B to any particular variable is arbitrary. That is, either variable could be Factor A or Factor B, and the results would not change. The isolated effects of each factor are called main effects in factorial designs. Main effects are simply the comparison of the two means associated with each level of Factor A (e.g., the mean for all students viewing an expert compared with all students viewing a peer) and, separately, the two means associated with Factor B (e.g., the mean for all students hearing factual messages compared with all students hearing narrative messages).

Although testing for main effects can answer a number of theoretical questions, the ANOVA procedure is also used to test for interaction effects. For instance, the procedure permits the comparison of the four means created through the combinations of message form and source (experts using factual messages, peers using factual messages, experts using narrative, and peers using narrative). In this case, the interaction effect is fixed, which means that the combination of two variables can be examined as it affects values of the dependent variable—this is what is referred to as an interaction effect.

Hopefully, you noticed that the ANOVA procedure has a somewhat unique set of terms to describe various elements of the procedure. For instance, you noticed that independent variables are often referred to as factors. Students new to more advanced procedures often confuse factors in ANOVA with factors created from a survey through exploratory or confirmatory factor analyses. There is some conceptual similarity—both uses of the term *factor* are referring to variables. The difference is that in ANOVA, the variables/factors are typically chosen by the researcher, whereas with surveys, the term usually refers to groups of questions that form specific variables. In addition, researchers often use simple notations to describe a factorial design. For instance, when talking about an experiment, the researcher might refer to a two-way, three-way, or four-way ANOVA—the numbers in these phrases simply tells you the number of independent variables (i.e., factors) in the design. Jennifer's study was a two-way ANOVA because it had two factors/independent variables. By the way, a ONEWAY ANOVA is called "ONEWAY" because it has only one factor in the design.

A final piece of shorthand often found in reference to ANOVA designs is when researchers use actual numbers to represent both the number of factors and the number of levels within each factor: for example, a 2×2 ANOVA, a 3×2 ANOVA, or a $3 \times 2 \times 4$ ANOVA. The description provides two important pieces of information about the ANOVA design. Counting the numbers will tell you how many variables are being used: 2×2 and 3×2 indicate a two-way ANOVA, and the $3 \times 2 \times 4$ ANOVA indicates the use of three variables. The actual numbers tell you how many groups or treatments are associated with each variable. A 2×2 ANOVA indicates two variables, each with two levels. A 3×2 ANOVA indicates two variables where one variable has three levels and the other has two. A $3 \times 2 \times 4$ ANOVA indicates three variables with three levels for the first, two for the second, and four for the last. By levels, we simply mean the number of treatments. In Jennifer's 2×2 study, she had two variables, each with two treatments or levels. An item to note is that you can multiply the levels and figure out the number of cells (or separate combinations of treatments in the analysis). A 2×2 ANOVA has 4 groups, a 3×2 ANOVA has 6 groups, and a $3 \times 2 \times 4$ ANOVA has 24 groups.

CALCULATING A FACTORIAL ANOVA

This section acquaints you with the process of calculating an ANOVA for a two-way design. The following example is based on Jennifer's exercise message study described previously. Understanding how various calculations occur will help you "read" the computer output intelligently. Consider the following data set for Jennifer's study. The numbers in the table represent how likely each participant is to engage in daily exercise—in this study, there are 12 participants. Higher values suggest that the participant is more likely to exercise daily.

Message Form	Source Expert	Peer
Factual	23	35
	25	38
	27	32
Narrative	41	50
	45	55
	19	60

When you calculate an ANOVA, you actually are calculating statistics for each main and interaction effect. To begin, you must obtain means, or averages, for each level of each variable as well as averages for each combination of levels.

Calculate the Grand Mean = 40 (mean of all scores)

Mean for all Factual = 30

Mean for all Narrative = 50

Mean for all Expert = 35

Mean for all Peer = 45

Mean for all Expert/Factual = 25

Mean for all Expert/Narrative = 45

Mean for all Peer/Factual = 35

Mean for all Peer/Narrative = 55

Using these means, you are able to begin calculating values that will be used in the ANOVA summary table. First use the sum of each score minus the mean squared to calculate the total sum of squares (see Formula 5.1).

$$SS_T = \Sigma\,(X - M)^2. \tag{5.1}$$

Or

$(23 - 40)^2$	289
$(25 - 40)^2$	225
$(27 - 40)^2$	169
$(32 - 40)^2$	64
$(35 - 40)^2$	25
$(38 - 40)^2$	4
$(41 - 40)^2$	1
$(45 - 40)^2$	25
$(49 - 40)^2$	81
$(50 - 40)^2$	100
$(55 - 40)^2$	225
$(60 - 40)^2$	400
Total SS =	1,608

The second step is to calculate the SS for Factors A (message form) and B (source) using Formula 5.2. Using this formula, you take the mean for each level of the variable and subtract the grand mean, square that, and then multiply by the sample size of that group. You repeat this calculation for each main effect.

$$SS_A = \Sigma\,(M_A - M_G)^2 * n. \tag{5.2}$$

For Factor A, message type, this formula results in the following:

$$SS_A = \quad (30 - 40)^2 * 6 \qquad 600 \qquad \text{Factual mean}$$

$$(50 - 40)^2 * 6 \qquad \underline{600} \qquad \text{Narrative mean}$$

$$1{,}200$$

The process is repeated for the next variable, type of source, or Factor B:

$$SS_B = \quad (35 - 40)^2 * 6 \qquad 150 \qquad \text{Expert}$$

$$(45 - 40)^2 * 6 \qquad \underline{150} \qquad \text{Peer}$$

$$300$$

The third step is to calculate the *SS* due to individual differences, or the error term, as more popularly called. Using Formula 5.3, you subtract each score from the mean for that cell and square the result. Once you do this for each score in the cell, you add the results to arrive at the overall error sums of squares.

$$SS_E = \Sigma\Sigma\ (X - M_{AB})^2. \tag{5.3}$$

In Jennifer's study, the following calculations were done; the total error sums of squares is determined by adding $8 + 32 + 18 + 50 = 108$.

The Expert/Factual		The Expert/Narrative	
$(23 - 25)^2$	4	$(41 - 45)^2$	16
$(25 - 25)^2$	0	$(45 - 45)^2$	0
$(27 - 25)^2$	4	$(49 - 45)^2$	16
	8		32

The Peer/Factual		The Peer/Narrative	
$(32 - 35)^2$	9	$(50 - 55)^2$	25
$(35 - 35)^2$	0	$(55 - 55)^2$	0
$(38 - 35)^2$	9	$(60 - 55)^2$	25
	18		50

The fourth step is to calculate the effect for the interaction, which is done by taking the SS_T and subtracting out all the other effects: $1,608 - 1,200 - 300 - 108$ or zero for $SS_{A \times B}$.

Once you have calculated the various sums of squares, the final steps are relatively easy. The df is calculated using the following formulas:

Total df: Total number of participants $- 1$.

Main effect df: Number of groups $- 1$.

Interaction df: Multiply the df for each factor together.

Error df: Total df – all main effect df – interaction df.   (5.4)

The mean square is the SS divided by the df; for A, this is $1,200/1$ or $1,200$. The F ratio is the MS of the effect divided by the MS of the error. For Factor A, the MS is $1,200/13.5$ or $F = 88.88$. The resulting F value should be compared to a table of critical F values to determine if it is significant at the .05 level. These calculations result in the following:

Effect	SS	df	MS	F	η^2
A	1,200	1	1,200	88.88	.75
B	300	1	300	22.22	.19
A × B	0	1	0	0.00	.00
Error	108	8	13.5		
Total	1,608	11			

Notice that the headings in the table are the same as for the ONEWAY ANOVA. The difference is the number of rows. The last column, labeled η^2, shows the effect size for each effect. The η^2 estimate is calculated using Formula 5.5. We will warn you here and later that you should calculate η^2 by hand, even if you use SPSS to do your factorial ANOVA. The reason for this is that SPSS provides an estimate of partial η^2, which is not ideal for reporting purposes (see Levine & Hullett, 2002).

$$\eta^2 = \frac{SS_{effect}}{SS_{total}}.$$ (5.5)

Once you have created the ANOVA summary table, the write-up of results is relatively straightforward. Typically, ANOVA results report the F value for each effect—in this case, both of the main effects and the interaction effect. In addition, degrees of freedom, significance levels, and effect size estimates are reported.

ASSUMPTIONS OF FACTORIAL ANOVA

Chapter 4 discussed the "big three" assumptions present in all ANOVA designs—independence, normality, and homogeneity of variance. Those assumptions apply to the factorial ANOVA in the same way—there are no unique additional assumptions.

USING COMPUTER PROGRAMS
TO CALCULATE FACTORIAL ANOVAS

Statistical programs are commonly used to calculate ANOVA procedures because the size of most data sets makes hand calculation impractical. To use computer programs like SPSS, you will typically need to identify the independent and dependent variables and select certain options to make the interpretation and write-up easier. In the example study used for this chapter, message form and message source would be entered as fixed factors in the design, and propensity to exercise would be entered as the dependent variable. Under the Options button, you can select the option to have descriptive statistics reported. This option is important because it will give you the overall mean and standard deviation as well as those statistics for each main effect and each cell in the design. Such statistics are commonly reported in a table, whereas the actual F values are reported in the text of the manuscript.

You can ask SPSS to provide post hoc tests to examine significant main effects—the interpretation of these tests is identical in both ONEWAY and factorial ANOVA. To interpret significant interaction effects, you must ask for simple effects comparisons. Unfortunately, there are no ways to accomplish this using dialogue boxes in SPSS—you must add a line to the syntax. Once you have selected all other necessary options, press "Paste" rather than "Run" in the main dialogue box. Once the syntax has opened, insert the bold-faced command in Figure 5.2.

```
UNIANOVA

    exercise BY source evidence

    /METHOD = SSTYPE(3)

    /INTERCEPT = INCLUDE

    /PRINT = DESCRIPTIVE

    /CRITERIA = ALPHA(.05)

    /emmeans=Tables (source by evidence) compare (evidence)

    /DESIGN = source evidence source*evidence
```

Figure 5.2   Command Syntax for Factorial ANOVA With Simple Effects Tests

The EMMEANS command directs SPSS to calculate simple effects comparisons between all levels of the source variable separately for each level of the evidence variable. Such information will allow you to draw conclusions about whether the effects of evidence type differ depending on whether a peer or a celebrity is presenting the message. This approach, although requiring basic knowledge of syntax, is preferable to the method advocated by Ho (2006), who suggests that each group in the design be recoded into a single variable and analyzed in the ONEWAY procedure using standard post hoc tests (see pp. 63–64).

INTERPRETING THE RESULTS
OF A SIGNIFICANT ANOVA

The interpretation of a factorial ANOVA is essentially the same as for the ONEWAY procedure in the sense that a significant F value indicates significant differences between means. Researchers typically refer to this as omnibus F. If there are only two groups or means, you can simply examine the means and determine the nature of the difference (as is the case with t tests). When more than two groups are involved, post hoc tests must be used (as in ONEWAY). This process of interpretation extends naturally to a factorial design where more than two independent variables are present. Figure 5.3 provides an example write-up with explanation.

"The ANOVA resulted in a significant main effect for mode, $F = 88.88$ (1, 8), $p < .05$, $\eta^2 = .75$, as well as a significant main effect for source, $F = 22.22$ (1, 8), $p < .05$, $\eta^2 = .19$. The interaction term was not significant."

$F = 88.88$	This is the actual F value you obtained from the ratio of the mean squares effect divided by the mean squares error.
(1, 8)	The values in parentheses show the degrees of freedom for both the effect/between group (1) and error/within group (8).
$p < .05$	The significance or probability level is governed by convention in the social sciences. In this case, there is less than a 5% chance of obtaining an F value this large by mere chance rather than some actual effect.
$\eta^2 = .75$	The eta squared estimate of effect size is reported using the Greek symbol for eta.

Figure 5.3   Deciphering the Write-Up of Factorial ANOVA

NOTE: The second main effect is interpreted in the same way. If the interaction term was significant, a third set of values would be reported and, in many cases, are reported even if not significant.

In 2×2 designs, interpretation of effects is relatively easy. If a significant F ratio is observed for a main effect, you can compare the means associated with that effect and see which mean is higher than the other—in this instance, the main effect F tells you that the two means are significantly different from one another and is basically the same as a t test. If you have a significant interaction effect, you can compare the levels of one variable at each level of the other to determine which are larger. More advanced factorial designs (e.g., 2×3, 3×3) require additional steps.

Main effects involving factors with three or more levels require post hoc tests to be calculated. These post hoc tests are interpreted in the same way as in ONEWAY because for main effects, only one variable is being analyzed. When significant interactions are observed, you must explore more specific effects. A significant interaction effect suggests that the main effect, even if significant, conceals much of what is happening in the model. Thus, to obtain a complete "story" of what is happening, you must go beyond the main effects and look at combinations of both variables simultaneously. In essence, you must tell SPSS to provide post hoc tests probing the simple effects present when you compare specific cells in the design against one another. For instance, you might want to know if a celebrity using narrative evidence is as effective at promoting exercise behavior among college students as is a peer using testimony from experts. Simple effects tests basically allow you to test whether the effects of one factor differ within various levels of another factor. Recall from Chapter 4 that when using either planned comparisons or post hoc tests, you should consider the need to adjust alpha levels to compensate for running multiple tests at the .05 level of significance and thus inflating the overall Type I error rate.

In addition to calculating simple effects, you should also plot interaction effects on a graph. By using separate lines for one variable and separate spots on the horizontal axis for the other variable, you can depict how the means for various groups can be plotted for the dependent variable (on the vertical axis). The interaction graph shown in Figure 5.4 shows how students score on a quiz depending on whether the teacher uses PowerPoint or not and whether the teacher cues students to take notes or not. As you can see, the effects of PowerPoint differed depending on whether the teacher used note-taking cues: In the no-cues condition, there was little effect for PowerPoint. However, in the cues condition, the use of PowerPoint had a substantial effect. The graph, coupled with simple effects tests, provides a robust explanation for significant interactions.

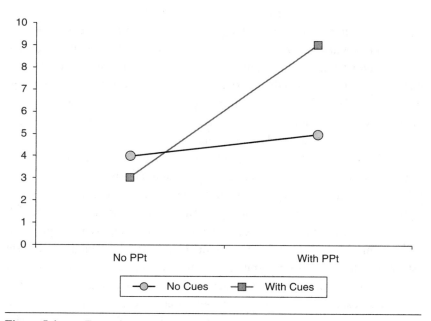

Figure 5.4   Example Interaction Graph

THE FACTORIAL ANOVA
IN COMMUNICATION RESEARCH

Kang, Y., Capella, J., & Fishbein, M. (2006). The attentional mechanism of message sensation value: Interaction between message sensation value and argument quality on message effectiveness. *Communication Monographs, 73,* 351–378.

Persuasion research has traditionally drawn a distinction between the content and format of persuasive messages. Message content refers to the topics, themes, and other substantive elements of the message, whereas format is the way in which those content features are presented. For example, a public service announcement (PSA) might use narratives to discuss the need to protect against sexually transmitted diseases (content) while making use of dramatic camera techniques to promote identification with the person telling the narrative (format). Generally speaking, persuasion scholars are interested both in the main effects of message content and message format as well as the interaction between the two.

Following this tradition of research, Kang and colleagues explored the persuasiveness of message content and message format in public service announcements aimed at preventing drug use (marijuana) among teenagers. Specifically, the study explored one message content element, argument quality, and one message format feature, message sensation value (MSV). Argument quality simply refers to a well-constructed message to which the listener is likely to respond favorably. Using elaboration likelihood theory, Kang and colleagues reason that when listeners are called to process messages on a deep rather than superficial level, arguments higher in quality will be more likely to have positive effects.

Message sensation value refers to features of a message that elicit sensory, affective, and aroused responses from listeners. Various MSV features include both video (e.g., cuts, edits, and special effects) and audio (e.g., music, sound effects, and voiceovers) as well as content format features (e.g., talking head vs. acting out, a surprise ending). Based on the theory behind MSV, those messages that include such elements should heighten attention. However, previous research exploring the effects of MSV features has been inconclusive: Whereas effects have been observed for specific elements of MSV individually (e.g., edits, visual graphics, and emotionally intense messages), data about the composite effects of MSV features are limited.

Kang and colleagues use two theories to make predictions about the interaction between MSV and argument quality. First, the activation model of information exposure suggests that high MSV messages should heighten

attention; in conditions of heightened attention, people will process information on a deeper level, and the effects of argument quality should be greater. In
low MSV conditions, people are expected to give less attention to the message
and will more likely use peripheral processing, in which case, the effects of
argument quality could be natural or even possibly reversed.

> Hypothesis 1: MSV interacts with argument quality on ad effectiveness, such
> that strong arguments are more effective than weak arguments for high MSV
> ads, whereas weak arguments are equally or more effective than strong argu-
> ments in low MSV ads.

A competing explanation stems from elaboration likelihood theory,
which suggests that MSV features might require a larger amount of cognitive
resources. Thus, messages high in MSV might overwhelm listeners and cause
them to process messages more superficially, in which case lower argument
quality would be more effective. Alternatively, messages low in MSV would
require fewer cognitive resources for processing; hence, the needs for high-
quality arguments might be higher.

> Hypothesis 2: MSV interacts with argument quality on ad effectiveness, such
> that strong arguments are more effective than weak arguments for low MSV
> ads, whereas weak arguments are equally or more effective than strong argu-
> ments for high MSV ads.

If you compare Hypotheses 1 and 2, you will notice that they are mutually
exclusive. Both predict an interaction effect, yet the nature of the interaction is
opposite for the two hypotheses.

The study was conducted using secondary data obtained from an antidrug
PSA archive housed at the Annenberg School at the University of Pennsylvania.
Three types of responses were analyzed in the study: adolescents' perceptions
of the ad's effectiveness, liking, and positive/negative thoughts about the ads.
In addition, data were obtained for each ad to categorize its argument effectiveness (high vs. low); trained coders were also used to assess the MSV for
each ad (high vs. low). A total of 601 adolescents rated the effectiveness of the
ads. The respondents were not randomly assigned to conditions because of the
procedures used to collect the initial data; thus, the study should be considered
nonexperimental, and causal conclusions are not justified.

The 2×2 (low vs. high argument quality by low vs. high MSV) resulted
in a significant interaction for one of the three dependent variables. The

interaction was significant for positive versus negative thought valence, $F(1, 56) = 7.00$, $p = .01$, partial $\eta^2 = .11$, but not for perceived ad effectiveness $F(1, 56) = 2.90$, $p = .09$, partial $\eta^2 = .09$, or for liking, $F(1, 56) = 3.94$, $p = .06$, partial $\eta^2 = .06$. Across all three interactions, a similar pattern was observed: Ad effectiveness was lower in high MSV conditions and low argument quality conditions. Conversely, as MSV decreased and argument quality increased, ad effectiveness increased. Interaction graphs are presented in Figures 5.5 to 5.7 for each interaction. The pattern of results is more consistent with the elaboration likelihood theory represented in Hypothesis 2.

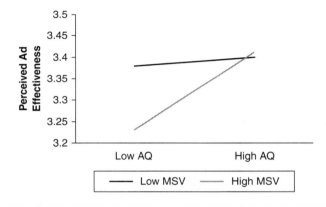

Figure 5.5   Interaction Between MSV and Argument Quality for Perceived Ad Effectiveness

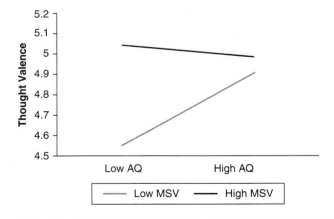

Figure 5.6   Interaction Between MSV and Argument Quality for Ad Liking

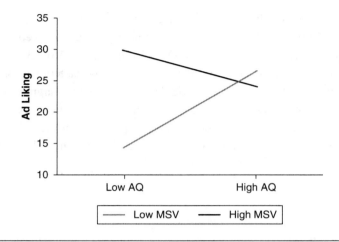

Figure 5.7   Interaction Between MSV and Argument Quality for Thought
                   Valence

REFERENCES

Ho, R. (2006). *Handbook of univariate and multivariate data analysis and interpreta-
    tion with SPSS.* Boca Raton, FL: Chapman & Hall.
Levine, T. R., & Hullett, C. R. (2002). Eta squared, partial squared, and misreporting
    of effect size in communication research. *Human Communication Research, 28,*
    612–626.
McNemar, Q. (1960). *Psychological statistics* (4th ed.). New York: John Wiley.

◈ Sample SPSS Printouts ◈

Sample output is provided for a study comparing relationship satisfaction (called RELSAT) for people in one of two relationship types (romantic or friendship) and who primarily use one of three message design logics (conventional, instrumental, and rhetorical). The study was a 2 × 3 design. The first box shows the SPSS syntax with the EMMEANS command inserted (recall that this must be manually inserted to test simple effects in higher order interactions). That command is in bold to highlight the syntax; bold is not necessary in SPSS.

```
UNIANOVA
    relsat  BY rel mesdes
    /METHOD = SSTYPE(3)
    /INTERCEPT = INCLUDE
    /PLOT = PROFILE( mesdes*rel )
    /EMMEANS = TABLES (rel by mesdes) compare (rel)
    /PRINT = DESCRIPTIVE HOMOGENEITY
    /CRITERIA = ALPHA(.05)
    /DESIGN = rel mesdes rel*mesdes .
```

Descriptive Statistics

Dependent Variable: relsat

rel	mesdes	Mean	Std. Deviation	N
Friendship	Conventional	2.716	1.37021	25
	Instrumental	4.8413	1.10971	23
	Rhetorical	3.1165	1.00811	23
	Total	3.4482	1.53772	71
Romantic	Conventional	2.8492	1.10199	25
	Instrumental	7.8067	.97924	24
	Rhetorical	4.0738	1.08538	24
	Total	4.8816	2.36458	73
Total	Conventional	2.6604	1.24529	50
	Instrumental	6.3555	1.82031	47
	Rhetorical	3.6053	1.14412	47
	Total	4.1749	2.11893	144

Levene's Test of Equality of Error Variances[a]

Dependent Variable: relsat

F	df1	df2	Sig.
1.315	5	138	.261

Tests the null hypothesis that the error variance of the dependent variable is equal across groups.

a. Design: Intercept+rel+mesdes+rel * mesdes

Test of Between-Subjects Effects

Dependent Variable: relsat

Source	Type III Sum of Squares	df	Mean Squares	F	Sig.
Corrected Model	469.245[a]	5	93.849	74.947	.000
Intercept	2528.978	1	2528.978	2019.611	.000
rel	73.881	1	73.881	59.000	.000
mesdes	347.423	2	173.711	138.724	.000
rel * rnesdes	44.143	2	22.071	17.626	.000
Error	172.805	138	1.252		
Total	3151.893	144			
Corrected Total	642.050	143			

a. R Squared = .731 (Adjusted R Squared = .721)

Pairwise Comparisons

Dependent Variable: relsat

mesdes	(I)rel	(J)rel	Mean Difference (I-J)	Std. Error	Sig.[a]	95% Confidence Interval for Difference[a]	
						Lower Bound	Upper Bound
Conventional	Friendship	Romantic	−.378	.317	.235	−1.003	.248
	Romantic	Friendship	.378	.317	.235	−.248	1.003
Instrumental	Friendship	Romantic	−2.965*	.327	.000	−3.611	−2.320
	Romantic	Friendship	2.965*	.327	.000	2.320	3.611
Rhetorical	Friendship	Romantic	−.957*	.327	.004	−1.603	−.312
	Romantic	Friendship	.957*	.327	.004	.312	1.603

Based on estimated marginal means

*. The mean difference is significant at the .05 level.

a. Adjustment for multiple comparisons: Least Significant Difference (equivalent to no adjustments).

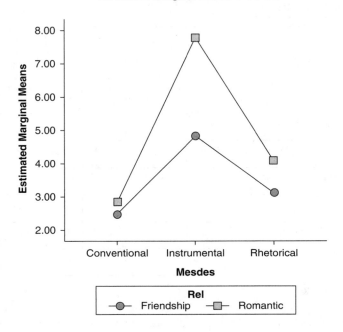

Estimated Marginal Means of RELSAT

⊰ SIX ⊱

ANALYSIS OF COVARIANCE

———•◆•———

A group of health communication researchers wanted to test the effectiveness of three types of public service announcements (PSAs) designed to reduce high-risk drinking behavior among college students. They designed an experiment with a control group and three experimental groups—one experimental group for each of the public service messages. To determine the effects of the PSAs, participants were asked to record how many drinks they had for 1 week after the experiment. The problem facing the researchers is that some students in the study were heavy drinkers and others avoided drinking at all. Although the students were randomly assigned to the various conditions, the differences in drinking habits prior to the study essentially created within-group variance that would make it more difficult to observe significant differences between the groups. To overcome this problem, the researchers used the number of drinks each student had during the week preceding the experiment as a covariate. By taking the covariate into account, the ensuing analysis of postexperiment drinks would be more precise.

The analysis of covariance (ANCOVA) is an extension of the ONEWAY or factorial ANOVA discussed in other chapters. Although more complex, interpretation of ANCOVA results is basically similar to other types of ANOVA procedures. What makes ANCOVA unique is that it attempts to reduce error variance by controlling for variance associated with a covariate, or what is also generally referred to as a concomitant variable. As you will learn, the ANCOVA procedure can provide important advantages if used appropriately. Specifically, the procedure allows you to increase precision and power, thereby reducing the risk of Type II error. Unfortunately, misapplication of the procedure can lead to faulty conclusions; accordingly, you will learn appropriate ways to use the procedure as well as approaches to avoid.

Unlike other chapters, this one will not contain calculation examples because there are many different applications of this procedure, and space does not permit a complete consideration of a sufficient number of examples to provide adequate understanding of the technique. You should consult Pedhazur (1997) for examples of the many different applications of this technique as well as an extensive discussion of the value and limitations of the procedure. This chapter will focus on the conceptual reasons for using ANCOVA and approaches for interpreting output.

UNDERSTANDING THE ANALYSIS OF COVARIANCE

When conducting experiments, researchers are often interested in controlling for extraneous variables. In fact, the key to designing effective experiments is finding ways to reduce or eliminate the potential effects of any variable not part of the study—this type of control is called experimental control and is essential for making any type of causal claim based on the results of the experiment. A second type of control is statistical control. Statistical control is where you identify and account for extraneous variables. While statistical control cannot necessarily help you make causal arguments, statistical control can help you account for what would normally be error variance, thus reducing the chance of Type II error. This chapter focuses on two issues: (a) how you can use ANCOVA to obtain statistical control and (b) why you should not use ANOVA to compensate for a lack of experimental control.

ANCOVA is appropriate to use when another variable, called a *covariate,* is part of the theoretical model but not explicitly identified as an independent variable. A covariate is any continuous variable hypothesized to have a direct relationship with the dependent variable—an ANCOVA design can include more than one covariate. Analysis of covariance is a form of analysis of variance that tests for significant differences between means by adjusting or controlling for initial differences in the data due to some other variable.

Although using ANCOVA to correct for nonrandom assignment (we discuss this inappropriate use of the procedure later in this section) is an inappropriate use of the procedure, there are other instances when ANCOVA is justified. Even when participants are randomly assigned to conditions, an analysis of covariance can be employed to parcel out the effects of some extraneous variable so that a more precise estimate of the independent variables' effects can be analyzed. In other words, because random assignment of individuals to groups leaves open the impact of naturally occurring variables (e.g., reading ability, verbal ability, communication apprehension, tolerance for ambiguity), you may want to control for the effects of those variables before testing hypothesized relationships. The steps for performing an analysis of covariance are summarized in Figure 6.1.

The key to appropriately using ANCOVA is identifying meaningful covariates to include in the analysis. Some covariates become identified on the basis of past research demonstrating the existence of some kind of association. For example, suppose from past research we know that age is related to perspective taking such that older children demonstrate greater ability to take the perspective of another person. If we are comparing two groups and the average age of one group is older than another, any result demonstrating a difference between the two groups using a dependent measure of perspective taking could have stemmed from this other known relationship rather than our treatment. The reason for this is that the difference in perspective taking between groups

---

1. Use literature and/or well-reasoned hunches to identify covariates that should have meaningful relationships with the dependent variable but not the independent variable. Collect data on the covariate prior to conducting the experiment.

2. Enter data so that each participant is coded for the condition he or she was in for each categorical independent variable followed with his or her score on the covariate(s) and dependent variable.

3. Test for the "big three" assumptions as well as assumptions unique to ANCOVA. Make corrections if necessary.

4. Calculate the overall mean, the mean associated with each level of each independent variable, and means associated with each combination of independent variables in your design, adjusting or controlling for values of the covariate.

5. After entering the covariate(s) into the model, perform, interpret, and write up the analysis using the same procedures that you would use for an ANOVA.

Figure 6.1   Steps in the Analysis of Covariance

can be the result not of the feature of interest (or an experimental manipulation or intervention) but instead be generated on the basis of the difference in age between the groups. Under these conditions, the use of a covariate analysis is warranted because one can adjust the means of the two groups on the basis of the difference in age as it relates to perspective taking. By removing the influence of age in the analysis, comparison of the adjusted means provides a test of the data where the groups are equivalent on the covariate. The resulting test is both more precise and more powerful.

Engaged Research

Assume that you and your classmates are conducting an experiment testing the effects of negative political advertising. You are specifically interested in the effects of two independent variables, positive versus negative ads and sex of the participant, on favorability ratings for the candidate sponsoring the ad. As you prepare the experiment, you should consider what other variables should be taken into consideration as covariates in this design. Using your own understanding of the issues as well as any research material that you have available, list at least five potential covariates that you could reasonably include in the study.

For another example, suppose we wish to examine whether students perform differently on speeches depending on whether the teacher uses primarily lecture, peer workshops, or discussion-based teaching strategies. Naturally, there should be differences in speech grades depending on how the teacher approaches the class. However, there is also a likely relationship between speech grades and public speaking anxiety; the more anxious a person is about speaking, the more likely that person is to score lower on speech grades. If you want to assess the effects of teaching approaches on speech grades, you probably need to account for students' public speaking anxiety. The ANCOVA provides a technique of examining and removing (or accounting for) the influence of one or more variables (e.g., public speaking anxiety) that would affect an estimation of the relationship between other variables (e.g., teaching strategies and speech grades). Of course, in this design, you would need to find a way to randomly assign students to classes, which could easily be done at the beginning of a term if multiple sections were scheduled at the same time.

The term *covariate* is often referred to as a "control" variable because the analysis is conducted after accounting for the effects of the covariate on the dependent variable. The ANCOVA procedure provides the basis of removing pretreatment variation (as measured by the covariate) prior to the testing of the differences caused by the treatment. The conceptual process of using ANCOVA to control the effects of a covariate is illustrated by the Venn diagram in Figure 6.2. The analysis and interpretation essentially proceed very similar to the standard ANOVA procedures in terms of the *F* test and post hoc analysis for comparing means. The only difference is that the means (and the variance) have been adjusted on the basis of the covariate.

One use of ANCOVA, though not recommended, is to adjust for nonrandom assignment of participants to groups. Participants are normally randomly assigned to conditions in experiments. The process of random assignment provides a basis for believing that the different experimental groups are equivalent. The equivalency in the groups becomes the justification for arguing that any observed difference in the dependent variable reflects an outcome caused by the differences in experimental stimulus. When random assignment is not possible, some researchers attempt to substitute statistical control for experimental control.

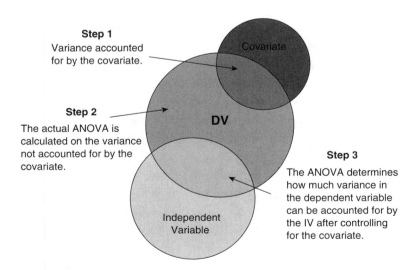

Step 1
Variance accounted for by the covariate.

Step 2
The actual ANOVA is calculated on the variance not accounted for by the covariate.

Covariate

DV

Step 3
The ANOVA determines how much variance in the dependent variable can be accounted for by the IV after controlling for the covariate.

Independent Variable

Figure 6.2   A Venn Diagram of ANCOVA

Suppose a researcher wants to compare the impact of a learning module in an interpersonal communication class. Specifically, the experiment investigates whether the use of a Student Response System (clickers) in a 300-person mass lecture class improves students' grades on exams. Clickers are handheld devices that students use to answer questions shown on a PowerPoint slide; students' responses are recorded by the computer, and a summary of those responses is displayed in a PowerPoint graph. The collective set of responses is displayed and can serve as a focal point for discussion by the instructor. Clickers provide a means of active participation and method for recording attendance. However, the system is relatively expensive when considering the cost for the equipment, software, and the purchase of the clickers. The investigator is interested in examining whether the use of clickers affects the scores of the midterm or final exam. The mass lecture occurs at 9 a.m. and 11 a.m. on Monday. The design is relatively simple: 9 a.m. students use the clickers, and the 11 a.m. students do not. Do students in a section that employs the technology score better on standardized tests or not?

The question is whether any difference in the dependent variable reflects a difference due to employing clickers (the manipulation between the groups) or some other difference between the groups. The use of a 9 a.m. and 11 a.m. mass lecture requires the use of existing intact groups as part of the investigation. The assignment to particular sections is not random but represents very much a self-selection as well as other institutional and potentially systematic factors. For example, suppose upper classes register first; the sections may differ based on the number of seniors and juniors. Theoretically, seniors and juniors should be scoring better than sophomores because of experience, knowledge, and the fact that dropouts would generally have lower grades. What this means is that any difference between the two groups in this variable may affect the difference in the means between the two groups. The remedy is to adjust the means for equivalency prior to conducting the various tests. Unfortunately, the correction offered by the ANCOVA procedure cannot statistically "fix" a deficient design. Although you may be able to find ways to statistically control some aspects of the intact groups, you will not be able to control for all potential intervening variables created by the lack of experimental control—you will not be able to make causal arguments regardless of whether you identify and statistically control for any number of covariates.

ASSUMPTIONS OF ANCOVA

Like the ONEWAY and factorial ANOVA, the ANCOVA procedure assumes that there is a normal distribution of values on the dependent variable, that there is independence between groups, and that there is homogeneity in the variance between groups. Strategies for preventing, identifying, and correcting for violations of these assumptions work the same way in ANCOVA as they do in other ANOVA procedures. In addition to the "big three" assumptions, ANCOVA has two additional assumptions: homogeneity of regression and a linear relationship between the covariate and the dependent variable.

First, you should think of the covariate as having a quantifiable statistical relationship with the dependent variable (DV) in the analysis (in Chapter 10, you will learn about a regression coefficient called *beta weights,* which are used to quantify such relationships). If you were to calculate the statistics describing the covariate-DV relationship for each group in the study, homogeneity of regression assumes that each value will be approximately equal. Or, more simply stated, the relationship between the covariate and the dependent variable should remain roughly similar from one group to the next. So long as the group sizes are roughly equal, the ANCOVA is robust even when this assumption is violated. However, violating this assumption raises potentially interesting possibilities.

To test for homogeneity of regression, you should calculate an ANOVA using the independent variables in the study but substituting the covariate for the dependent variable. If the resulting F tests are significant, the homogeneity of regression assumption is violated. If the relationship between the covariate and dependent variable changes from one condition to the next, this raises a possibility that some interaction is occurring between the covariate and the independent variable(s) in terms of values for the dependent variable. That being the case, you should create groups from your covariate and include them as a part new blocking variable in the analysis so that you can further explore and account for the interaction (we discuss "blocking" in more depth later).

Second, most ANCOVA techniques assume linear relations and fail to provide adequate analysis for nonlinearity, extrapolation, differential growth, or problems of measurement error. The problem is that most covariate procedures do not provide a means of assessment for any of these possibilities and, should they occur, provide the potential for misleading results in terms of both magnitude and direction. Great care must be taken and stress placed on whether any of these possibilities exist as well as any means to assess the existence of these problems. Using scatterplots or actual nonlinear tests can help you determine whether the linearity assumption was met. If the assumption is violated, you should use the regression procedure to perform the analysis using a nonlinear term for the covariate and effect coding for the independent variable(s).

INTERPRETING RESULTS OF ANCOVA

Because the ANCOVA is basically an ANOVA with covariates added, the procedures for calculating and interpreting analyses remain essentially the same. The ANCOVA provides two types of significance test results: (a) results about the importance or significance of the covariate and (b) results of the test removing the influence or taking into consideration the influence of the covariate.

The first test provides information on the impact of the covariate; the higher the correlation of the covariate with the dependent variable, usually the greater the impact of the covariate. In the ANOVA summary table obtained from the analysis, the covariate will have a separate line and will have F values, effect size estimates, and so on. Visually, the covariate will look like a main effect in the summary table. Because the covariate is not the primary variable of interest, the effect of this variable is typically unimportant so long as it is significant. If the covariate does become of interest, such as when homogeneity of regression is violated, you should create a blocking variable from the covariate and treat it like any other variable in the model.

The second type of test relates to the independent variable(s) in the design. As with the ANOVA, the summary table for ANCOVA provides a main effect for each variable as well as an interaction effect if the design is factorial in design. The F values, degrees of freedom, and effect size should be reported as explained in Chapter 4. The ANCOVA printout will typically provide two tables for descriptive statistics by group. You should use the table with adjusted means, which implies that the means and standard deviations are calculated after the covariate is controlled for or taken into account. Text in Figure 6.3 provides a sample write-up for a ONEWAY ANCOVA using a covariate. The example assumes that the researcher was exploring whether sex (i.e., male vs. female) and partner's use of nonverbal immediacy (high, moderately high, moderately low, and low) affect satisfaction in a relationship when holding constant the amount of time that the couple has been together.

"The covariate, time in relationship, was significantly related to relationship satisfaction, $F = 12.99$ (1, 41), $p < .05$, r = .36. After accounting for time in relationship, there was a significant main effect for sex, $F = 5.73$ (1, 41), $p < .05$, $\eta^2 = .01$, as well as a significant main effect for use of nonverbal immediacy, $F = 146.86$ (3, 41), $p < .05$, $\eta^2 = .79$. The interaction between sex and nonverbal immediacy was also significant, $F = 6.68$ (3, 41), $p < .05$, $\eta^2 = .04$."

$F = 12.99$	F values should be reported for each main effect and for the covariate.
(1, 41)	The values in parentheses show the degrees of freedom for both the effect/between group (1 or 3) and error/within group (41).
$p < .05$	The significance or probability level is governed by convention in the social sciences. In this case, there is less than a 5% chance of obtaining an F value this large by mere chance rather than some actual effect.
$\eta^2 = .79$	The eta squared estimate of effect size is reported using the Greek symbol for eta.
$r = .36$	The correlation between the covariate and dependent variable was reported. It would also be appropriate to report eta squared.

Figure 6.3   Deciphering the Write-Up of ANCOVA

CONCLUDING COMMENTS ON ANCOVA

The benefits of ANCOVA are greatest when you want to statistically control for some variable that is related to the dependent variable but not the independent variable. Typically, such control is useful in studies where *traits or other preexisting individual differences* could influence values on the dependent variable. Covariates work best when their data are obtained prior to any sort of experimental manipulation and random assignment is used to place participants in conditions. In those situations, the ANCOVA procedure can statistically control for variance in the dependent variable associated with the covariate—variance typically found within groups, otherwise known as error variance. The end result can be a more precise and powerful test of the independent variable.

Second, as with any statistical procedure, variables included in the ANCOVA should be generated by theory. Going on a "fishing expedition" with numerous covariates can actually be harmful. Although one or two carefully planned covariates can dramatically improve the precision and power of an analysis, each covariate also uses up one degree of freedom. Covariates that have little or no relationship with the dependent variable offer no advantage and actually make finding significant results more difficult. As a rule of thumb, ANCOVA works best when the correlation between the covariate and the dependent variable is at least $r = .40$ or higher.

Finally, it should be noted that both Anderson (1963) and Lord (1969) argue against the use of covariate analysis to equate groups. They suggest that instead of adjusting for the covariate, the covariate should be made an explicit part of the analysis, as is the case with a blocking variable (for a discussion of blocking variables, see Keppel & Wickens, 2004, pp. 228–232). Researchers create blocking variables by dividing values for a continuous variable into ordinal categories, much like what is done with income on many surveys (i.e., rather than asking for an exact amount, respondents are asked to indicate where their income fits within a range of values). By creating an ordinal blocking variable, you can then include that variable as another factor in the analysis. The advantage of this approach is that you can explore interaction effects while still gaining the advantage of having what would have been error variance be part of the specified model. Recasting the covariate as a blocking variable is appealing because it allows conclusions to be drawn about how, exactly, the covariate works in the model. A related approach, and one that would be even more precise, is to use effect coding and perform the analysis using regression (for a discussion of effect coding, see Pedhazur, 1997). The advantage of using either a blocking variable or the regression approach is that the covariate is explicitly part of the theoretical model.

THE ANCOVA IN COMMUNICATION RESEARCH

Warren, J., Hecht, M., Wagstaff, D., Ndiaye, E., Distmans, P., & Marsiglia, F. (2006). Communicating prevention: The effects of the *Keepin' it REAL* classroom videotapes and televised PSAs on middle school students' substance use. *Journal of Applied Communication Research, 34,* 209–227.

Given the significant evidence concerning the negative effects of substance abuse early in life, communication researchers are interested in discovering health messages to promote healthier behavior and to curb underage drinking, drug use, and tobacco use. The objectives of these researchers are to (a) create age-appropriate health messages, (b) test the effectiveness of those messages, and (c) determine the most effective modality for those messages (e.g., peer-to-peer communication, public service advertisements, Web pages).

Jennifer Warren and her colleagues specifically wanted to test a particular set of health messages created by the Drug Resistance Skills Project called Keepin' it REAL (kiR). The kiR program was designed as a school-based program to curb drug use among culturally diverse teenagers. Messages used in the program coalesced around four resistance skills associated with the acronym REAL: refuse, explain, avoid, and leave. The messages of the kiR program are disseminated through two mediums: school-based videotapes and public service announcements (PSAs). Previous research had focused on the outcomes of the overall program, but Warren and her colleagues were most interested in determining the effects, both combined and in isolation, of the PSAs and classroom videos. They generated and tested two hypotheses:

Hypothesis 1: Intervention students who report seeing PSAs at least once will demonstrate smaller increases in substance use than those who did not.

Hypothesis 2: Intervention students who report seeing at least four videos will demonstrate smaller increases in substance use than will intervention students who report seeing fewer videos. In turn, the latter will report less substance use than will control students.

Data were obtained from nearly 5,000 middle school students who participated in the larger kiR program. For the larger kiR project, students were randomly assigned to one of the experimental groups or the control group. Students' self-reported substance abuse was collected before the project began and once later after the program had been in operation. During the second round of surveys, students were asked to indicate how many classroom videos they had watched as well as how many PSAs containing the kiR messages they had seen.

Because the authors were interested in learning whether there were changes in students' substance use as a result of the kiR program, they had to account for students' initial substance abuse reports when determining whether the program caused a positive or negative change in substance abuse. For example, whether or not taking drugs one fewer times per week is important only if you know how many times people did drugs per week before the program started. If they took drugs seven or more times, one fewer is not all that impressive; if they only did drugs once per week, one less time per week means they stopped, which is important. Thus, the ANCOVA was necessary because it allowed Warren and her colleagues to take into account students' previous drug use.

Classroom videos emerged as an effective medium for disseminating the kiR messages. All students increased their substance abuse over the course of the study. However, for students who saw the videos four or five times, results showed that, after adjusting for initial substance abuse, increases in substance abuse were smaller than for those who saw the videos fewer than four times. There were also no significant differences in substance abuse between students depending on how many PSAs they reported having seen.

Warren and her colleagues conclude that the classroom videos are more effective than the PSAs for curbing or reducing substance abuse among teenagers. The kiR program had its greatest and only significant effect when students saw the classroom videos at least four times; fewer than that did not produce significant effects.

REFERENCES

Anderson, N. H. (1963). Comparison of different populations: Resistance to extinction and transfer. *Psychological Review, 70,* 162–179.

Keppel, G., & Wickens, T. D. (2004). *Design and analysis: A researcher's handbook* (4th ed.). Upper Saddle River, NJ: Pearson.

Lord, F. M. (1969). Statistical adjustments when comparing preexisting groups. *Psychological Bulletin, 72,* 336–337.

Pedhazur, E. (1997). *Multiple regression in behavioral research: Explanation and prediction* (3rd ed.). New York: Holt, Rinehart & Winston.

❧ Sample SPSS Printouts ❧

The output shown for this chapter is related to a study comparing relationship satisfaction (RELSAT) for depending on sex (male or female) with the amount of nonverbal involvement (NIV) of the relational partner. A covariate, time in the relationship (RELTIME), was included because it was assumed that those in relationships longer would naturally develop satisfaction levels that are different from those in relationships for shorter periods. Thus, the objective was to test the sex-by-involvement effects while accounting for and holding constant the amount of time in the relationship. The key question guiding this study is whether relationship satisfaction differs depending on the sex of the person and the amount of nonverbal involvement of his or her relational partner while controlling for time in relationship. The pattern of SPSS output is roughly the same; however, the EMMEAN command provides a set of means and standard deviations that are adjusted for the covariate.

Tests of Between-Subjects Effects

Dependent Variable: relsat

Source	Type III Sum of Squares	df	Mean Square	F	Sig.
Corrected Model	763.655[a]	8	95.457	65.598	.000
Intercept	6783.483	1	6783.483	4661.602	.000
reltime	18.902	1	18.902	12.989	.001
niv	641.121	3	213.707	146.859	.000
sex	8.348	1	8.348	5.736	.021
niv *sex	29.175	3	9.725	6.683	.001
Error	59.662	41	1.455		
Total	7857.958	50			
Corrected Total	823.318	49			

a. R Squared = .928 (Adjusted R Squared = .913)

Estimates

Dependent Variable: relsat

				95% Confidence Interval	
sex	nonverbal involve	Mean	Std. Error	Lower Bound	Upper Bound
Male	low	5.291[a]	.494	4.292	6.289
	Moderate Lod	9.866[a]	.496	8.864	10.868
	Moderate High	12.847[a]	.545	11.746	13.948
	High	17.865[a]	.638	16.576	19.153
Female	low	8.385[a]	.493	7.389	9.380
	Moderate Lod	11.237[a]	.484	10.261	12.214
	Moderate High	13.509[a]	.456	12.588	14.430
	High	16.027[a]	.477	15.063	16.991

a. Covariates appearing in the model are evaluated at the following values: reltime = .8810.

Pairwise Comparisons

Dependent Variable: relsat

sex	(I) nonverbal Involve	(J) nonverbal involve	Mean Difference (I-J)	Std. Error	Sig.[a]
Male	low	Moderate Lod	−4.575*	.697	.000
		Moderate High	−7.557*	.722	.000
		High	−12.574*	.826	.000
	Moderate Lod	low	4.575*	.697	.000
		Moderate High	−2.981*	.718	.000
		High	−7.999*	.833	.000
	Moderate High	low	7.557*	.722	.000
		Moderate Lod	2.981*	.718	.000
		High	−5.018*	.929	.000
	High	low	12.574*	.826	.000
		Moderate Lod	7.999*	.833	.000
		Moderate High	5.018*	.929	.000
Female	low	Moderate Lod	−2.853*	.685	.000
		Moderate High	−5.125*	.671	.000
		High	−7.643*	.691	.000
	Moderate Lod	low	2.853*	.685	.000
		Moderate High	−2.272*	.663	.001
		High	−4.790*	.712	.000
	Moderate High	low	5.125*	.671	.000
		Moderate Lod	2.272*	.663	.001
		High	-2.518*	.662	.000
	High	low	7.643*	.691	.000
		Moderate Lod	4.790*	.712	.000
		Moderate High	2.518*	.662	.000

*Based on estimated marginal means

Estimated Marginal Means of Relat Satis

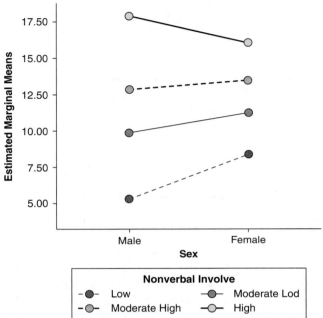

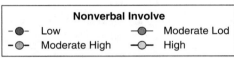

SEVEN

MULTIVARIATE ANOVA

—————◆●◆—————

Suppose that you wanted to determine whether the sex and verbal aggressiveness of a supervisor interacted to influence employees' perceptions of supervisor effectiveness and their job satisfaction. To try and answer this question, you design an experiment where participants watch a short video of a supervisor giving employees recorded directions for completing some task. In some situations, the supervisor is a man; in others, the supervisor is a woman. You also manipulate the script for the videos to include either high or low levels of verbally aggressive behaviors. After randomly assigning participants to one of the various conditions in the 2 (male vs. female supervisor) × 2 (high vs. low verbal aggressiveness) design, participants watched the video and completed two scales—one measuring their perceptions of the supervisor's communication competence and another measuring how satisfied they would likely be with their job. This experiment does not differ substantially from the basic ANOVA discussed previously—the main difference is the two dependent variables being used in the study.

Complex research designs often explore how one or more independent variables might affect multiple dependent variables. The simple ANOVA procedure discussed earlier can easily be expanded to include more than one dependent variable; such an approach is called a multivariate analysis of variance, or MANOVA. The MANOVA is part of a broader family of statistics known as multivariate statistics, which generally means that effects of independent variables are being explored on the linear combination of more than one dependent variable. Although slightly more complex, multivariate designs are economical because more information can be gained from the same sample. Previous chapters addressed univariate statistics such as the *t* test, ONEWAY ANOVA, and factorial ANOVA, which provide results when only one dependent measure is considered.

Of course, you could design a study with multiple dependent variables and examine each variable separately using the previously mentioned univariate statistics. However, multivariate analysis provides an option of considering all dependent variables, at least initially, at the same time. The use of multivariate designs is justified for three general reasons. First, theory typically suggests that any experimental manipulation or naturally occurring independent variable will affect more than one outcome variable. Consequently, simultaneously testing the effects of an independent variable on more than one dependent variable may be required for theoretical reasons alone. Second, as will be explained later, the multivariate ANOVA allows you to test multiple dependent variables while at the same time providing protection against Type I error. Finally, there are some types of procedures, such as within-subject or repeated-measure designs, that require the use of multivariate statistics.

This chapter, for the sake of clarity, will use the term *repeated measures* when the design uses the same measures across time with the same participants and the term *multivariate* analysis when considering the issues of multiple dependent measures. Although it is possible to combine the use of repeated measures and multiple dependent variables, those more complex designs are not considered here but are discussed at length in more advanced texts (see Stevens, 2002).

MULTIVARIATE DESIGNS

Multivariate techniques probably are the most misunderstood and misused statistical technique. The reporting of the technique often is incomplete and difficult. The result is sometimes a variety of suggestions and options that appear contradictory or inconsistent. This section describes reasons for using multivariate designs, identifies the assumptions underlying the procedures, and offers advice on how to report the results of multivariate analyses.

Why Use Multivariate Designs?

Typically, multivariate analysis is justified using one of three general broad justifications: (a) repeated measures, (b) familywise protection, and (c) desire to generate classification using a combination of predictors. The first justification for use of multivariate analysis is when an investigation uses the same instrument over time. The use of a measure at multiple times means there exists a dependency or correlation between the measurement periods. The repeated-measures analysis is described in detail later in the chapter.

The second justification involves an experimenter that has used multiple dependent variables and wants to examine each one independently. The problem is that the use of multiple ANOVA tests risks the capitalization on chance, or Type I, error. The challenge is to provide a means of reducing or holding constant Type I error so that the *p* value of .05 (or whatever value the investigator is using) remains constant. Multivariate statistics provides a means of maintaining an acceptable familywise error rate. You will learn about this issue of familywise alpha inflation later when you read about the topic of intercorrelation between the dependent variables.

The third and final justification provides a means of creating combinatorial vectors or functions that combine the variables in the use of prediction. The most popular of these techniques is canonical or discriminant analysis. Essentially, these forms of analysis create vectors (lines) that are a combination of variables in order to separate groups or classify individual entries into groups.

Consider the problem of a person finding a piece of pottery in South America. The person wants to find out which native tribe made the piece. Each tribe has a combination of distinct characteristics involving materials, color, measurement, and so on that can be combined and, when applied to the individual piece, permit the classification of the pottery as produced by a particular tribe. Notice that in this case, the goal for the use of the technique is to provide a means of eventually taking an individual example and classifying that example into an appropriate group. The equation is intended to literally "discriminate" the probability of group membership given information about a particular example. What this means is that the employment of the multivariate technique in this example is to provide a means of measurement for future research, and the analysis, while interesting, does not constitute a meaningful end in and of itself.

The best-known example of this in communication is the Relational Dimension Instrument (RDI) developed by Mary Anne Fitzpatrick (1988). The RDI was developed as a series of subscales that a person fills out relating to interaction and other assumptions about marriage. Then the answers are put into an equation that predicts the relational type that this person falls into: (a) traditional, (b) independents, and (c) separate. The classification into types permits the analysis for future research because each type involves a set of assumptions and evidence of difference. Notice that the goal of the research is to take information generated by a person and to use the equation to classify the individual into the categorical system. Researchers can then use the resulting classification as the basis for subsequent analysis. The result of the original investigations was the development of the measurement device that has a precise equation that others can use to classify individuals filling out a particular scale.

Statistical Assumptions of Multivariate Designs

The following assumptions apply to the use of multivariate analyses presented in this chapter: (a) There are no causal structures among the variables, (b) there exists an expectation of interrelationships among the dependent variables, and (c) there is homoscedasticity, or a roughly equal amount of covariance among the dependent variables. Each assumption involves a set of theoretical expectations that should be evaluated by the investigator.

The first question to ask before using a multivariate design is whether there is an expectation or prediction of causality between any of the independent or dependent variables. Generally, if there is an expectation of causality, this group of multivariate designs is inappropriate. Importantly, causality requires an examination using some form of structural equation modeling (path analysis). It is only after such an expectation is dismissed that multivariate techniques should be employed for the analysis. The best way to proceed is to examine the variables in terms of the theoretical model used to generate the design. If the theory specifies or expects causality among the variables, the multivariate design will produce misleading results. The set of mathematics assumes, implicitly, that there exists a lack of causality among any of the variables.

Causality can be thought of as a means of setting an ordered structure among the set of relations. MANOVA assumes that such an ordering does not exist. A general criticism of reliance on MANOVA is the atheoretical assumptions that you must accept to use the technique. While the technique is useful, you must make some sacrifices in order to employ the technique, and careful evaluation should be made before whether or not such procedures are appropriate.

Second, the reason for multivariate analysis is the desire to consider possible intercorrelation between the dependent variables. The impact of the intercorrelation usually makes the univariate analyses of each separate dependent variable problematic given the following two statistical concerns: (a) inflation of Type II error and (b) correlated results. Consider that multiple univariate analyses, each using an alpha level of .05, have a greater than 5% error rate considering multiple tests. What happens is that the 5% alpha level assumes that there exist a limited or fixed number of tests or chances. When you begin to run more tests, each one with a 5% Type I error, the probability of generating a randomly significant result becomes greater than 5%. That is why there are various corrections imposed or suggested in ANOVA for multiple tests.

But when the dependent variables are correlated, the impact of multiple tests can be significantly divergent from the expected error. The expectation of correlations between the variables suggests correlations (which could be positive or negative, as well as small or large) among the various significance tests. Essentially, the various tests no longer function as independent tests but share some measure of nonindependence in terms of significance probability. The result generates potentially misleading results and provides the basis for the use of multivariate testing to maintain the fidelity of the alpha level (it should be noted that such outcomes will increase the level of Type II error—which is a serious consideration when deciding to use any multivariate procedure).

Finally, the MANOVA assumes that there is homoscedasticity or roughly equal covariance between the dependent variables. Homoscedasticity simply means that the correlations between the various dependent variables in the design should be roughly similar. Although the MANOVA is relatively robust against violations of homoscedasticity so long as group sizes are equal, you should use the Box M test to examine whether this assumption has been met. If the Box M test is significant, the assumption of homoscedasticity has been violated, and you should use a corrected significance test to report results. The Box M test is highly sensitive to violations of normality, and consequently, you should use $p < .001$ as your significance test level when interpreting the test. If the test shows a violation at this more conservative level, you should use a more conservative test such as Pillai's trace. If the Box M test is not significant, Wilks' lambda is commonly reported. Steps in conducting the multivariate analysis are described in Figure 7.1.

1. Enter data by providing both categorical and at least two or more dependent variables for each person. The dependent variables need not be repeated measures.

2. Identify the independent and multiple dependent variables to calculate the analysis. In most programs, such as SPSS, you can include covariates if you like (the analysis would become a MANCOVA, or multivariate analysis of covariance).

3. Use the Box M test to determine whether homoscedasticity has been met. If it has, report Wilks' lamda; if not, use Pillai's trace.

4. Report the multivariate effect. If there are significant multivariate effects (either a main effect or an interaction), examine each dependent variable for univariate effects and perform standard follow-up procedures as necessary.

5. Use other advanced procedures such as discriminant analysis if you are interested in exploring multivariate vectors in the dependent variables by group.

Figure 7.1   Steps in Conducting a MANOVA

Reporting Requirements

One aspect of multivariate statistics makes reporting difficult. The multivariate function is the result of a process that considers the intercorrelation of the existing variables. Changing the number of variables, by definition, changes the function and can do so very radically, depending on the correlation of whatever variable is added or deleted. Therefore, the report of any multivariate analysis should include a zero-order correlation matrix that reports the mean, standard deviation, and reliability for each variable. The failure to include this information makes comparison to other multivariate analyses impossible because the resulting multivariate equation contains different assumptions (based on a zero-order set of associations) that cannot be derived from the multivariate function.

Reporting requirements differ based on the particular statistic and the number of dependent measures. If you are using multiple dependent variables, you should report an overall multivariate F test of significance, often an F test. The normal procedure includes the omnibus test, if significant, followed up by univariate F tests for each variable. The argument for this is that the multivariate F test provides for protection against familywise error rate. Under these conditions, the resulting analysis is a two-step, multivariate F followed by univariate

F tests. The resulting univariate *F* tests are reported and interpreted as standard ANOVA results. However, Pedhazur (1997) recommends against this procedure because it "ignores the intercorrelations among the dependent variables and thereby subverts the very purpose of doing MANOVA in the first place" (p. 957). In order to correct for this, he suggests that a significant multivariate *F* be "followed by a [discriminant analysis] for the purpose of shedding light on the nature of the dimensions on which the groups differ" (p. 959); although this practice is rarely followed in favor of separate univariate analyses, we recommend that you explore this approach in further detail when running a MANOVA. A sample write-up for a MANOVA is provided in Figure 7.2.

If your objective is to create a mulitvariate vector, you should follow a different approach. This analysis is focused on the creation of either some type of canonical analysis or CA (discriminant analysis is a subtype of CA and

To determine whether there are significant differences in willingness to communicate and self-perceived communication competence among people who have attended only high school, some college, college, and graduate school, a MANOVA was calculated. The Box M test was significant, Box M = 191.71, $F = 20.34$ (9, 73342.77), $p < .001$, and subsequently, the multivariate test showed significant differences, Pillai's trace = 1.21, $F = 40.69$ (6, 160), $p < .001$, partial $\eta^2 = .60$. Follow-up univariate tests showed that there were significant differences between the four groups on both dependent variables: willingness to communicate, $F = 142.97$ (3, 80), $p < .001$, partial $\eta^2 = .84$, and self-perceived communication competence, $F = 8.54$ (3, 80), $p < .001$, partial $\eta^2 = .24$. Post hoc tests on both dependent variables showed that high school graduates and those who have attended some college had significantly lower willingness to communicate and self-perceived communication competence than did college graduates and those with graduate degrees.

Box M = 191.71, $F = 20.34$ (9, 73342.77), $p < .001$	The Box M test was significant at the more conservative $p < .001$ level and therefore homoscedasticity was violated.
Pillai's trace = 1.21, $F = 40.69$ (6, 160), $p < .001$	Pillai's trace should be used when the Box M test is violated. Otherwise, use Wilks' lambda.
$F = 142.97$ (3, 80), $p < .001$, partial $\eta^2 = .84$	Univariate tests for each dependent variable are reported to follow the significant multivariate test.

Figure 7.2   Example MANOVA Write-Up

generates the same results). The CA provides a vector of variables in order to maximize the correlation between independent and dependent variables. The overall correlation should not be interpreted in terms of variance accounted for (Pedhazur, 1997, p. 929) but instead as a set of associations between two sets of variables.

What should be reported is the equation; in that respect, it is much like the reporting of a multiple regression. However, it is possible to generate multiple significant functions or roots and provide estimates of the ability to correctly classify individuals scores on one set of variables (or one predictor) using the linear combination of the other variables. Essentially, one can take the combination of dependent variables to predict a value on the independent variable or some other means of classification. The loadings or weights for variables are the correlation between the variable and the function used for prediction. In other words, the significant variables in the equation, when combined in the manner specified in the equation, will produce predictability or classification accuracy as provided. What should be reported, therefore, is the necessary information about the value of the equation and the variables (multiple R_c, significance of that, and the value and significance for each predictor). If classification is used (often for a discriminant function), then that information should be provided. These tests assume normal distributions, and that should be tested and any deviation reported.

REPEATED MEASURES

Suppose you wanted to conduct a study to determine whether there is a short-term change in people's perceptions of violence after repeated exposure to violent media content. You design a study where you collect baseline data, then show a violent television show and take measurements at 15-minute intervals during the show and 15 minutes after the show is over. For a 30-minute show, this means that you will have a total of four data points for each person, including the baseline assessment, two administrations during the show, and one after. Your objective in the study is to determine whether there are significant changes in participants' perceptions of violence during and after the show when compared with their baseline data. The repeated-measures design provides a way of answering that question.

This repeated-measures design has measurement at multiple times, using the same participants. The simplest form of this involves the correlated or within-person *t* test, usually referred to as the "paired" *t* test. This design measures a person at Time 1 and Time 2 using the same measure. The comparison is whether or not change occurs between Time 1 and Time 2 based on the individual's scores. This design is obviously appropriate for longitudinal designs often associated with interventions for treatment of some condition or education.

Why Use Repeated Measures?

The advantage of the repeated-measures design is that it provides a more powerful technique to detect differences between scores. The advantage comes from the assumption that differences between Time 1 and Time 2 are probably related to the existence of the intervention. Because the same person is completing the measure, the reasonable assumption is that any change from Time 1 to Time 2 must have come because of the intervention. For example, if you were one of the people in the experimental group viewing the violent programming, any change from your baseline assessment to one of the other time intervals likely would have been caused only by the violent programming that you watched. The argument is that any change took place for some reason, and the most likely reason is the intervention or experimental manipulation (obviously there exist a number of potential threats to this claim that require assessment).

An entire set of experimental design specifications, known as the "Solomon Four Group," deals with this kind of design and the potential threats to internal validity and potential means of assessing or eliminating those threats to the interpretation of the results. These design options were mentioned briefly in Chapter 1; for more information, you should consult Campbell and Stanley's (1963) work. In addition to using good design options, many of the threats to internal validity could be assessed mathematically, and when present, the results can be corrected.

Whereas the paired sample *t* test compares only two points in time, more advanced procedures can include multiple (i.e., more than two) measurements. A longitudinal design can have a pretest, immediate posttest, 3-month delayed posttest, 6-month delayed posttest, and so on. If the number of assessments is large and regular, a different set of statistics, known as time series (one type of autoregressive integrated moving average [ARIMA] model), may be appropriate.

An example of this would be analyzing weekly television ratings for 1 year or longer. If the number of measurement periods is relatively small, you can use the repeated-measures analysis.

Interpretation and Assumptions

In practice, the repeated-measures analysis functions much like a traditional ANOVA—you have an overall (i.e., omnibus) value that determines whether significance exists and then test the differences between time periods using some type of post hoc analysis. In addition, the analysis can be tailored to consider various trends or decay possibilities. Suppose, for example, you have participants engage in some activity designed to reduce communication apprehension. The comparison from the pretest to the immediate posttest provides one measure of improvement. If the design has two additional measurements, 1 and 2 years later, the total number of measurements for participants is four.

The analysis could examine several possibilities. Assuming that the treatment was successful, there could be a significant decline in pretest to posttest scores. If the treatment declines in effectiveness over time, you can model a trend from the immediate to 1-year delayed to 2-year delayed measurement. Alternatively, suppose the theory expects the treatment to increase in effectiveness over time (because the impact of declining apprehension is increased effectiveness and confidence is contagious); you can then propose the assessment of a model to assess that particular outcome. Obviously, the number of measurement periods permits more sophisticated and complete models to be considered.

Engaged Research

Suppose that you wanted to conduct a research project exploring how communication behaviors change in a relationship over time. Take a moment to operationalize what type(s) of relationship(s) you would want to study. Then, identify what variables you would want to explore (e.g., self-disclosure, conflict, supportive communication). How long of a period of time would you want to use? How many measurements would you want to collect? How could you design the study to collect information on these variables several times? As you consider these questions, what do you think the strengths and weaknesses/drawbacks are of this approach?

When interpreting results of a repeated-measures design, several issues should be considered. First, the dimensionality and reliability of the instrument(s) used should be reported for each time period. In other words, if you are using a unidimensional scale, the same dimensions should occur for each time period, and the reliability should be similar for each measurement. Significant departures in either dimensionality or reliability provide some concerns, and additional analyses should examine the reasons for the differences.

Second, mortality provides a significant issue for longitudinal designs. Generally, one can provide a test for each time period using only those participants who were measured at each time period. The question is whether any differences associated with dropping out affect the observed measurement. One possible method of assessment is to compare the means of those remaining in the investigation with those dropping out to determine if there is any difference in the observed mean level of participants. This, combined with any other analysis for the basis of the mortality, can serve to assess the degree to which this threat is a problem. The challenge is to understand whether any systematic reason exists for persons not to complete all measurements and evaluate the degree to which that reason influences the outcomes observed.

Last, the repeated-measures analysis has the same assumptions underpinning other ANOVA procedures and one new one, called *sphericity*. Sphericity assumes that the correlations between values at the various times are homogeneous, or roughly equal. So, for instance, in the mediated violence study, the correlation between the baseline measurement and the last measurement should be roughly similar to the correlation between the two middle measurements. In practice, the correlations are never identical, and sphericity is violated in every study to some degree. A step-by-step explanation of the process used in a repeated-measures analysis is shown in Figure 7.3.

In SPSS and other statistical packages, the repeated-measures analysis provides multiple F values, each with different degrees of freedom. Typically, those values are labeled *sphericity assumed, Greenhouse-Geisser, Huynh-Feldt,* and *lower bound.* To determine which set of values you should report, you need to know whether you have violated sphericity. A test called the Mauchly test of sphericity can be calculated in SPSS to tell you whether sphericity has been violated.

If the Mauchly test is not significant and therefore sphericity has not been violated, use the "sphericity assumed" values for F. If the Mauchly test is significant and you have evidence that sphericity has been violated, you should examine the other three values. If the "lower-bound" test, which is the

---

1. Collect data for each participant using at least two or potentially more points in time. You may classify participants according to other variables if you want to run a combined within-subject and between-subjects design (also called a split-plot design).

2. When entering the data and prior to performing the overall analysis, you will need to assign in SPSS which order the repeated measures come in. For example, you would need to know which came first, second, and so on.

3. Test the data for normality and other abnormalities that could affect the precision of the test.

4. Test for sphericity using the Mauchly test described later.

5. Calculate the within-subjects test. If the sphericity assumption is met, use the "sphericity assumed" values; if the assumption is not met, use other corrected values.

6. Use follow-up tests to probe significant within-subjects effects. You can test for both linear and nonlinear trends in the data depending on how many data points (or points in time) you collect.

Figure 7.3   Steps in the Repeated-Measures Analysis

---

most conservative, shows a significant F, the matter ends, and you have evidence to reject the null. If the sphericity assumed and lower-bound F tests are contradictory, you should rely on the Greenhouse-Geisser test to make a final determination. Practically speaking, the four tests often yield similar results.

To report within-subjects or repeated-measures designs, you should provide an indication of whether the sphericity assumption was met and then report the appropriate F values. In the example provided in Figure 7.4, Mauchly's test of sphericity indicated that the sphericity assumption was violated. Both the sphericity-assumed F value and the Greenhouse-Geisser-adjusted F value (notice the adjusted degrees of freedom for that F) showed that there was a significant interaction between the within-subjects variable and the sex variable. In this example, the researchers were interested in learning whether the trends between men and women differed in terms of self-disclosure; the follow-up tests reported as part of the analysis showed that the trends differed between men and women. You will notice that the write-up is very similar to the standard ANOVA in terms of reporting the F value, degrees of freedom, and so on (see Figure 7.4). The one difference is the Greenhouse-Geisser epsilon correction reported in the second F value; you obtain that value from the same table that contains Mauchly's test of sphericity if you are using SPSS.

To determine whether self-disclosure patterns differ among men and women over the course of a relationship, we calculated a split-plot analysis with one within-subjects factor (self-disclosure measured at four points in time) and one between-subjects factor (sex). Mauchly's test suggested that the sphericity assumption was violated, $\chi^2 = 60.10$ (5), $p < .001$, and consequently, various estimates of epsilon were used to correct and test within-subjects effects. A significant self-disclosure by group interaction was observed, $F = 6.75$ (3, 144), $p < .001$, and subsequent corrected tests supported the initial results, Greenhouse-Geisser = .54, $F = 6.75$ (1.63, 78.19), $p < .05$. Follow-up tests indicated that a quadratic trend best fits the data for men, $F = 18.40$ (1, 24), $p < .05$; however, for women, a linear trend best fits the data, $F = 203.67$ (1, 24), $p < .05$. Whereas women tend to continue increasing their self-disclosure over the course of a relationship, men tend to be best described by a ceiling effect where their rates of self-disclosure level off as the relationship progresses.

$\chi^2 = 60.10$ (5), $p < .001$	The significant Mauchly's test tells you that sphericity was violated. This indicates that you should use a more conservative multivariate test.
$F = 6.75$ (3, 144), $p < .001$	This value reports the uncorrected multivariate F.
Greenhouse-Geisser = .54, $F = 6.75$ (1.63, 78.19), $p < .05$	The Greenhouse-Geisser-corrected F (notice the corrected df) is more conservative and corrects for the sphericity violation.
$F = 18.40$ (1, 24), $p < .05$	Both of the other F values are univariate results (notice the single df for each dependent variable).

Figure 7.4   Example Within-Subjects Write-Up

THE MANOVA IN COMMUNICATION RESEARCH

Schrodt, P., & Witt, P. (2006). Students' attributions of instructor credibility as a function of students' expectations of instructional technology use and nonverbal immediacy. *Communication Education, 55,* 1–20.

Instructional communication researchers have long recognized that teachers, like other types of speakers, must create and sustain credibility. Previous research on this topic has shown that teacher credibility is characterized by three dimensions, including competence, trustworthiness, and perceived caring. Schrodt and Witt designed a study to determine how teacher communication behaviors influenced students' perceptions of teacher credibility.

Specifically, they wanted to determine whether use of technology and immediacy by teachers affected students' perceptions of teacher credibility.

Using attribution theory, Schrodt and Witt reasoned that a teacher's use of
technology and immediacy would cause students to make attributions about
the teacher's competence, trustworthiness, and caring—the three dimensions
of credibility. Furthermore, because instructors' use of technology interacts
with their other communication behaviors to influence students' attributions,
Schrodt and Witt reasoned that technology use and immediacy would interact
to influence students' perceptions of their teachers' credibility. To test these
assumptions, they designed an experiment using hypothetical scenarios to test
the following hypothesis:

> Hypothesis 1: Levels of expected technology use will interact with levels
> of teacher nonverbal immediacy to influence students' initial attributions of
> instructor credibility (i.e., competence, character, and perceived caring).

A total of 549 students enrolled in a basic communication course took
part in the study. Participants were randomly assigned to one of eight experimental groups representing manipulations of technology use (no technology,
minimal technology, moderate technology, and complete technology) and
teacher immediacy (high or low). Instructor credibility was measured using
McCroskey & Young's Teacher Credibility Scale, which is a 12-item semantic
differential scale measuring the three dimensions of teacher credibility discussed earlier. This resulted in a 4×2 experimental design with three dependent variables: competence, trustworthiness, and caring.

The results of the experiment showed a significant multivariate interaction effect between technology use and immediacy for students' perceptions
of teacher credibility, Wilks' $\lambda = .930$, $F(9, 1311.94) = 4.41$, $\eta^2 = .07$, $p <
.001$. There were also significant multivariate main effects for both technol-
ogy use, Wilks' $\lambda = .813$, $F(9, 1311.94) = 12.93$, $\eta^2 = .19$, $p < .001$, and
nonverbal immediacy, Wilks' $\lambda = .537$, $F(9, 1311.94) = 154.92$, $\eta^2 = .46$, $p <
.001$. Subsequent univariate ANOVAs revealed significant interaction effects
for each of the separate dependent variables; there were also significant main
effects for technology use and immediacy on each of the dependent variables.
Additional analyses showed that the effects of technology use were curvilinear
and differed depending on whether the teacher was depicted as highly immediate or not.

Schrodt and Witt conclude that there is an interaction between anticipated technology use and immediacy on students' perceptions of teacher credibility. For instructor competence, there was a curvilinear effect where no technology and complete technology were perceived as lower in competence than minimal or moderate technology; this effect was more pronounced for highly immediate teachers than for teachers depicted with low immediacy. Similar patterns were observed for both other dimensions of teacher credibility. Schrodt and Witt conclude that teachers should incorporate some technology (i.e., not too much or too little) and should try to enact immediate behaviors. The combination of high immediacy and some to moderate use of technology consistently produced the highest credibility ratings across each of the three dimensions of teacher credibility.

REFERENCES

Campbell, D. T., & Stanley, J. C. (1963). *Experimental and quasi-experimental designs for research.* Boston: Houghton Mifflin.

Fitzpatrick, M. A. (1988). *Between husbands & wives: Communication in marriage.* Newbury Park, CA: Sage.

Pedhazur, E. J. (1997). *Multiple regression in behavioral research* (3rd ed.). New York: Harcourt Brace.

Stevens, J. P. (2002). *Applied multivariate statistics for the social sciences* (4th ed.). Mahwah, NJ: Lawrence Erlbaum.

❧ Sample SPSS Printouts ❧

The output shown is for a basic MANOVA where two dependent variables (job satisfaction or JOBSAT and job tenure or JBTENURE) are analyzed. The independent variables are sex of the employee (male or female) and job type (supervisor or subordinate). After providing the descriptive statistics for both dependent variables, the Box M test is reported and is followed by the multivariate tests and univariate tests.

Descriptive Statistics

	sex	job	Mean	Std Deviation	N
jobsat	male	supervisor	12.0892	.97799	100
		subordinate	14.0178	1.05965	100
		Total	13.0535	1.40321	200
	female	supervisor	2.9347	1.09721	100
		subordinate	5.8728	.96003	100
		Total	4.4037	1.79621	200
	Total	supervisor	7.5119	4.70439	200
		subordinate	9.9453	4.20544	200
		Total	8.7286	4.61980	400
jbtenure	male	supervisor	4.4974	.94891	100
		subordinate	13.9474	2.49426	100
		Total	9.2224	5.09714	200
	female	supervisor	15.3349	.95823	100
		subordinate	2.7999	2.25973	100
		Total	9.0674	6.51737	200
	Total	supervisor	9.9162	5.51499	200
		subordinate	8.3737	6.07110	200
		Total	9.1449	5.84369	400

Box's Test of Equality of Covariance Matrices[a]

Box's M	325.839
F	35.874
df1	9
df2	1797081
Sig.	.000

Tests the null hypothesis that the observed covariance matrices of the dependent variables are equal across groups.

a. Design: Intercept+sex+job+sex * job

Multivariate Tests[b]

Effect		Value	F	Hypothesis df	Error df	Sig.
Intercept	Pillar's Trace	.987	14509.024[a]	2.000	395.000	.000
	Wilks' Lambda	.013	14509.024[a]	2.000	395.000	.000
	Hotelling's Trace	73.463	14509.024[a]	2.000	395.000	.000
	Roy's Largest Root	73.463	14509.024[a]	2.000	395.000	.000
sex	Pillai's Trace	.968	5908.458[a]	2.000	395.000	.000
	Wilks' Lambda	.032	5908.458[a]	2.000	395.000	.000
	Hotelling's Trace	29.916	5908.458[a]	2.000	395.000	.000
	Roy's Largest Root	29.916	5908.458[a]	2.000	395.000	.000
job	Pillar's Trace	.792	751.210[a]	2.000	395.000	.000
	Wilks' Lambda	.208	751.210[a]	2.000	395.000	.000
	Hotelling's Trace	3.804	751.210[a]	2.000	395.000	.000
	Roy's Largest Root	3.804	751.210[a]	2.000	395.000	.000
sex * job	Pillai's Trace	.946	3432.454[a]	2.000	395.000	.000
	Wilks' Lambda	.054	3432.454[a]	2.000	395.000	.000
	Hotelling's Trace	17.380	3432.454[a]	2.000	395.000	.000
	Roy's Largest Root	17.380	3432.454[a]	2.000	395.000	.000

a. Exact statistic

b. Design: Intercept+sex+job+sex * job

Levene's Test of Equality of Error Variances[a]

	F	df1	df2	Sig.
jobsat	1.235	3	396	.296
jbtenure	30.334	3	396	.000

Tests the null hypothesis that the error variance of the dependent variable is equal across groups.
a. Design: Intercept+sex+job+sex * job

Tests of Between-Subjects Effects

Source	Dependent Variable	Type III Sum of Squares	df	Mean Square	F	Sig.
Corrected Model	jobsat	8099.414[a]	3	2699.805	2568.273	.000
	jbtenure	12323.839[b]	3	4107.946	1249.912	.000
Intercept	jobsat	30475.558	1	30475.558	28990.821	.000
	jbtenure	33451.678	1	33451.678	10178.238	.000
sex	jobsat	7481.818	1	7481.818	7117.311	.000
	jbtenure	2.402	1	2.402	.731	.393
lob	jobsat	592.119	1	592.119	563.272	.000
	jbtenure	237.931	1	237.931	72.394	.000
sex * job	jobsat	25.477	1	25.477	24.236	.000
	jbtenure	12083.506	1	12083.506	3676.610	.000
Error	jobsat	416.281	396	1.051		
	jbtenure	1301.489	396	3.287		
Total	jobsat	38991.252	400			
	jbtenure	47077.006	400			
Corrected Total	jobsat	8515.695	399			
	jbtenure	13625.328	399			

a. R Squared = .951 (Adjusted R Squared = .951)

b. R Squared = .904 (Adjusted R Squared = .904)

EIGHT

CHI-SQUARE STATISTIC

For several years, Marie has worked to improve the lives of women in rural Appalachian counties in Ohio and West Virginia. For a research project in a research methods class, Marie was interested in exploring whether rural Appalachian newspapers had a disproportionate bias toward showing certain ages and sexes in front-page pictures. She collected a representative sample of front pages of local newspapers for a 5-year period and classified each front-page picture according to sex (male vs. female) and probable age (child, adolescent, adult, elderly). After classifying the pictures, Marie tabulated the distribution and compared her observed distribution with what would have been expected if the distribution was random. The chi-square indicated that the observed distribution was significantly different than a random distribution, and the cross-tabulation table allowed Marie to conclude that adult men were pictured at a much higher rate than were females of any age group or males of nonadult age groups.

Researchers are often interested in learning whether an observed distribution of data significantly differs from what they expected to find. In such instances, the chi-square statistic coupled with a cross-tabulation table can be a very useful analytical technique.

UNDERSTANDING THE CHI-SQUARE STATISTIC

The chi-square statistic is a comparatively easy statistic to calculate by hand. Sometimes called a "goodness-of-fit" statistic, the chi-square allows you to compare an observed set of data against an expected set of values to see how well the observed data fit what was expected. In Marie's project, she was using the chi-square statistic to measure the discrepancy between the pictures she coded and what she expected to find. In some cases, what you expect is a theoretically defined set of outcomes; in other cases, the outcome you expect is random. In Marie's study, she expected that the pictures on front pages of Appalachian newspapers would be random—reflecting the seemingly random nature of news in small-town Appalachia. The question driving Marie's research was, "To what extent, if any, did front-page pictures in rural Appalachian newspapers depart from a random distribution?" The following steps, identified in Figure 8.1, are used to complete the chi-square test.

In Marie's study, a significant chi-square indicated that the observed distribution of pictures was not random. Recall that Marie was coding for two variables: sex and age. Sex was coded as a nominal, two-level variable, and age was coded as an ordinal, four-level variable. Marie's design is typical of the type of instance where you would normally use a chi-square—to test associations between two categorical (i.e., nominal or ordinal) variables.

CALCULATING A CHI-SQUARE

The following cross-tabulation table shows the distribution of pictures observed by Marie. Each value in the center, nonshaded cells represents the number of pictures for that combination. For example, there were 8 adolescent males shown and 21 elderly females shown. The shaded cells on the right and

---

1. Enter data so that each case is coded for two or more categorical variables.

2. Create a cross-tabulation table (also called a contingency table) specifying one variable as columns and the other as rows. Observed counts for each cell in the table should be identified.

3. Calculate the expected value for each cell using Formula 8.1.

4. Calculate the chi-square statistic using Formula 8.2.

5. Calculate the degrees of freedom using Formula 8.3.

6. Compare the calculated chi-square against the critical value of chi to determine if it is significant.

7. Write up results.

Figure 8.1   Steps in the Chi-Square Test

bottom show totals for rows and columns. For example, there were 66 males and 53 females shown, and there were 77 adults shown when adding both sexes together. Finally, the value in the lower right cell shows that there were a grand total of 119 pictures coded for the study.

Sex	Age				Total
	Child	*Adolescent*	*Adult*	*Elderly*	*Total*
Male	2	8	50	6	66
Female	3	2	27	21	53
Total	5	10	77	27	119

Values in the cross-tabulation table are the actual or observed set of data. To calculate the chi-square statistic, Marie needed to compare the observed data with what would be expected if the distributions are random. The formula for generating an expected frequency is as follows:

$$(\text{Row Total} \times \text{Column Total})/\text{Grand Total}. \qquad (8.1)$$

The expected frequency formula must be calculated for each cell in the cross-tabulation matrix. The bolded values in the table below show the expected frequency for each cell.

Sex	Age				Total
	Child	*Adolescent*	*Adult*	*Elderly*	*Total*
Male	$(66 \times 5)/119$ **2.77**	$(66 \times 10)/119$ **5.54**	$(66 \times 77)/119$ **42.70**	$(66 \times 27)/119$ **14.97**	66
Female	$(53 \times 5)/119$ **2.22**	$(53 \times 10)/119$ **4.45**	$(53 \times 77)119$ **34.29**	$(53 \times 27)119$ **12.03**	53
Total	5	10	77	27	119

You should notice that if you add the row or column entries for the expected frequencies, they will total the actual column and row totals. This is an excellent way to check your work. The expected values in the cells show what would have been expected if the distribution of pictures was random with respect to age and sex.

Once Marie was able to create a cross-tabulation table of observed frequencies and then calculate the expected frequencies for those values, she calculated a chi-square statistic to determine if the observed frequencies were significantly different from the expected frequencies. The formula for chi-square is as follows (for further discussion of this formula, see Williams, 1979):

$$\chi^2 = \sum \frac{(\text{Observed} - \text{Expected})^2}{\text{Expected}}. \tag{8.2}$$

In short, this formula takes the observed score and compares it with the expected score. If the observed and expected scores are equal, then the difference (Observed – Expected) would be zero. If the difference between the observed and expected values becomes larger, a significant chi-square becomes more likely. For Marie's study, she had a 2 × 4 design (as indicated by the levels for each variable) and, consequently, had to calculate difference scores for eight cells. Marie's calculations are shown in Figure 8.2.

After calculating the chi-square statistic, Marie's next step was to test whether that statistic was significant. To do that, she had to calculate the degrees of freedom:

$$df = (\text{number of rows} - 1) \times (\text{number of columns} - 1). \tag{8.3}$$

Calculating the Chi-Square

Sum of
$(2-2.77)^2/2.77$	=	.59/2.27	=	0.26
$(8-5.54)^2/5.54$	=	6.05/5.54	=	1.09
$(50-42.7)^2/42.7$	=	53..29/14.97	=	3.56
$(6-14.97)^2/14.97$	=	80.46/14.97	=	5.37
$(3-2.22)^2/2.22$	=	4.93/2.22	=	2.22
$(2-4.45)^2/4.45$	=	6.0/4.45	=	1.35
$(27-34.29)^2/34.29$	=	53.14/34.29	=	1.55
$(21-12.03)^2/12.03$	=	80.46/12.03	=	6.69

(This is the sum or χ^2): 22.09

Figure 8.2

In Marie's case, the calculations for her study reflected the 2 × 4 design employed in her study:

$$df = (4 - 1) \times (2 - 1) \text{ or } 3 \times 1 = 3.$$

After determining the degrees of freedom, the final step is to use the degrees of freedom and desired significance level to obtain the critical value for chi. Using those values, you would need to use a chi-square table to look up the critical value. Using a desired probability value of .05 and 3 degrees of freedom, the critical value for chi is 7.82. The critical value of chi is necessary because it tells you that values greater than 7.82 are significant and values less than 7.82 are not. Marie's value of 22.09 clearly met the critical value test, and consequently, she concluded that the distribution of observed values significantly departed from a random distribution.

ASSUMPTIONS OF THE CHI-SQUARE STATISTIC

It is important that you understand the assumptions of the particular statistical form you are using and the implications of these assumptions for the data distribution. First, the chi-square statistic often involves the use of categorical variables. In the examples you have read about in this chapter, the chi-square was used to analyze relationships between two categorical variables (i.e., sex, which is nominal, and age, which is ordinal). Although this is a very common use of the chi-square and thus implies a certain assumption about the data, chi-squares are also used in very advanced procedures such as path analysis, confirmatory factor analysis, and structural equation modeling; in more advanced statistical procedures, the variables could also be continuous in nature (i.e., interval or ratio).

Engaged Research

Conduct a simple survey to see whether people who pick certain majors are more or less likely to enroll in classes emphasizing service learning. For your project, create a short course description for an interdisciplinary service learning class (e.g., "Understanding Community Formation Through

(Continued)

(Continued)

Service Learning"). After showing the course description to other students, ask them their major and whether or not they would be willing to take such a class. After interviewing 30 people, create a cross-tabulation chart and use a chi-square to determine whether the response pattern is random.

Second, the chi-square statistic assumes that there is a proportional distribution among the expected values for various cells. In other words, the expected values in the cells should reflect variance and should be proportionally distributed. In the previous section, we mentioned a warning from the computer program indicating that the expected count (or distribution) for one or more cells in the study was less than 5; that warning is really indicating that this assumption was violated. What this violation means is that the expected distribution fell outside the normal parameters of the statistic. While it is possible to have an actual or observed distribution of zero in a particular combination (cell), an expected value of less than 5 can negatively affect the interpretation of the statistic. Remember, it is the expected distribution that is the value used to determine whether the conditions are met for the statistic.

The assumption that expected cell counts should reflect naturally expected variance is similar to other types of statistical assumptions. In a very real sense, all statistics assume various kinds of distributions or presume them in order to work effectively. In this case, the assumption of a random distribution is met if there is sufficient variance in the expected values. This assumption is similar to the assumptions of homogeneity of variance necessary for ANOVA or normal distributions for correlations or the t test. However, these statistics are robust to violations (which translates as the distribution has to depart significantly for the significance test to be inaccurate).

USING COMPUTER PROGRAMS
TO CALCULATE A CHI-SQUARE

In order to calculate this statistic using a computer program, you will need to provide the following: (a) the classification variables and (b) the beginning and ending values for the variables. In Marie's study, the variables are (1) age and (2) gender. For the age variable, pictures were coded numerically: (1) child, (2) adolescent, (3) adult, and (4) elderly. For gender, the pictures were coded as follows: (1) male and (2) female. Using this technique of specification, you can opt to only include certain combinations in the chi-square analysis. For instance, you could specify that you wanted to calculate a chi-square to specifically test the relationship between males and females for adult and elderly. In other words, you do not have to include all levels of a variable in a particular analysis. Most computer programs will allow you to select whatever combination of values that you would like to include, and consequently, the results can be tailored to include or exclude various combinations of levels of variables.

The selection of values represents a practical choice when considering the distribution of the values across the various combinations (cells). Suppose, for example, that you conducted a study looking at sex (male or female) and television sports viewing habits (football, soccer, baseball, basketball, bowling). The results might generate some combinations (female/bowling) that are extremely low in frequency in a row or column (bowling). Under those conditions, the expected frequency calculated by the formula might be very small (under 5 usually), and the computer program will provide you a warning message or even refuse to calculate the parameter. What the program is saying is that most formulas assume that the minimum frequency for use of the calculation has not been met by the data. This represents a problem for use of the statistic.

There are several options as this point. First, you could exclude the low-frequency variable (bowling) from the analysis. A second option would be to combine that variable with another one, creating a new category (combining poker and bowling into something called "blue-collar games"). If all else fails, you can label the new category "other." When making these changes, make sure that the methods section for your manuscript appropriately reflects the change and the reason for the change. A third option is that there are alternative formulas for chi-square that can handle lower expected frequencies, but these may or may not be labeled or available on statistical packages, and you should find an appropriate reference or consultant to see that new set of assumptions is met.

INTERPRETING THE RESULTS
OF A SIGNIFICANT CHI-SQUARE

Assuming that the assumptions of the chi-square statistic are met and the value is significant, the last question is how to interpret the results. A significant chi-square tells you that the observed distribution differs significantly from the expected distribution. By examining the differences between the observed and expected counts within each cell, you can draw conclusions about which cell(s) contributed most to the significant chi-square. The difference values for each cell provide some basis for interpretation; however, most scholars prefer a more direct and systematic test.

In the case of a chi-square statistic where the degrees of freedom is 1, or what is basically a 2 (number of rows) × 2 (number of columns) design, the data can be interpreted as a point biserial correlation. The particular structure of a 2 × 2 design permits an easy interpretation of the association generated by the outcome. Think of the question as, "If I know the value of one variable, how accurately can I predict the value of the other variable?" In this case, if you know the value of the first variable (e.g., sex, where you have only two choices), is the value of the second variable more likely to be one choice or the other? A nonsignificant chi-square means that you do not have evidence for predicting the value of the second variable based on the first variable. Essentially, the system should be considered random and no association exists. If knowing the value of the first variable permits a 100% accurate prediction of the second variable, then the correlation is 1.00 or −1.00. If the value is significant but not 1.00, then you can make some guess about the value of the second variable if you know the value of the first variable.

Consider what happens if you do not have a 2 × 2 design (e.g., 2 × 4, 5 × 6, etc., where the number of rows and/or columns is greater than 2). In such cases, a significant chi-square tells you that the distribution is not random but provides little direct information about any set of associations that does exist. There are a variety of post hoc techniques (recall from Chapter 4 that *post hoc* is the term used to describe tests used after an omnibus test such as a chi-square or F test in ONEWAY ANOVA). Much like the approaches used in analysis of variance procedures, you must select a particular approach to identify the nature of the various differences that may exist in the design between any combination of cells, rows, or columns.

There are a variety of kinds of approaches to generating and testing models (log linear, prediction analysis, analysis of residuals, etc.). A comprehensive listing of these possibilities is found in Cochran's (1954) article in *Biometrics,* "Some Methods for Strengthening the Common χ^2 Tests." One approach for following up a significant chi-square test is to conduct specific chi-square tests within the larger contingency table. So, if you started with a 3 × 3 design and observed a significant chi-square, you might subdivide your design into one or more smaller designs. You can specify such follow-up procedures a priori or test many possible combinations as post hoc tests. With either approach, you may want to use a Bonferroni adjustment for alpha to correct for possible familywise Type I error.

> "There is a significant relationship between sex and age in terms of the types of people depicted in front-page pictures in rural Appalachian newspapers, $\chi^2 = 22.09$ (3, $N = 119$), $p < .05$."

$\chi^2 = 22.09$	This value is the actual chi-square value that you calculated using the first two formulas presented in this chapter.
(3, $N = 119$)	The values in parentheses show the degrees of freedom (3), which is obtained by using Formula 8.3, and the total number of cases (119).
$p < .05$	The significance or probability level is governed by convention in the social sciences. In this case, there is less than a 5% chance of obtaining a chi-square value this large by mere chance rather than some actual effect.

Figure 8.3   Deciphering the Write-Up of Chi-Square

In addition to subdividing your contingency tables into smaller tables for planned or post hoc analyses, you can also perform residual analyses to determine which cells contributed to the significant chi-square. Using SPSS or other software packages, you can specify that standardized residuals be provided for each cell in your design. Standardized residuals are the difference between the observed and expected counts for each cell in the design converted to z scores (i.e., standardized values). Positive standardized residuals represent cells where there was a positive departure from what was expected, and negative standardized residuals represent cells where there was a negative departure from expected. Standardized values greater than ±1.96 are significant departures from expected ($p < .05$). An example of how to write up the results of a chi-square is found in Figure 8.3.

THE CHI-SQUARE IN COMMUNICATION RESEARCH

Dailey, R. (2006). Confirmation in parent-adolescent relationships and adolescent openness: Toward extending confirmation theory. *Communication Monographs, 73*, 434–458.

As adolescents begin to attain independence, they exhibit decreased closeness, less family time, more conflict, and more topic avoidance with their parents. Although they do develop stronger ties with peers, continued closeness with parents remains critical for effective development. An important element in maintaining parental ties is the extent to which adolescents remain open when communicating with parents. Previous research has linked parental communication style with adolescent openness. To extend that research, Dailey investigated the link between parents' confirmation in the parent-adolescent relationship and their adolescents' openness. Confirmation is the extent to which adolescents' need for validation is met by others—in this case, their parents.

Scholarship has concluded that confirming messages validate others as unique, valuable, and worthy of respect. Moreover, confirming messages can be categorized as recognizing, acknowledging, or endorsing others, whereas disconfirming messages are indifferent, impervious, and/or disqualifying. Research also suggests that the frequency and consistency of such messages is important because they work collectively to foster a certain climate in a relationship. Because family communication literature points to the need for confirmation in family relationships, Dailey hypothesized that the following:

> Hypothesis 1: Parental confirmation is positively related to adolescent openness with parents.

Because families are systems, Dailey questioned whether the mutually reinforcing nature of confirmation messages between parents and adolescents and adolescents and parents would combine to influence adolescents' openness:

> Research Question 1: Do parent and adolescent confirmation behaviors combine to predict adolescent openness with parents?

Finally, Dailey questioned whether sex of the parent or adolescent would be a moderating factor in these relationships:

> Research Question 2: Is the relationship between confirmation in parent-adolescent relationships and adolescent openness moderated by parent or adolescent sex?

A total of 59 parent-adolescent dyads took part in a videotaped interaction where they discussed various moral and ethical dilemmas and also completed survey questions about demographics, family structure, and, for adolescents, perceived parental confirmation and openness with parents. The videotaped interactions occurred in a room staged to resemble a living room. Videotaped interactions were divided into messages from parents ($n = 1,787$) and messages from adolescents ($n = 1,544$). Each message was rated for confirmation by a trained coder using a scale of disconfirming (–4) to confirming (4). Negative values represent disconfirming messages, whereas positive values represent confirming messages.

The hypothesis and second research question were explored using a regression analysis, which is discussed in more detail in a later chapter. Generally, the regression showed that parental confirmation positively predicted adolescent openness. A significant interaction did emerge between adolescents' confirmation messages and openness such that confirming messages and openness were positively related for females but not for males.

To answer the first research question about interactions, Dailey coded messages into 2,480 message sequences, where each response message was coded as a disconfirming or confirming response to either a confirming or disconfirming initial message. Results of this coding procedure generally showed that the most likely sequence was a confirming message given in response to another confirming message—66.6% of the sequences fit this pattern, and there was little variance when dividing the 2,480 response sequences by parent ($n = 1,244$) and adolescent ($n = 1,236$) responses. Dailey then calculated the probability that a particular type of message (e.g., a confirming message from an adolescent) would follow another type of message (e.g., a disconfirming message from a parent). Table 8.1 shows the probabilities for various response patterns divided by whether the adolescents reported less or more openness in their relationship with their parent, as determined by a median split on the openness scale.

Using a less conservative significance level ($p < .10$), Dailey found that adolescents reporting greater openness, as compared with those reporting less openness, were more likely to engage in the sequence of parent confirmation followed by adolescent confirmation, $\chi^2(1) = 3.84$, $p = .06$, but less likely to exhibit the sequence where parent confirmation is followed by adolescent disconfirmation, $\chi^2(1) = 7.80$, $p < .01$. In addition, when adolescents report greater openness, they are less likely than those reporting less openness to exhibit the sequence where adolescent disconfirmation is followed by parent confirmation, $\chi^2(1) = 4.05$, $p = .06$. Dailey concludes that adolescents reporting greater openness are more likely to reciprocate confirmation from parents than are adolescents reporting less openness.

Table 8.1   Probability Values for Various Response Patterns

	Disconfirmation	Confirmation
	Parent Response	
Adolescent message		
Less open		
Disconfirmation	.16	.84
Confirmation	.03	.97
More open		
Disconfirmation	.21	.79
Confirmation	.02	.98
	Adolescent Response	
Parent message		
Less open		
Disconfirmation	.76	.24
Confirmation	.40	.60
More open		
Disconfirmation	.77	.23
Confirmation	.20	.80

REFERENCES

Cochran, S. (1954). Some methods for strengthening the common χ^2 tests. *Biometrics, 10,* 417–451.

Williams, F. (1979). *Reasoning with statistics* (2nd ed.). New York: Holt, Rinehart & Winston.

❧ Sample SPSS Printouts ❧

Assume that you collected data for a political party in your town to determine whether there are sex differences in how likely voters affiliate with particular political parties. The output shown here first provides a cross-tabulation table showing the actual counts within the sex-by-party (2 × 2) contingency table— percentage values are also reported for rows, columns, and percent of total for each cell. The chi-square statistic is reported in the next table.

sex * party Crosstabulation

			party Democrat	party Republican	Total
sex	Male	Count	3	6	9
		% within sex	33.3%	66.7%	100.0%
		% within party	25.0%	75.0%	45.0%
		% of Total	15.0%	30.0%	45.0%
	Female	Count	9	2	11
		% within sex	81.8%	18.2%	100.0%
		% within party	75.0%	25.0%	55.0%
		% of Total	45.0%	10.0%	55.0%
Total		Count	12	8	20
		% within sex	60.0%	40.0%	100.0%
		% within party	100.0%	100.0%	100.0%
		% of Total	60.0%	40.0%	100.0%

Chi-Square Tests

	Value	df	Asymp. Sig. (2-Sided)	Exact Sig. (2-Sided)	Exact Sig (1-Sided)
Pearson Chi-Square	4.848[b]	1	.028		
Continuity Correction[a]	3.039	1	.081		
Likelihood Ratio	5.032	1	.025		
Fisher's Exact Test				.065	.040
N of Valid Cases	20				

a. Computed only for a 2 × 2 table

b. 2 cells (50.0%) have expected count less than 5. The minimum expected count is 3.60.

NINE

SIMPLE BIVARIATE CORRELATION

Kevin is a communication student who has recently developed an interest in the research regarding the fear of communicating with others. In order to fulfill the requirements of an assignment in his research methods class, Kevin decided to examine whether there is any relationship between income and communication apprehension. It is possible, Kevin reasoned, that the wealthier an individual is, the more confidence she or he is likely to have generally, and therefore the less communication apprehension she or he should experience. He collected a small sample of individuals in his community and analyzed the data using the correlation coefficient. The results of Kevin's data analysis revealed no statistically significant relationship between income level and communication apprehension.

The simple correlation coefficient could be considered the workhorse driving many other statistics. Because many other procedures essentially compare variance and covariance, the correlation could be viewed as the fundamental building block for other procedures—even the *t* test and ANOVA. The correlation helps answer a fundamental question about the relationship of two variables: "If I know the value of the first variable, how accurately can I predict the second variable?" If you apply this simple question to other statistical procedures you have learned about (e.g., *t* test, ANOVA, chi-square), you can see why we call the simple correlation a "workhorse."

UNDERSTANDING THE CORRELATION COEFFICIENT

A correlation describes a statistical relationship between two variables based on each observation (e.g., person, case). Each participant (or other type of unit of analysis) has two scores: one for the X variable and one for the Y variable. Suppose we want to find the correlation of height and weight. For each person (the unit of analysis), we would have a score for both height and weight. The correlation measures the relationship between the two variables. A scatterplot depicting this relationship is shown in Figure 9.1. Notice that the data set includes 18 people, each represented by an "X" on the graph. The line in the graph simply shows a visual representation of the correlation—a positive

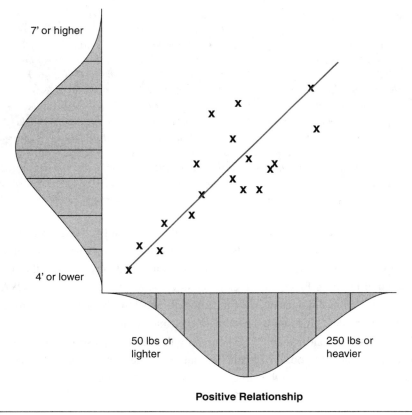

Positive Relationship

Figure 9.1   A Scatterplot of a Positive Correlation

relationship between height and weight. Both the *X*- and *Y*-axes for the plot are depicted as normal bell curves to show that the correlation procedure basically examines the variance in one variable in relation to the variance in another. Importantly, the term *relationship* does not necessarily imply causation.

Correlations range from +1.00 to −1.00 (both of these values indicate perfectly correlated variables). If the two variables are not correlated (or you do not have the data to be able to observe the correlation), the correlation value will be zero. The values in between, which are more commonly observed, indicate some less than perfect ability to predict the value of one variable based on the value of the other. Not surprisingly, the more accurate the prediction, the larger the correlation (i.e., closer to either 1 or −1); correspondingly, the smaller the correlation (i.e., closer to zero), the less accuracy in the prediction. A positive correlation indicates that as one value increases, the value for the other variable also increases (as height increases in persons, so does the average weight). A negative correlation indicates that as one value for a variable increases, the value of the other variable diminishes (as smoking tobacco increases, life expectancy diminishes). The size of the correlation value indicates the accuracy of the prediction in the direction indicated—larger correlations indicate greater accuracy.

CALCULATING THE CORRELATION COEFFICIENT

The correlation coefficient is a comparison (in a ratio form) of the covariance of the two variables to the total amount of variability. In other words, the correlation is a comparison, and when the covariance and variance are equal, the ratio is 1.00 (or −1.00). The formula below describes the relationship of covariance (the degree to which the two variables vary together) as it relates to the total amount of variability across both variables. Covariance means that as the values of one variable change, the value of the other variable changes in a predictable direction. As *X* increases, so does the corresponding value of *Y*, or as *X* increases, the value of *Y* decreases. For instance, consider the data reported in Table 9.1 comparing income (*X*) and level of communication apprehension (*Y*). Looking just at the *X* and *Y* columns, you can see that there is some degree of variability and that the two values share some degree of covariance. The purpose of the correlation procedure is to quantify the extent to which the covariance between *X* (income) and *Y* (communication apprehension) is greater than the overall variance in the sample.

Table 9.1 Computing the Correlation Coefficient

Applying the data from two measures completed by each of 10 individuals, we find the following:

Respondent	X	Y	$X-\bar{X}$	$Y-\bar{Y}$	$(X-\bar{X})^2$	$(Y-\bar{Y})^2$	$(X-\bar{X})(Y-\bar{Y})$
1	10,000	60	−22,500	0	506,250,000	0	0
2	15,000	79	−17,500	19	306,250,000	361	−332,500
3	20,000	65	−12,500	5	156,250,000	25	−62,500
4	25,000	66	−7,500	6	56,250,000	36	−45,000
5	30,000	51	−2,500	−9	6,250,000	81	22,500
6	35,000	73	2,500	13	6,250,000	169	32,500
7	40,000	52	7,500	−8	56,250,000	64	−60,000
8	45,000	31	12,500	−29	156,250,000	841	−362,500
9	50,000	59	17,500	−1	306,250,000	1	−17,500
10	55,000	60	22,500	0	506,250,000	0	0
Total, Sum, or Σ	325,000	596	0	0	2,062,500,000	1,578	−825,000

Means:
$$\bar{X} = \frac{325,000}{10} = 3,250 \qquad \bar{Y} = \frac{596}{10} = 60$$

142

The computational formula for the correlation coefficient is shown in Formula 9.1 (McNemar, 1960). The numerator of the formula calculates the overall variability in the sample of values for the two variables, whereas the denominator calculates the shared variance between the two variables. The denominator is typically larger than the numerator, which results in a value between −1 and 1.

$$r = \frac{\sum (X - \bar{X})(Y - \bar{Y})}{\sqrt{\left[\sum (X - \bar{X})^2\right]\left[\sum (Y - \bar{Y})^2\right]}}. \tag{9.1}$$

In Kevin's study, he was interested in the relationship between income and level of communication apprehension. More specifically, he expected that income level would be negatively associated with communication, such that as income level increased, communication apprehension would decrease. Figure 9.2 presents the steps that are used to compute the correlation coefficient.

Applying the formula for a correlation based on the sample data above reveals the following:

$$r = \frac{\sum (X - \bar{X})(Y - \bar{Y})}{\sqrt{\left[\sum (X - \bar{X})^2\right]\left[\sum (Y - \bar{Y})^2\right]}}$$

$$r = \frac{-825,00}{\sqrt{[(1578)][(2,062,500,000)]}}$$

$$r = \frac{-825,000}{1,803,883}$$

$$r = -.46$$

1. Enter the data for each participant using the format shown in Figure 9.2 (use a column format to avoid confusion).

2. Complete calculations to obtain information for each column.

3. Calculate the sums of each column in the bottom row.

4. Calculate the correlation coefficient using information from the table to complete Formula 9.1.

5. Test the significance of the correlation.

6. Write up results.

Figure 9.2   Steps in Computing the Correlation Coefficient

You should remember that correlation coefficients are always between -1.00 and $+1.00$. If you end up with a coefficient that is larger than $+1.00$ or -1.00, you have made a calculation error.

Importantly, before Kevin can claim that the relationship between income and communication apprehension is generalizable to the general population, he needs to determine how likely it is that he would have observed a correlation coefficient that high by chance. In order to determine whether a correlation coefficient is statistically significant, use the table in Appendix D. You will also need to determine your degrees of freedom, which is simply the number of pairs of data in your sample minus 2. Applying this simple formula to Kevin's data, we can easily determine that he had 8 degrees of freedom $(10 - 2 = 8)$.

Kevin's coefficient of $-.46$ had 8 degrees of freedom. Looking in Appendix D, you will find a table titled "Critical Values for the r Statistic." Using the degrees of freedom (8), the level of risk you are willing to take (typically .05), and a one-tailed test (because Kevin specified the direction of his hypothesis), the critical value is .5494. So, is Kevin's correlation coefficient of $-.46$ statistically significant at the .05 level? In this case, the obtained value of $-.46$ (ignore the negative or positive sign when you examine the critical value) does not exceed the critical value (.5494), so the correlation is not significant. Of course, the effect size (the value of the correlation) is relatively large, and with a slightly larger sample, assuming the pattern continued, the correlation coefficient could exceed the critical value.

In larger samples where you have greater degrees of freedom, you will need to use a more extensive table of critical values or a computer program to determine significance. Whereas the critical value tells you whether the observed correlation is unlikely due to chance, an alternative approach is to consider the confidence interval (CI) for the obtained correlation. The confidence interval, most commonly considered at the 95% level, helps you determine a range of values around your observed value that represents the likely actual correlation. Although you can estimate the 95% CI for the correlation using Formula 9.2, the distribution of Pearson's r is not normal, and consequently, you are better served by using an online calculator that converts the r to Fisher's z and then calculates the 95% confidence interval. An example of such a calculator can be found at http://faculty.vassar.edu/lowry/rho.html. To illustrate the process, however, we will continue with the formula.

$$95\% \, \text{CI} = \frac{(1-r^2)*t}{\sqrt{(N-1)}}. \qquad (9.2)$$

Applying this formula to the previous example reveals

$$95\% \, \text{CI} = \frac{(1-.21)*2}{\sqrt{(10-1)}}$$
$$95\% \, \text{CI} = \frac{.79*2}{3}$$
$$95\% \, \text{CI} = .53$$

After obtaining the value of the 95% CI, your next task is to use that value to determine the upper bound limit and the lower bound limit. In this case, the lower limit of the confidence interval is −.46 − .53 or −.99, and the upper limit is −.46 + .53 or .07 (zero is included in the confidence interval).

The 95% confidence interval shows the values of r that would fall within one standard deviation above and below the reported value. In this case, the confidence interval ranges from .07 to −.99; thus, you would have confidence that the actual correlation would fall somewhere between −.99 and .07. Because the confidence interval is so large and includes the possibility of no correlation at all (i.e., a correlation of zero), we must place less confidence in the initial correlation of $r = -.46$. In other words, under these circumstances, there is a 95% chance that the correlation could range anywhere between .07 and −.99—the observed −.46 could, in fact, be spurious based on this large confidence interval. You will notice that the easiest way to improve the confidence interval (i.e., shrinking the interval and likely moving it away from zero) would be to increase the sample size.

ASSUMPTIONS OF THE CORRELATION COEFFICIENT

The first assumption of the correlation coefficient is that your data on both variables are measured on either an interval or ratio scale. Recall that interval scales are those that have equal intervals between points on the scales but do not have a true zero point. On the other hand, ratio scales have both equal intervals between points on their scale and do have a true zero point. The correlation coefficient also assumes that the traits you are measuring are normally distributed in the population. In other words, you should be confident that if you collect data from the entire population, the results will be normally distributed.

Engaged Research

Many universities have adopted newspaper readership programs in an effort to help students become more aware of current political and civic issues. For your project, create a simple survey assessing the extent to which individuals read the paper as well as a measure of their political knowledge. Administer this survey to at least 30 people and use the correlation coefficient to determine if there is any relationship between newspaper readership and political knowledge.

The correlation coefficient discussed in this chapter also assumes that any relationship between two variables is linear. If you were to plot the variables on a scatterplot, you should be able to clearly see a clear trend from the lower left to the upper right (a positive relationship) or from the upper left to the lower right (a negative relationship). If the relationship changes directions somewhere in the middle, you have a curvilinear relationship. The correlation coefficient presented in this chapter is not the best type to use to test curvilinear relationships.

In addition, homoscedasticity is assumed in computing this statistic. Homoscedasticity simply refers to the assumption that scores on the Y variable are normally distributed across each value of the Y variable. If the scores are not distributed in this way, the correlation coefficient becomes a misleading average of points of lower and higher correlation. You can spot this easily by plotting your variables on a scatterplot and making sure that the dots are spread out relatively equally along the entire length of the distribution.

USING COMPUTER PROGRAMS TO CALCULATE CORRELATION COEFFICIENTS

Computer printouts provide a wealth of information. You are most interested in the size and direction of the correlation, whether or not the correlation is significant, and the sample size used to compute the correlation. SPSS will often default to using a listwise deletion for the calculation of individual correlations. What this means is that missing data in any element delete the case, but only for the calculation of that particular correlation. As a result, the sample size will vary slightly from one correlation to the next. This feature is something to pay close attention to, because if you believe that you have no missing data, then the inconsistent sample size between correlations indicates possible problems that should be further considered.

Examine the means and variability for each variable (standard deviations/variance). Make sure that the values of these parameters are what one would normally expect for the variables. For instance, if you observe too little variability, the size of the correlation could be artificially inflated. Alternatively, if you have too much variability, you may not be able to detect any covariation, and your correlation will be artificially low. Since the correlation is ultimately a ratio, a change in the values of any of the fundamental parameters may greatly affect the calculation of the association. If you are using a commonly used scale, previous research should provide a basis for assessing whether the measures of both central tendency and dispersion are within what one would expect given the history of the use of that scale. If substantial differences are observed, you may have reason to suspect the accuracy of your findings.

Importantly, a significant correlation simply indicates that zero is not included in the confidence interval. As a result, a confidence interval can potentially range from .01 to .99. The larger the sample size, the smaller the confidence interval, and therefore the more accurate the estimation of the parameter. Also, a significant correlation indicates that the expected value of the relationship is either positive or negative, rather than indicating a particular value. Clearly, the size of the correlation (.10, .50, .90) can indicate the expectation of the size of the association, but that estimate will usually have substantial sampling error, unless the sample size is large (in excess of 1,600 in most cases).

INTERPRETING THE RESULTS OF A CORRELATION

The interpretation of a correlation is dependent on the context and application for the correlation. What would in one context be a very significant effect would be very disappointing in another context. For example, a professional basketball player making 50% of shot attempts would not be surprising; a professional baseball player getting a hit 50% of the time at bat would be astonishing. The question is, to fulfill the theoretical expectations, what should be the direction and size of the correlation? Part of the answer, of course, considers what past research results would predict.

You should remember that the correlation fits within a context of theory or a set of structures under investigation. In the case of more complex analyses, such as structural equation modeling, the correlation is viewed in the context of how that association fits within a pattern of results. The interpretation and application of any correlation should always be thought of as the answer to the following question: "Given an association, what conclusions does the association permit?" In the case of a correlation that is inconsistent with prior research and/or theories, the results call into question previous findings. The development of explanations for the differences in outcome can provide the basis for further investigation.

The key element for you to remember is that a correlation simply provides an answer to the following question: Given information about one variable, how accurately can the value of the second variable be predicted? The interpretation should therefore focus on how strongly the two variables are related and what conclusions can be drawn from that specific relationship. When the assessment is framed in those terms, the impact of any significant correlation can be addressed. It is also critical to keep in mind that the fact that two variables are related does not mean that one causes the other. Put simply, correlation is not causation. An example of how to write up the results for the correlation coefficient can be found in Figure 9.3.

CORRECTING FOR VARIOUS ARTIFACTS

Various artifacts can occur, affecting the calculation of any statistical parameter. By *artifact*, we mean that there are statistical abnormalities that could affect the precision of your correlation estimate. For example, when you use scales that have less than perfect reliability (as all do), the error associated with unreliability has the effect of reducing your ability to detect covariance and adds to the overall variability; these actions reduce the size of the observed correlation.

The impact of various artifacts (restriction in range, attenuation, dichotomization of a continuous variable) systematically reduces the size of the correlation and therefore increases the probability of finding a nonsignificant

"There exists no significant correlation between income and communication apprehension, $r(8) = -.46$, $p > .05$ for this data set."

$r = -.46$	This represents the actual value of the correlation coefficient that Kevin calculated using the formula presented in this chapter.
(8)	This is the number of degrees of freedom, which was obtained by subtracting 2 from the total number of pairs.
$p > .05$	As noted previously, the significance or probability level is governed by convention in the social sciences. In this case, the correlation coefficient is not statistically significant.

Figure 9.3   Deciphering the Write-Up Correlation Coefficients

correlation. Consider, for instance, what happens when you have a restricted range of values. Assume that you conducted a survey with college students exploring the relationship between the amount of time spent in a romantic relationship and the amount of perceived conflict that occurs with the romantic partner. Because you are sampling college students, you will not be able to include many long-term (e.g., 20 years or longer) romantic relationships. This artifact restricts the range on the "time in relationship" variable. Because the range is restricted, the potential observed covariance will be smaller, which will result in a smaller than expected correlation. As you can see from this example and the discussion of unreliability above, there is some advantage if you can determine the amount of imprecision due to these artifacts and correct your correlation estimate to account for the problems. A full discussion and information on correction is available in Hunter and Schmidt (1990). As you become more familiar with the correlation procedure, you may want to explore various corrections for artifacts so that the precision of your findings can be improved.

Statistical packages vary in their ability to handle and incorporate the various artifacts. For example, LISREL, in the default mode, automatically corrects for attenuation in the correlation (as does AMOS). Most SPSS routines are not able to correct for artifacts, and therefore the estimates are inaccurate (the level of inaccuracy is a function of the size of the unreliability for the variables). If you are interested in performing analyses with corrected data, you should explore using more advanced statistical programs that may be available on your campus. Also, whereas we briefly discussed the impact of artifacts on correlations, these artifacts occur for all statistics.

THE CORRELATION COEFFICIENT
IN COMMUNICATION RESEARCH

Perry, S. D. (2007). Tsunami warning dissemination in Mauritius. *Journal of Applied Communication Research, 35,* 399–417.

On December 26, 2004, a massive earthquake off the coast of Indonesia generated an enormous tsunami that resulted in the death of approximately 230,000 people in the Indian Ocean basin. As Stephen Perry notes, postdisaster communication surveys are essential in cases like this as a means of improving future disaster warning efficiency. In particular, following a disaster event, authorities need to assess how warnings were disseminated to the public. Unfortunately, Perry establishes that such assessments have been largely ignored by communication scholars. This gap in the literature is especially problematic given the potential of applied communication scholarship to help prevent the loss of life in future environmental disasters. Perry addresses this gap in the literature by examining warning dissemination in the Republic of Mauritius following the 2004 Indonesian earthquake.

Initially, Perry notes that, although scholars have widely examined news diffusion and dissemination, few have studied the process of warning a population following a tsunami. In fact, the only study reviewed by Perry that did examine tsunami warnings failed to include measures of the time it took to alert at-risk populations. Also, few scholars have examined news diffusion in an international context by studying how news diffusion flows through multiple channels in different societies. Based on such differences and news diffusion research, Perry poses the following research question:

Research Question 1: How quickly did warnings/news about the tsunami spread, to whom, and through what channels?

Other factors, such as the severity of an individual's last experience with a particular crisis as well as his or her emotional and behavioral responses to media coverage of a crisis, are critical issues to examine as a means of understanding how people are likely to react to a warning. Experience with a crisis was an especially salient issue in Mauritius as most of its citizens had not experienced a tsunami in their lifetime. As a result, the following research question was explored:

> Research Question 2: What are the behavioral, attitudinal, and emotional responses of people to the tsunami warning and information?

Finally, any study of crisis communication should be concerned with the myriad avenues through which people seek additional information on the events that have transpired following a disaster. In order to assess different sources of information and their perceived utility to participants, the following research question was advanced:

> Research Question 3: Where did people turn to seek additional information after learning about the tsunami, and how useful did they perceive that information to be?

Participants in this study included 319 residents of Mauritius who responded to a brief telephone survey. The survey included measures of how individuals responded to the tsunami warning (e.g., "I phoned friends or family to warn them"), perceived usefulness of the warning information, perceived seriousness of the tsunami threat, the medium through which respondents first encountered the warning (e.g., telephone, radio, television), items asking whether respondents sought more information, and questions assessing how worried participants were. Before considering the results of this study, it is important to note that Perry used a number of statistics to analyze the research questions posed in this study; however, we will focus here on the author's analyses of the simple bivariate correlations.

Demographic factors were examined in order to answer the first research question. Specifically, correlations were computed between the time it took a person to hear the tsunami warning and six respondent characteristics, including gender, age, education, time spent watching TV, time spent listening to the radio, and distance lived from shore. Interestingly, Perry found significant correlations between only two factors. Age was negatively correlated with information speed ($r = -.14, p < .05$), indicating that as age increased, elapsed time before the warning decreased. Television viewing was also negatively related to warning speed ($r = -.14$, $p < .05$) in that as TV consumption increased, elapsed time before hearing the warning decreased.

The second research question examined respondents' behavioral, attitudinal, and emotional responses to the tsunami warning. Correlations were computed to explore relationships between participants' level of worry and perceived seriousness of the event and demographic and media use variables. As shown in Table 9.2, perceptions of danger to family, friends, self, and others were positively related to level of worry and perceived seriousness.

The final research question examined respondents' information-seeking behavior. Correlations revealed that the earlier people found out about the tsunami, the more sources they pursued to acquire additional information ($r = -.14$, $p < .05$). Respondents who perceived that their family and friends had been affected also sought more information from a variety of sources ($r = .11$, $p < .05$). Finally, perceived danger to self was positively related to information seeking ($r = .32$, $p < .05$). In other words, as perceived danger increased, so did participants' use of multiple sources for additional information.

According to Perry, the results of this study provide a number of practical applications of communication research to future disasters. For example, given the large reliance on television in Mauritius, Perry argues that the medium must be made more responsive by developing broadcast warnings that can be displayed immediately in the event of a crisis. Given the international scope

Table 9.2   Correlations Between Perceptions of Danger, Perceived Seriousness, and Level of Worry ($n = 52$)

	Worry	*Seriousness*
Thought family/friends might be affected	.46***	.35*
Perceived danger to self	.35*	.56***
Perceived danger to others in Mauritius	.39**	.28*

NOTE: The sample for Research Question 2 is smaller than the overall sample because only 52 participants reported thinking the wave was still approaching when asked these questions. In other words, those who thought the wave had already passed would not have had the same behavioral, attitudinal, and emotional responses to the warning information.

$*p < .05$; $**p < .01$; $***p < .001$.

of the 2004 tsunami, Perry also advocates the advent of a multilingual warning system. Ultimately, the development of effective warning dissemination practices will be critical to reducing death tolls in future disasters.

REFERENCES

Hunter, J. E., & Schmidt, F. L. (1990). *Methods of meta-analysis: Correcting error and bias in research findings.* Newbury Park, CA: Sage.
McNemar, Q. (1960). *Psychological statistics* (4th ed.). New York: John Wiley.

✂ Sample SPSS Printouts ✂

Correlation output typically comes in the form of a matrix where you are examining correlations among a set of variables. The correlation matrix below contains four variables obtained from students' grades and self-reports in a public speaking class: grade for Quiz 1, self-reported effort in preparing for Speech 1, self-reported interest in the Speech 1 topic selected, and their actual grade on Speech 1. The correlation matrix shows Pearson's r, two-tailed significance level, and pairwise n used in calculating the r for that cell. Coefficients proceeded by a negative sign are negative correlations; others are positive. Also note that significant correlations are marked or "flagged" with one or two asterisks to indicate $p < .05$ or $p < .01$, respectively.

Correlations

		quiz1	effort	interest	speech 1
quiz 1	Pearson Correlation	1	.307*	.115	−.037
	Sig. (2-tailed)		.034	.427	.800
	N	50	48	50	50
effort	Pearson Correlation	.307*	1	−.624**	−.246
	Sig. (2-tailed)	.034		.000	.092
	N	48	48	48	48
interest	Pearson Correlation	.115	−624**	1	.058
	Sig. (2-tailed)	.427	.000		.688
	N	50	48	50	50
speech1	Pearson Correlation	−.037	-.246	.058	1
	Sig. (2-tailed)	.800	.092	.688	
	N	50	48	50	50

*Correlation is significant at the 0.05 level (2-tailed).
**Correlation is significant at the 0.01 level (2-tailed).

TEN

MULTIPLE REGRESSION

———◆◆◆———

Stan is enrolled in a communication research course and is interested in variables that predict attitude change when audiences are exposed to persuasive appeals. In order to fulfill a course assignment, Stan designed a study to explore the extent to which the perceived credibility of the speaker and the quality of arguments used predict audience attitude change. Using multiple regression, based on a sample of 60 respondents, Stan was able to determine that both credibility and argument quality acted as significant predictors of attitude change.

In the previous chapter, you learned about the simple correlation procedure, which explores relationships between two variables. Although the correlation was called the "workhorse" of statistical procedure, we are often interested in models that are more complex than two variables being related. Regression, a natural extension of the correlation, allows you to explore the relationship between a dependent, or criterion, variable, and one or more independent variables.

UNDERSTANDING MULTIPLE REGRESSION

A correlation coefficient provides you with the ability to quantitatively describe the relationship between one variable and another variable. Whereas the correlation coefficient only provides an estimate describing the strength of the relationship, the regression procedure goes further and provides an estimate of how much variance in the dependent variable is accounted for by variance in the independent, or predictor, variable. Regression has a variety of uses in research, ranging from developing predictive models to use in practical situations (e.g., How much return in profit can you expect for each dollar spent on advertising?) to testing hypothesized theoretical relationship among multiple variables (e.g., Which communication variables have the greatest influence in a model predicting job stress and burnout?).

Although the term *regression* applies to a broad family of procedures (similar to how *ANOVA* can actually be used in reference to ONEWAY, factorial, analysis of covariance, etc.), we will distinguish here between simple regression and multiple regression. Using a simple regression, you can determine the predictive value of one variable for another. In calculating the simple regression, you will obtain an unstandardized beta value, which tells you how many units of X must change to achieve one unit of change in Y. Using the beta value, you can predict a certain value of Y based on knowledge of a constant (which is basically error) and a given value for X. Consequently, the simple regression is useful because it not only provides an estimate of the relationship between variables, just like a correlation does, but it also provides information that can be useful for prediction.

The value of a regression procedure was actually first introduced to you in the previous chapter. If you recall, the correlation was illustrated using a scatterplot with values depicting the intersection of respondents' height and weight. Also on the graph was a line. The line shown on the scatterplot is actually a regression line. Using the beta value generated in the regression, we can accurately place the line on the graph and use it to predict, for a given value of X, what the value of Y should be—you simply select your value for X on the X-axis, follow it up to the regression line, and then note the corresponding value for Y on the Y-axis. Rather than using a scatterplot to predict, it is actually easier to use the following simple linear equation:

$$Y = a + bX + e.$$

The a is the intercept, the b is the slope or regression coefficient, and the e is the error term. Assuming that the intercept is set to zero (which is often the case in regression), you simply need to insert values for X, the beta coefficient, and error. With such information, you can then predict values for Y. Thus, prediction is an important outcome for regression.

So, why would a researcher use multiple regression instead of simply looking at the relationships between two variables (i.e., bivariate correlation or simple regression)? Recall from our introductory example that Stan designed a persuasion experiment and hypothesized that the amount of attitude change in the audience (dependent variable) is predicted by the credibility of the communicator and the quality of the arguments (both of these are predictor variables). If credibility of the communicator and the quality of arguments are independent (i.e., unrelated to each other or $r = .00$), the standardized regression coefficient is the same as the zero-order correlation (*zero order* refers to the simple bivariate correlation not controlling for any other influences). But suppose that the perception of the credibility of a communicator is correlated with the perception by the audience of the quality of the argument. In this case, the correlation between credibility and attitude change, as well as argument quality and attitude change, overlaps and shares some common elements. Multiple regression allows you to calculate a partial correlation, which is the correlation between a predictor variable and a dependent variable when holding constant another variable or variables. Thus, the regression extends beyond the bivariate correlation because it allows you to test a multiple-variable model and gives you comparatively more information about the relationship between each variable in the model and the criterion variable.

Multiple regression uses multiple predictors in the regression equation to predict a value for a single dependent (also called *criterion*) variable. The formula for the multiple regression equation can be found in Formula 10.1 (for more information, see Pedhazur, 1997).

$$Y = \beta_1 X_1 + \beta_2 X_2 + \beta_3 X_3 \cdots + \beta_i X_i + C. \tag{10.1}$$

In this formula, the predictor variables are denoted by X (the subscript number denotes different predictors), and C represents a constant (also the *y*-intercept in linear algebra). This regression equation is for raw scores and is useful if the goal is to predict a particular value that has meaning or application beyond the scale (like predicting income). Thus, one use for multiple regression, particularly in finance and economics, is to make predictions about a particular outcome (i.e., Y) based on a particular input (i.e., X) or set of inputs.

Whereas prediction is an important use of regression, social scientific researchers are typically more interested in developing and testing hypothesized models. For prediction to be meaningful, the value being predicted must have some real-world meaning or implication. When predicting income, for instance, any increase or decrease in actual income levels has real meaning—literally in dollars and cents. This is often not the case in research. For example, the Personal Report of Communication Apprehension–24 (PRCA-24) measures the level of anxiety felt about communication. The PRCA does a very good job of eliciting reliable and useful information; however, the particular score (50, 55, or 60) has no meaning outside of the metric of the particular scale.

In the social sciences, because the real meaning of specific values is arbitrary, researchers are typically more interested in figuring out some way of comparing various independent variables to determine which are "more important" than others in predicting values for a dependent variable. Using unstandardized betas is not the solution because they cannot be compared—one unit of value on the PRCA-24 is not equivalent in any way to a unit of value associated with giving a public speech or having a communication class. Thus, to compare multiple predictor variables to determine which are "more important," you must find a way to represent the influence of all predictor variables using a common metric for comparison. The term *common metric* just means using a value that, for each variable, represents the same unit of measurement.

The multiple regression aids your ability to compare variables by taking two steps. First, standardized regression removes the *y*-intercept; therefore, there is no constant to the equation. As a result, the line will pass through the origin (coordinates 0,0). This step provides an easily interpretable starting point for the regression to easily compare the influence of various predictors. The second step is to express the influence of each predictor variable in standardized units. What this means is that the units of change in each predictor are divided by the overall standard deviation for that predictor; the resulting value tells you how much each variable must change to achieve one unit of change in the dependent variable.

The equation produces the following two important terms for consideration: (1) the weight or contribution of the individual elements and (2) the overall accuracy of the prediction of the equation. The standardized beta coefficient describes how important one variable is in relation to another in terms of predicting values for the dependent/criterion variable. Variables with larger standardized betas (either positive or negative) have more predictive power than variables with smaller beta weights. In a given regression model, you can directly compare standardized beta weights to determine the relative importance of particular variables in the equation.

CALCULATING A MULTIPLE REGRESSION

Stan's first step in analyzing attitude change was to select the predictor variables. As he considered the multiple factors that likely affect the attitude of an audience, Stan followed a few simple criteria that ultimately led him to choose argument quality and speaker credibility. Initially, Stan's review of literature in this area revealed that both variables had theoretical significance. Stan also knew that both variables had been examined separately in research exploring attitude change in the past. In addition, Stan was confident that speaker credibility and argument quality were not so highly correlated as to produce a multicollinearity problem (for additional guidelines for avoiding multicollinearity problems, see Dizney & Gromen, 1967; Heise, 1969). All of the steps for computing a multiple regression are summarized in Figure 10.1.

As you have learned throughout this text, gathering a representative and adequate sample is critical to ensuring accurate estimations of any statistical procedure. When conducting a multiple regression, statisticians recommend that you select at least 15 events for each predictor variable and attempt to keep sample sizes equal across the measurement of all variables (see Stevens, 2002).

Although computer programs are typically used to calculate multiple regression coefficients, Stan calculated these by hand using Formula 10.2. This formula provides the proportion of variance in the dependent variable (Y) that is shared with the independent variables (R^2_{Y2}). As you can see, the formula includes squared correlations for each dependent variable with the independent variable (r^2_{Y1} and r^2_{Y2}) as well as the squared correlation of

---

1. Select predictor variables.

2. Select an adequate sample.

3. Compute the multiple correlation coefficient using Formula 10.2.

4. Test the significance of the correlation coefficient using Formula 10.3.

5. Calculate the beta weights for each predictor variable using Formula 10.4.

6. Test the significance of the beta weights for each predictor variable using Formula 10.5.

7. Write up results.

Figure 10.1   Steps in Calculating a Multiple Regression

the two independent variables with each other (r^2_{Y2}). Pearson correlations for all of Stan's variables can be found in Figure 10.2.

$$R^2_{Y12} = \frac{r^2_{Y1} + r^2_{Y2} - 2r_{Y1}r_{Y2}r_{12}}{1 - r^2_{12}}. \tag{10.2}$$

	Argument Quality (X_1)	Credibility (X_2)	Attitude Change (Y)	Standard Deviation
Argument quality (X_1)	1.0	.38	.64	8.8
Credibility (X_2)		1.0	.52	7.8
Attitude change (Y)			1.0	6.8

Figure 10.2   Correlations for Argument Quality, Credibility, and Attitude Change

Applying the formula for the multiple correlation coefficient to Stan's data reveals the following:

$$R^2_{Y12} = \frac{(.64)^2 + (.52)^2 - 2(.64 * .52 * .38)}{1 - .14}$$
$$R^2_{Y12} = \frac{.41 + .27 - 2(.08)}{1 - .14}$$
$$R^2_{Y12} = \frac{.52}{.86}$$
$$R^2_{Y12} = .60$$

In order to determine if the observed multiple correlation coefficient is statistically significant, compute Formula 10.3. This formula uses the F distribution and includes the squared multiple correlation coefficient (R^2), the number of predictor variables (m), and the number of events in the study (n). This test is entered with m degrees of freedom in the denominator and $n - m - 1$ degrees of freedom in the numerator.

$$F_{m, n-m-1} = \frac{R^2}{1 - R^2} \left(\frac{n - m - 1}{m} \right). \tag{10.3}$$

When Stan's data are inserted into the formula, the result is (recall that Stan sampled 60 individuals)

$$F = \frac{.60}{1 - .60}\left(\frac{60 - 2 - 1}{2}\right)$$

$$F = 1.5 * 28.5$$

$$F = 42.75$$

In order to determine whether this value is statistically significant, consult the critical values for the F distribution provided in Appendix C. Stan set his alpha level at .05 and calculated 2 ($m = 2$ predictor variables) and 57 ($60 - 2 - 1$) degrees of freedom. Given that the test statistic (42.75) is larger than the critical value (3.150), Stan concluded that the multiple correlation coefficient is significant.

The next step in multiple regression analysis is to calculate beta weights in order to determine the relative contribution of each predictor variable (see Formula 10.4).

$$\beta_1 = \frac{r_{Y1} - r_{Y2}r_{Y12}}{1 - r_{12}^2}$$

$$\beta_2 = \frac{r_{Y2} - r_{Y1}r_{Y12}}{1 - r_{12}^2} \tag{10.4}$$

The result for the first beta weight, based on Stan's data, follows:

$$\beta_1 = \frac{.64 - (.52 * .38)}{1 - .14}$$

$$\beta_1 = \frac{.44}{.86}$$

$$\beta_1 = .51$$

The result for the second beta weight is:

$$\beta_2 = \frac{.52 - (.64 * .38)}{1 - .14}$$

$$\beta_2 = \frac{.28}{.86}$$

$$\beta_2 = .33$$

A version of the *t* test is used to determine if the beta weights are statistically significant (see Formula 10.5).

$$t = \frac{\beta}{s_\beta}$$

$$s_\beta = \sqrt{\frac{1 - R^2}{(n - k - 1)(1 - r_{12}^2)}}$$

(10.5)

Note: S_β is the standard error of beta, k is the number of variables, and r_{12}^2 is the squared multiple correlation coefficient of the predictor variables.

Applying Formula 11.5 to Stan's data reveals the following:

$$\beta_1 = t = \frac{.51}{.09} = 5.67$$

$$\beta_2 = t = \frac{.33}{.09} = 3.67$$

The degrees of freedom, using Stan's data, are 57 ($n - m - 1$ or $60 - 2 - 1$). Using the procedures outlined in Chapter 2, Stan was able to determine that both *t* values are significant.

ASSUMPTIONS OF MULTIPLE REGRESSION

For the mathematical logic of multiple regression to work, the following assumptions must be met: (a) Multicolinearity should be kept to a minimum, (b) no causal connections should exist among variables, and (c) the relationships between the variables are linear (unless you believe that there are nonlinear relationships, in which case there are different methods to handle that process for multiple regression).

Multicolinearity, or just colinearity, occurs when two or more of the independent variables are highly correlated with one another. Images in Figure 10.3 visually show the concept of colinearity. Suppose in a public speaking class, we were trying to predict students' grades based on their three speech grades and exam grades. If colinearity is absent, none of the predictor variables should share variance; however, if colinearity is present, the predictor variables will overlap and share variance. Colinearity is present in every set of predictors to some degree. So, like many statistical assumptions, it is not "if" you have violated the assumption that colinearity should be absent but, rather, by how much and with what effect. To detect colinearity, you should ask SPSS to provide you with tolerance and VIF values (do this by checking "colinearity diagnostics" under options). If the VIF value is less than 1 or the VIF value is greater than 4, you may have colinearity problems. If such problems are present, overall model statistics (R^2 and F) are not affected; however, the regression coefficients for each variable are not reliable estimates. If you have colinearity, you have several potential options. First, you could simplify your model and eliminate problematic variables; this is the best solution. In some cases, you might be able to combine variables. For instance, if you have several factors from the same scale, you might be justified in treating the scale as one-dimensional rather than multidimensional. Third, you could center variables, which involves subtracting the mean from each person's value to create a new, centered version of the variable. This process makes explanations slightly more complicated but should eliminate any colinearity problem. Finally, the addition of more people/cases can sometimes reduce colinearity because the standard error for each variable is diminished.

The second condition posits that if you have A, B, and C as predictor variables for X, there is no expectation of a causal relationship between A and B. Multiple regression is a simple form of structural equation modeling or path analysis that simply has no indirect paths. In other words, all of the assumptions of causal modeling must be met. If, for example, you believe that

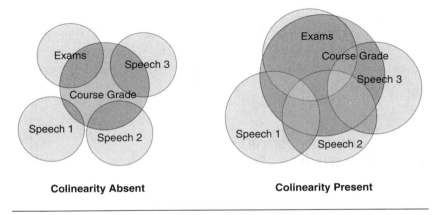

Figure 10.3   Visual Representation of Colinearity

A causes *B*, which in turn causes *X*, the multiple regression is inappropriate and you should use path analysis instead.

Engaged Research

You have likely come across reports of research indicating that a sense of humor is important to a number of health outcomes. For your project, use multiple regression to test the hypothesis that humor orientation as well as the ability to cope using humor negatively predict perceived stress. You will find it useful to review the published results of Nathan Miczo's (2004) research on humor, published in *Communication Studies,* for access to measures for all of these variables.

Finally, the default assumption is that linear relationships exist among all the variables. If you believe there are interactions or any other form of non-linearity, you should either transform the relationships so they are linear or conduct some other analysis that will consider this set of relationships. There are methods for including interaction terms in multiple regression; however, experts differ about how to model this in the analysis. Some authors argue that multiple regression is a special case of ANOVA (ANOVA does not assume that the relationships among variables are linear). ANOVA is often used to test nonlinear relationships and/or power functions. However, multiple regression, by assuming linearity among the variables, makes an additional requirement. The value of the multiple *R* in multiple regression should be identical to the value of omega in ANOVA (in theory), if the conditions for multiple regression were met and an ANOVA was run instead. This relationship is one reason persons using meta-analysis can convert either ANOVA or multiple regression results back and forth.

USING COMPUTER PROGRAMS
TO CALCULATE REGRESSION

After selecting your dependent and predictor variables, the other major decision in setting up the SPSS program is variable entry. SPSS provides several different options for how variables are entered into the regression model. We discuss three here: (a) forced entry, (b) forward entry, and (c) hierarchical. Forced entry, much like it sounds, requires the computer to enter all the variables in the equation at the same time, regardless of importance. This produces a multiple R that uses the values of all variables to predict the dependent variable. You need to examine the significance tests for the individual predictors to determine which ones, if any, provide significant predictive power.

Forward entry starts with the variable that has the largest contribution to estimating the dependent variable. After one iteration, the variables are entered in turn as long as the contribution of the variable is significant (as measured usually by a t test of the standardized coefficient) or a significant improvement in the value of the predictability using the multiple R. As soon as the next entry is not significant, the analysis stops and the multiple R at that point is the final point of analysis. You will need to decide how much additional prediction in terms of the multiple R is necessary or desirable in order to determine when to stop adding variables as a means of improving the predictability of the dependent variable. In addition to forward entry, there are also options for stepwise and backward entry. Because these methods for entering variables lack theoretical grounding in specific research contexts, we advise against using them.

A third option is to use hierarchical regression. The hierarchical technique can technically use either forced or forward entry but specifies that various independent variables should be entered in sequential blocks. For instance, suppose theory tells you that several demographic variables unimportant to your study influence the dependent variable. Using blocks, you can enter all relevant demographic variables first in one block and then your predictor variables of interest in a second block. In SPSS and other computer programs, you can obtain not only overall statistics for the resulting model but also "change statistics" for each step in the process. For instance, you can see if the addition of the independent variables in the second block caused a significant change in the variance accounted for by the model (i.e., not only that the variance accounted for by the model was significant but that the CHANGE in variance accounted for was significant). When writing up the result of change statistics, you should highlight them with the "Δ" symbol: for example, $\Delta R^2 = .23$, $\Delta F = 5.7$, $p < .05$.

As you analyze the data, keep in mind that the resulting equation/model is what is important. A good equation may reflect a theoretical set of premises and, whether the equation works or fails, you may produce results that have significant ramifications for a theory. At the same time, a good equation may provide a means of prediction that generates some practical application such as a solution to a problem or the estimation of some important parameter. A caution is therefore warranted: Regression models that do not have both theoretical and practical support should be questioned. In many ways, regression should be the perfect combination of theory and practice. Theory should guide the identification of a model, and the resulting model should have meaningful practical implications. In other words, your regression equation should be informed by both theory and practical circumstances.

The computer program you are using may contain other items not mentioned in this chapter, such as shrinkage correction. Shrinkage refers to the fact that as you add variables to the equation, the multiple R gets bigger. The problem with the growing multiple R is that some variables add very little to predictability but add substantial noise to the equation because of the poor contribution of the variables. There is a correction for this, known as shrinkage correction, where the multiple R is corrected on the basis of the additional variable. So you have the multiple R as it exists in a kind of raw form and then an *adjusted* multiple R, corrected for the addition of the marginal contribution of an individual variable. In SPSS, both the uncorrected and adjusted R are reported; you should use the adjusted R when analyzing and reporting results.

INTERPRETING THE RESULTS
OF A MULTIPLE REGRESSION

Assuming the assumptions are met, the goal of multiple regression is the generation of an equation that will include multiple predictors. The multiple R is a special kind of correlation. Recall that a normal bivariate correlation explores estimates of one variable based on the value of another variable. Multiple regression goes further to create an equation that, provided the values of the predictors variables, predicts the value of the dependent variable. In short, the goal of the equation is to take the values of the predictor variable and estimate an expected value. The multiple R is the correlation between the actual value of the dependent variable and the predicted value based on the equation. The value of multiple regression is that the multiple R should be larger than any of the single bivariate correlations. If a bivariate correlation is larger than the multiple R, then the prediction of the single variable is better than the equation using multiple variables.

It is also important to note that the multiple R will always be positive, not negative. The value of any particular standardized coefficient may be positive or negative (and it is the absolute size of the standardized coefficient that should be considered, not the direction in terms of the contribution to the estimation of the dependent variable); however, the multiple R should always be positive. Individual predictor variables may or may not be significant and, if significant, might be positively or negatively related to the dependent variable. When interpreting the way that specific variables contribute to the equation, in addition to paying attention to the value of the unstandardized beta weight, you should also consider the sign when describing what the model tells you.

An example of how to write the results for a multiple regression is provided in Figure 10.4. If your results are being submitted for publication, include a complete zero-order correlation matrix that provides the means, standard deviations, and reliabilities for all variables. This information preserves the data for subsequent meta-analyses and establishes baseline measurements for all variables of interest.

"Hypothesis 1 predicted that argument quality and speaker credibility would predict attitude change. A multiple regression produced a significant model, $F(2, 57) = 42.75$, $p < .05$, $R^2 = .60$. Argument quality ($\beta = .51$, $t(57) = 5.67$, $p < .05$) and speaker credibility ($\beta = .33$, $t(57) = 3.67$, $p < .05$) served as positive predictors of attitude change."

$F(2, 57) = 42.75$	This is the F value Stan obtained from the test of the multiple correlation coefficient. The degrees of freedom were calculated based on Formula 10.3.
$R^2 = .60$	This is the multiple correlation coefficient (see Formula 10.2).
$\beta = .51$, $\beta = .33$	These are the beta weights for each of the predictor variables (see Formula 10.4).
$t(57) = 5.67$, $t(57) = 3.67$	These are the t tests Stan used to determine the significance of the beta weights (see Formula 10.5).
$p < .05$	The p value reflects the significance levels for the tests performed.

Figure 10.4   Deciphering the Write-Up of a Multiple Regression

You should also provide the final standardized equation in your write-up (the raw form should be provided if you are expecting direct application to some problem of interest). The multiple R, the coefficients, and the associated information for the statistical tests should also be provided. Usually the form of the tests is F, t, or z and therefore should follow the reporting for those particular statistics with regard to format (see ANOVA, t test, or z for format of reporting).

MULTIPLE REGRESSION
IN COMMUNICATION RESEARCH

Knobloch, L. K. (2006). Relating uncertainty and message production within courtship: Features of date request messages. *Human Communication Research, 32,* 244–273.

Research has shown that relational uncertainty—the degree of confidence people have in their perceptions of involvement within interpersonal relationships—is strongly related to the use of various communication strategies such as the ways people express jealousy and the ways people communicate about unexpected events. At the level of specific messages rather than strategies, uncertainty is related to question asking and intimacy during initial interactions, but the role of uncertainty in how messages are produced in longer term relationships is relatively unknown. Knobloch addresses this gap by exploring how relational uncertainty influences message production when one person asks another person for a date.

On the basis of the rationale that relational uncertainty might make message production more difficult because it limits the ability to plan and increases the potential risk of face-threatening responses, Knobloch reasons that higher levels of relational uncertainty should be negatively related to the fluency (smooth, fluid, and free of speech errors) of the request (Hypothesis 1), affiliativeness (degree of liking conveyed by a message) of the request (Hypothesis 2), the extent to which the request focuses on the relationship (Hypothesis 3), the explicitness of the request (Hypothesis 4), and the perceived effectiveness of the request (Hypothesis 5). In addition, reasoning that our own perceptions of our message effectiveness might be more stringent than the evaluation of others, Knobloch assessed the extent to which relational uncertainty and perceived effectiveness were related after controlling for the perceptions of others (Hypothesis 6). Finally, one research question probed whether relational uncertainty predicts future date requests when controlling for the length of the relationship.

A total of 248 participants were recruited from communication courses to take part in the study. Participants, who ranged in age from 18 to 41 years old, completed a survey instrument assessing relational uncertainty (self, partner, and relationship uncertainty were separated out as distinct dimensions) and then were asked to engage in a date request. After completing the surveys, each participant entered a room with a phone and was asked to imagine that he or she was calling a romantic partner and leave a message on that person's answering machine asking for a date—those messaged were recorded for later analysis. Following the recording, each participant also rated the self-reported effectiveness of the date request as well as how realistic he or she thought the date request was. Independent judges also rated the recorded date requests for fluency, affiliativeness, relationship focus, explicitness, and effectiveness. The total length of each message request was also determined by counting the number of words in the request.

For space reasons, only results for Hypothesis 5—there is a negative relationship between relational uncertainty and perceived effectiveness of a date request—are summarized here. Two hierarchical regressions, one with raters' evaluations of date request effectiveness and the other with self-reported effectiveness as dependent variables, were calculated. The first step of the regression included two variables, perceived realism and message length, considered as covariates to be controlled for when assessing the predictive influence of uncertainty. Table 10.1 shows results of the regressions.

As you can see from the table, perceived realism was positively related to self-reported effectiveness but not independent ratings of effectiveness; this pattern was reversed for message length. After controlling for the covariates, each dimension of uncertainty accounted for significant variance in both independent and self-reported effectiveness. We should note that to balance the risk of Type I and Type II error, Knobloch set alpha to .10 for hypothesized associations—thus, the standardized beta coefficients for each uncertainty dimension and effectiveness ratings by independent judges were deemed significant but not at the standard $p < .05$ level. Knobloch concludes that the results are consistent with a conclusion to reject the null hypothesis.

Table 10.1   Regression of Independent and Self-Reported Effectiveness Onto
Relational Uncertainty

	Rated Effectiveness	Self-Reported Effectiveness
R^2 Step 1	.06***	.10***
Realism β	.09	.32***
Message length β	.23***	.00
R^2 Δ Step 2	.03***	.05***
Self uncertainty β	−.17**	−.22***
R^2 Δ Step 2	.01*	.04**
Partner uncertainty β	−.11*	−.19**
R^2 Δ Step 2	.01*	.04**
Relationship uncertainty β	−.11*	−.19**

* $p < .10$; ** $p < .01$; *** $p < .001$.

REFERENCES

Dizney, H., & Gromen, L. (1967). Predictive validity and differential achievement on three MLA comparative language foreign language tests. *Educational and Psychological Measurement, 27,* 1127–1130.

Heise, D. R. (1969). Problems in path analysis and causal inferences. In E. F. Borgatta (Ed.), *Sociological methodology* (pp. 38–73). San Francisco: Jossey-Bass.

Miczo, N. (2004). Humor ability, unwillingness to communicate, loneliness, and perceived stress: Testing a security theory. *Communication Studies, 55,* 209–226.

Pedhazur, E. P. (1997). *Multiple regression in behavioral research: Explanation and prediction.* New York: Harcourt Brace.

Stevens, J. P. (2002). *Applied multivariate statistics for the social sciences* (4th ed.). Mahwah, NJ: Lawrence Erlbaum.

✄ Sample SPSS Printouts ✄

The printouts included here are for a regression calculated for a study trying to determine what variables predict whether or not a person will stop using tobacco. The dependent variable in the study is behavior change—the likelihood that a person will stop using tobacco in the next few days. The predictor variables are as follows: the number of years that the person has used tobacco, the age of the person, his or her intent to stop using, the number of logical appeals to stop using that the person has heard in the past month, and the number of fear appeals to stop using that he or she has heard in the past month. The researcher was interested in testing a model where age and years using was entered first in one block, intent to quit using was entered second, and both types of persuasive appeals were entered in a third block. SPSS output provides summary and change statistics for the model, the ANOVA table testing significance of the model, and regression coefficients. This printout also includes zero-order, part, and partial correlations with the regression coefficients.

Model Summary

Model	R	R Square	Adjusted R Square	Std. Error of the Estimate	Change Statistics				
					R Square Change	F Change	df1	df2	Sig. F Change
1	.648[a]	.420	.356	.74160	.420	6.519	2	18	.007
2	.998[b]	.996	.995	.06544	.576	2294.481	1	17	.000
3	.998[c]	.997	.996	.05932	.001	2.846	2	15	.090

a. Predictors: (Constant), yrsuse, age

b. Predictors: (Constant), yrsuse, age, int

c. Predictors: (Constant), yrsuse, age, int, logappeal, fearapp

ANOVA[d]

Model		Sum of Squares	df	Mean Square	F	Sig.
1	Regression	7.171	2	3.585	6.519	.007[a]
	Residual	9.900	18	.550		
	Total	17.070	20			
2	Regression	16.997	3	5.666	1322.924	.000[b]
	Residual	.073	17	.004		
	Total	17.070	20			
3	Regression	17.017	5	3.403	967.302	.000[c]
	Residual	.053	15	.004		
	Total	17.070	20			

a. Predictors: (Constant), yrsuse, age

b. Predictors: (Constant), yrsuse, age, int

c. Predictors: (Constant), yrsuse, age, int, logappeal, fearapp

d. Dependent Variable: behchange

Coefficients[a]

Model		Unstandardized Coefficients B	Std. Error	Standardized Coefficients Beta	t	Sig.	Correlations Zero-order	Partial	Part	Collinearity Statistics Tolerance	VIF
1	(Constant)	26.234	4.413		5.945	.000					
	age	.439	.163	.583	2.694	.015	.160	.536	.484	.688	1.454
	yrsuse	-.644	.184	-.757	-3.499	.003	-.432	-.636	-.628	.688	1.454
2	(Constant)	4.337	.600		7.222	.000					
	age	.015	.017	.020	.895	.383	.160	.212	.014	.499	2.005
	yrsuse	-.026	.021	-.030	-1.235	.234	-.432	-.287	-.020	.421	2.373
	int	.984	.021	.982	47.901	.000	.998	.996	.759	.597	1.674
3	(Constant)	3.663	.620		5.908	.000					
	age	.019	.017	.026	1.150	.268	.160	.285	.017	.412	2.428
	yrsuse	-.020	.021	-.023	-.950	.357	-.432	-.238	-.014	.341	2.933
	int	.978	.020	.976	48.638	.000	.998	.997	.698	.512	1.953
	fearapp	.004	.009	.007	.430	.673	-.039	.110	.006	.800	1.251
	logappeal	.040	.017	.036	2.356	.032	.256	.520	.034	.863	1.159

a. Dependent Variable: behchange

ELEVEN

FACTOR ANALYSIS

Joe was conducting a study of how teachers provide students with social and academic support. After carefully reviewing literature on the topic and interviewing teachers to understand their social support strategies, Joe constructed a survey with 30 questions. After having students complete the survey, Joe then needed to perform regression analyses to determine whether teachers' use of social support predicted students' learning in a class. But running 30 different regressions (one for each survey question) would be impractical. Joe needed to find a way of systematically reducing the 30 survey items to one or a few continuous variables. To do this, he used factor analysis.

In Chapter 1 and in subsequent chapters, you have learned that different statistical procedures require use of different types of variables. For instance, a ONEWAY ANOVA typically requires use of a categorical independent variable and a continuous dependent variable, a correlation requires continuous variables, and so on. Categorical variables are typically created by a researcher where groups of people are exposed to certain conditions representing qualitatively distinct values of the variable—for example, an experimental and control group. Continuous variables typically come from some sort of survey or scale where participants' responses to several survey questions are summed or averaged to arrive at a score representing a variable. Scales are the most commonly used method of obtaining continuous data used in communication research. Understanding how to turn several answers to specific survey questions into meaningful variables is essential in most research projects. This chapter teaches you about one technique for analyzing survey items—factor analysis.

THE PURPOSE OF FACTOR ANALYSIS

When completing surveys, you have probably noticed that some questions seem redundant—that is, they seem to ask the same question in slightly different ways. In fact, in a 20- to 24-item survey, you might observe several sets of questions that are similar. Surveys are intentionally constructed with groups of questions so that each survey can collect data on different factors or variables (in this context, the term *factor* means the same thing as *variable*). For surveys with a long record of use, such factors may already be identified in the literature. For instance, the Personal Report of Communication Apprehension–24 (PRCA-24), used to assess communication apprehension, has a well-recognized factor structure measuring communication apprehension (CA) in public, meeting, dyadic, and group contexts. If using that scale, you would actually collect data on four different variables (five if you count the summed "overall CA" value).

When using newer scales, you may not have information on what, if any, factors exist on the scale. In other words, you may not know whether you should average all of the questions to achieve values for one variable or whether there are two or more factors present in the scale, in which case you should average/sum questions relevant to each factor separately. This question is essentially asking about the measurement model appropriate for the scale you are using. To determine the appropriate measurement model, you should use factor analysis. Some researchers go so far as to suggest that you should determine the measurement model from scratch each time you use a scale because the model could change slightly from one sample to another.

Factor analysis is important to measurement because the analysis assists you in determining coherence or structure among items that are believed to measure a common variable. The question in any measurement context is that when you employ some measure (i.e., a survey, scale, index, or other measurement tool) to evaluate the quantity of something, would the same answers be generated if other measures were selected? With that question comes the associated question of whether something you wish to measure is made up of "parts" or "factors" that are said to make up some underlying construct.

Suppose you wish to measure survey participants' attitudes toward eating fruit. You construct the following scale using Likert-type statements to which respondents indicate agreement on a 1 (*strongly agree*) to 7 (*strongly disagree*) scale:

I like to eat strawberries.

I like to eat blackberries.

I like to eat blueberries.

I like to eat raspberries.

The content of each item represents a different fruit to which the person can indicate his or her desire to eat. As you review these questions, do you think that the survey provides a valid assessment of individuals' attitudes toward eating fruit? Probably not—the scale could be criticized because all the fruits identified in the questions are berries.

Here is the underlying issue: You are trying to measure a concept or construct. The variable you are interested in measuring requires that you understand and articulate what that variable means in terms of the possible examples. While it is easy to ask whether or not a person likes fruit, there are perhaps dozens and dozens of different kinds of fruit, each with separate species or types. I might like one species or type of berry and not like another. In addition, fruits come in a variety of types and include items grown on vines, bushes, and trees, for example. Think of it this way: Is my attitude about liking a fruit really made up of attitudes about particular kinds of fruit that represent separate categories?

Even more difficult is that some fruit is preferred and eaten raw and some is cooked, fried, dried, juiced, or fermented. A person may not like plums but love prunes. A person may not eat grapes whole but like wine. So when one asks about fruit, the difference between blueberry pancakes, blueberry pie, blueberry syrup, blueberry yogurt, and so on can provide a fundamental difference in reacting to the item. A person may like to drink orange juice but not like to eat an orange; measuring an attitude toward even a common fruit such as oranges provides for an interesting set of challenges. But, back to our original example: You believe that questions on berries are not enough to really measure the attitudes toward fruit, so you add the following items:

I like to eat bananas.

I like to eat apples.

I like to eat cherries.

I like to eat grapes.

Again, you look at the scale and discover there are no citrus fruits. The above fruits are all those that grow on trees or vines. But none of the fruits are considered citrus fruits that are high in citric acid, a particular type of substance. So you add the following:

I like to eat pineapples.

I like to eat oranges.

I like to eat limes.

I like to eat lemons.

Now, you look at the scale and you are relatively happy with the diversity of fruits covered. But then you go to the store to check out whether you really have captured the variety of fruits that exist. You walk up and down the aisles and find out that you have no exotic fruits. You again review your scale items and add the following:

I like to eat papaya.

I like to eat star fruit.

I like to eat mangos.

I like to eat ugli fruit.

We will stop there with those examples. Notice, for example, that pineapples and oranges can be sweet, but limes and lemons are generally not considered sweet. Also, we did not include all fruit (pears, coconut, etc.). But that is a fundamental problem in measurement: You usually cannot and probably should not include all examples in the scale. You will never be able to exhaust all possibilities because, if for no other reason, it will be difficult to get someone to respond to a survey asking about thousands of unique fruits.

Suppose we use the 16 items on the scale and have some number of participants complete the scale. Now here is what you do not know and wish to know: Are attitudes toward fruit something that is universal across all fruits, or are there clusters of questions that take the general attitude toward fruit and divide this up into various elements (factors)? For example, you might have the answers dividing up into different kinds of fruit (berries, citrus, known, exotic). If that is the case, then people's attitudes toward fruit are complex, and you are really dealing with four separate and distinct evaluations that a person is making about the various fruits. In this instance, we would call the scale multidimensional because there is a four-factor measurement model. Conversely, you might find that people's responses cluster depending on whether the fruit is sweet or sour; in that instance, you would have a multidimensional two-factor scale. Or, you may simply observe a one-dimensional construct of all attitudes toward fruit where no groupings are identified. In essence, people's attitudes may be split along any number of continuums or dimensions or may be relatively monolithic—this is exactly what you must determine before using your fruit scale in any sort of analysis.

To determine the dimensionality of a particular scale, you have two basic options: exploratory factor analysis and confirmatory factor analysis. As you will learn, exploratory factor analysis is more appropriate in situations where you have little theory or prior research to guide selection of a measurement model. The confirmatory factor analysis, as the name suggests, is used in situations where you already suspect that a particular measurement model should exist and you want to statistically verify that assumption.

Engaged Research

Identify several political and social issues and create a survey assessing participants' perceptions of how important each topic is to them. Ask respondents to react to each item by indicating how important each issue is using a 1 (*not important*) to 5 (*highly important*) scale. After obtaining at least 50 responses to the survey, use the information explained below to run an exploratory factor analysis. Based on results of the analysis, would you describe people's opinions about the importance of social issues as one-dimensional or multidimensional?

EXPLORATORY FACTOR ANALYSIS

The exploratory factor analysis (EFA) procedure uses statistics to identify an underlying structure among the various items that form a scale. The procedure attempts to generate vectors of items that produce a factor score (the terms *vector* and *factor* technically mean different things in this context; however, practically speaking, they are referring to the same outcome). The maximum number of possible vectors is limited to the number of items in the analysis—there could be, for instance, 24 vectors for a 24-item survey. Practically speaking, the procedure is used to try and determine the *minimum* appropriate number of vectors. Because each scale item is linearly contributing to a particular vector, each item has a specific factor loading value that represents its "contribution" to that vector. These loadings are like correlations—the farther the score is away from zero (and the closer to 1 or −1), the more that item is associated with that vector. The steps for an EFA are described in Figure 11.1.

The EFA procedure requires that you make some important decisions when interpreting results. The first decision is about the number of meaningful vectors that exists. Recall that the maximum number of possible vectors is equal to the number of questions included in the analysis. Using the maximum number of vectors would not be helpful, so the objective is to determine the fewest number of meaningful vectors. In other words, rather than having 24 different vectors where each item is a vector, it would be more desirable to have 2 or 3 vectors where multiple items contribute to each vector. Such a model would provide a more parsimonious and coherent set of variables.

The EFA assists you in making this decision because it provides statistics for determining which vectors account for the most variance in the scale.

1. Identify all items associated with a particular scale.

2. Use a predetermined criterion to select the number of factors/vectors to retain. The default in SPSS is to retain all factors with eigenvalues of 1 or higher.

3. Use a rotation method to assist in interpreting factor loadings. If you suspect the factors should be correlated, you should use oblique rotation methods such as promax; if you suspect that they are not correlated, you should use an orthogonal method such as varimax.

4. Interpret factor loadings using a predetermined criterion. A conservative criterion is to require a primary loading of .70 and no secondary loading higher than .30; a less conservative criterion is .60 and .40 for primary and secondary loadings, respectively.

5. Name the factor(s), calculate values for the factors that include (either summing or averaging) items for that factor, and then calculate reliability.

Figure 11.1   Steps in an Exploratory Factor Analysis

Usually, the process will involve some method of extracting vectors starting with the largest or most predictive and then, in turn, will generate vectors with less value in terms of predictability. The challenge is to determine which vectors are interpretable and important in terms of establishing the existence of dimensions or factors.

The question of how to generate factors and how to determine how many factors exist provides the subject of much discussion and differing views. One approach is to use eigenvectors (and the associated eigenvalues) as a basis for selecting of the number of factors. The eigenvector approach extracts factors until all the variance in the scale is accounted for; most typically, the number of factors generated will equal the number of items used in the exercise. After only a few factors, however, the relative amount of additional variance accounted for by the additional factors diminishes to decimal dust. By using the eigenvalues, you can determine a "cutoff" on factors. For instance, most researchers retain factors with eigenvalues of more than 1.00; another approach is to retain all factors until the gap between the eigenvalue of the factors is less than .50, retain all factors until a certain threshold of variance (e.g., 50%) is reached, and so on. What happens is that some rule system will be used to determine how many factors should be analyzed from the scale. By default, SPSS uses the eigenvalue criterion where all factors with eigenvalues of 1 or higher are retained. This approach is reasonable in most circumstances.

The second part of the procedure is determining which items belong to which factors. Most statistical programs, including SPSS, provide rotation methods to make identification of factor item loadings easier. Simply speaking, the vectors created and retained could be depicted using a complex multidimensional graph. Because each item has some contribution to the vector, all items on the scale, even in cases where their contribution is miniscule, would be depicted on the graph. As you might imagine, the graph could be difficult to interpret because there are many items and multiple vantage points. The rotation method is basically an attempt to find the best vantage point for seeing grouped items. You might think of this analogy. If you were asked to point to the transmission on your car while standing in the trunk, you could point in the general direction but not be very precise. If a mechanic lifted your car on jacks and you rotated your vantage point, you could easily see and identify the transmission. This is exactly what rotation is in EFA—the vectors are being rotated so you can see them easier. The process of interpretation is further aided by the fact that the loadings are represented by values rather than a graph. Although a visual image might seem appealing, it is actually easier to make decisions by using values and rules of thumb for interpreting those values.

For each vector, every item in the analysis will have a rotated loading coefficient. The most commonly used rotation methods are varimax (if you suspect the factors are not correlated) and promax (if you suspect the factors are correlated). Using the rotation coefficients, you must have some criteria for determining which items belong to which factors. The criteria most commonly used are 60/40 or 70/30. The more conservative of the two criteria requires that an item have a primary loading on one factor of at least .70 and no secondary loadings on other factors of greater than .30. The more liberal criterion requires a primary loading of at least .60 and no secondary loading higher than .40. These criteria help ensure that items have a sufficient primary loading (the higher of the two values) and do not load on multiple factors, which could confuse interpretation. Thus, the rotation brings clarity to your measurement model because you have statistical evidence to group certain items together on one variable, other items on another variable, and so forth. It should be noted that although these criteria are commonly recommended (see Stevens, 2002), much more liberal criteria are often found in research. Such practices are problematic because they result in unreliable measurement models and potentially increase error.

Once you have identified which items load on which factors, your next task is to name the factor. This is a fairly interpretive process—you must carefully consider all of the items loading on a particular factor and think about what those items, in total, are assessing. For instance, we might find that all "exotic" fruit load on one factor, all citrus fruit on another, and so on. Last, you must determine reliability scores for each factor and calculate the variables. You calculate reliability using only those items loading on the factor/variable in question (e.g., all of the exotic fruit items). To calculate the variable score for each person, you can add values for each question together to achieve a total score or you can average the values of each question. If sufficient reliability is achieved and after you calculate the variables, you can use the factor scores (also called composite scores) as variables in other analyses. For instance, you could explore whether there are significant differences between men and women on how much they like to eat exotic fruit, citrus fruit, and so on.

Unlike other statistical procedures you have read about, the EFA has few assumptions that must be met prior to conducting the analysis. Essentially, the primary assumption is that there are meaningful correlations among the items that you are considering as part of the EFA (for instance, the various items on a scale). If there are no meaningful correlations among the items, then there is practically no reason to suspect any sort of underlying structure among the variables. Besides exploring the overall correlation matrix for several meaningful correlations (say above .30), there are also specialized statistical tests available in SPSS and other packages to determine the assumption of whether some underlying structure is tenable. The Kaiser-Meyer-Olkin (KMO) test of sampling adequacy should be at least .60 or higher, and Bartlett's test of sphericity should be significant. If both tests are satisfied, the data meet the basic statistical assumptions common to EFA. In addition to the assumptions surrounding the correlation matrices, the EFA assumes that any underlying structure will involve linear relationships as well as normal distributions for both individual items and the overall factor. Finally, you should use common sense. The EFA provides something of a statistical fishing expedition for factors, and you should carefully compare results with theory and your understanding of the scale and underlying assumptions of validity before adopting any particular measurement model.

Finally, when using SPSS, you should take care to employ an appropriate form of exploratory factor analysis (see Park, Dailey, & Lemus, 2002). In the SPSS factor analysis routine, the default extraction method uses a principal components analysis. This approach assumes that extracted factors are uncorrelated, which is rarely the case. Rather than using principal components, you are better served in most instances using principal axis factoring. This option can be selected from a drop-down menu in the "Extraction" box.

CONFIRMATORY FACTOR ANALYSIS

Confirmatory factor analysis (CFA) is a procedure that requires you to define the measurement model, or factors, a priori, or before you perform the analysis. Recall that the EFA assists you in determining what, if any, underlying structure exists in the data. The EFA is most appropriate in situations where you have little guidance from theory or previous research. A confirmatory factor analysis, on the other hand, requires or expects particular items to be associated with a particular factor. Thus, rather than asking, "What are the factors?" as you would in an EFA, in CFA, you are asking, "Is this factor structure consistent with the data?" The advantage of CFA is that an investigator must develop a theory about the measurement of some concept and provide items that reflect that theory. A test of a measurement model in CFA is essentially the test of an underlying theory about the nature of the constructs. This contrasts with EFA, where the theory follows the outcome of the statistical test or association among the measures; in a sense, EFA is a grounded approach to construction of measurement instruments.

Strangely enough, CFA techniques predate and were developed long before EFA techniques, which require extensive application of computers to be useful. Procedures for CFA were developed as a means of providing evidence for measurement structure or coherence, and the calculations are simple enough to be conducted without extensive use of computers.

Some researchers suggest that a CFA can only be run after a successful EFA—that the CFA should be used to confirm the EFA. That assumption is both problematic and wrong. The techniques are simply different. The EFA approach provides an assessment of the mathematical relationships among items by creating vectors and assessing the relationship of the item to that vector (these relationships are referred to as *loadings*). A critical question is how one draws or creates the vectors (that is where the term *rotation* comes in), and for EFA, you have principal components analysis, varimax, equimax, and so on. A final part of this puzzle was whether the vectors should be mathematically independent (orthogonal) or to permit the vectors to be correlated (oblique). All of these issues are mathematical issues and generally require no specification in advance of what items go on which factors.

CFA differs from EFA by requiring the investigator to specify, in advance, what items are expected to load on what factor. The criteria for assessing the internal structure of a factor are (a) content homogeneity and (b) internal consistency. The steps involved in a confirmatory factory analysis are summarized in Figure 11.2.

Content Homogeneity. Content homogeneity or content validity is an assessment of the degree to which the underlying content of the items can be viewed as similar. The test is really a semantic test or association among the various items under consideration. Consider the previous example of measuring an attitude toward fruit.

The decision to make "fruit" the category argues that any fruit is the same in terms of attitude as any other fruit. If there is disagreement with that assumption, then theory must be generated to describe fruit similarity

---

1. Assess content validity. Because a CFA is testing a theorized measurement model, content validity must be present to guide creation of a theoretical model.

2. Calculate observed correlations among items.

3. Calculate item loadings (the correlation of a particular item with the overall total score of the factor) and reliability for the factor.

4. Calculate the expected correlation matrix.

5. Calculate the error matrix.

6. Calculate the chi-square and determine if it is significant. If it is not significant, the model fits well with the data; if it is significant, the data are significantly different from the expected model.

Figure 11.2   Steps in a CFA

and divide fruit according to some set of criteria (berries, citrus, tree/bush fruit, tropical, etc.). Such categories then provide a basis for testing whether the theory describing those categories is consistent with the perspectives of people filling out the scale. Essentially, the investigator is testing whether the divisions established by the researcher are shared by the participants in the study—whether the theorized measurement model is consistent with the data.

This level of analysis requires a fairly good knowledge of the participants' understanding about the nature of the issues in the construct. This understanding represents a form of measurement theory about variables and constructs. A successful CFA test indicates that the understanding of the content is shared between the investigator and the participants.

Internal Consistency Calculation. Suppose we have four items with the following correlation matrix among the items. The matrix shows that Item A has a .33 correlation with Item B, which has a .47 correlation with Item C and so on. The loadings explain how strongly each item contributes to the factor. So, Item D loads more strongly on the factor than does Item A, which has the weakest loading. The alpha reliability estimate for this factor is .73 with 145 people completing the survey. Although SPSS will not calculate the entire CFA for you, these values can be easily obtained from SPSS using the exploratory factor analysis procedure.

Actual Matrix

	A	B	C	D
A				
B	.33			
C	.45	.47		
D	.29	.38	.50	
Loading	.53	.61	.82	.60

Alpha is .73.

This is with 145
persons in the sample.

To calculate a CFA, you must have both an actual matrix and an expected matrix. The above matrix is the actual matrix. What we need to do is to calculate an expected matrix. To calculate a value of an expected matrix, you use the loadings. You multiply the loadings and get the expected matrix.

Expected Matrix Calculation

	A	B	C
A			
B	.53*.61		
C	.53*.82	.61*.82	
D	.53*.60	.61*.60	.82*.60

Or

Expected Matrix

	A	B	C
A			
B	.32		
C	.43	.50	
D	.31	.36	.49

After calculating the expected matrix, you can then calculate the error matrix, which is simply the difference between the actual and expected values.

Notice that the actual correlation between Items A and B is .33; if you subtract the expected correlation of .32, you are left with the .01 error shown in the matrix below.

Error Matrix			
	A	B	C
A			
B	.01		
C	.02	.03	
D	.02	.02	.01

After you have determined the actual, expected, and error matrices, you can then calculate a chi-square statistic. Recall from Chapter 8 that a chi-square is commonly used to determine whether the difference between an observed and expected set of values is significant. In Chapter 7, you learned to use the chi-square to determine whether there are significant differences between an observed and expected cross-tabulation/contingency table. In this instance, you are using the chi-square to determine whether there are significant differences between an observed and expected correlation matrix.

To calculate the chi-square, you use the following formula (Formula 11.1):

$$\chi^2 = \frac{\Sigma d^2}{2\sigma^2}. \tag{11.1}$$

The sum of d^2 is the sum of the squared values of the error matrix, or .0023.

The σ^2 is calculated using Formula 11.2:

$$\sigma^2 = \frac{(1 - \text{average } r^2)^2}{N - 1} \tag{11.2}$$

The average r is the average of the expected matrix.

Or, in this case, .40. So

$$\sigma^2 = \frac{(1 - .40^2)^2}{145 - 1}$$

or .0049.

Returning to our original formula, you end up with

$$\chi^2 = \frac{.0023}{.0098}$$

so $\chi^2 = .23$.

Finally, you must calculate the degrees of freedom using Formula 11.3:

$$df = (\text{number of correlations} - 1) = 5. \qquad (11.3)$$

Using a standard table for critical values of chi, you can easily determine whether the chi-square is significant. A nonsignificant chi-square indicates that the level of departure from the theoretical system is less than one would expect due to chance. Recall that a chi-square measures the deviation from what is expected or predicted. In this case, the prediction is the theoretical model. The chi-square numerator is a sum of the errors from the theoretical model (observed values minus expected values predicted by the model). What happens is that as the size of the error gets larger, the numerator becomes larger, and therefore the ratio or the chi-square becomes larger. The larger the chi-square, the more error or departure from the predicted model. A significant chi-square indicates that the difference between the actual data (observed) and the measurement model (predicted) is larger than chance. There is a significant difference between the data and the predicted measurement model: A significant chi-square indicates the model cannot predict the values and therefore does not work. In this case, the numerator is small, and consequently, the resulting chi-square is small and not significant. This means that the departure of the observed correlations from the expected correlations is small, and consequently, the model is a good fit with the data.

As suggested previously, the primary assumption guiding use of the CFA is that particular items are associated with a latent variable; that is, several items are hypothesized to be connected by some underlying structure. This implies that the a priori identification of a measurement model is a key assumption in CFA. Because the CFA tests linear relationships, a second assumption is that the relationship between each item and the latent variable is, indeed, linear rather than curvilinear. Finally, like many other procedures, the CFA assumes normality among the various distributions of both items and the overall variable.

FACTOR ANALYSIS IN COMMUNICATION RESEARCH

Palmgreen, P., Stepsehenson, M. T., Everett, M. W., Baseheart, J. R., & Francies, R. (2002). Perceived message sensation value (PMSV) and the dimensions and validation of a PMSV scale. *Health Communication, 14,* 403–428.

Research has found that people's tendency to seek sensation is linked to engaging in high-risk behavior such as drug use and a preference for messages high in sensation value. Messages that contain features that elicit sensory, affective, and arousal responses are referred to as high in message sensation value (MSV). Such messages tend to have audio, video, and other features that heighten psychological arousal toward the messages and have been shown to result in greater levels of attention, deeper levels of processing, and greater levels of behavioral change in response to the messages. Because MSV appears to be highly relevant for persuasive health messages, being able to use a valid and reliable scale assessing MSV should be an important objective for health communication, message effects researchers.

Everett and Palmgreen developed a scale assessing MSV; that scale was subsequently used to classify public service announcement (PSA) messages trying to prevent cocaine and marijuana use. Although the PMSV scale demonstrated high reliability and construct validity, little work had been done to assess the dimensionality of the MSV scale. The purpose of the current study was to develop additional validity evidence for the scale by determining a measurement model for the scale and to examine relationships between those dimensions and PSA processing measures, as well as measures of positive and negative affective reactions to the PSAs. In this summary, we will focus only on the research questions and results related to the question of dimensionality. The relevant research questions were as follows:

Research Question 1a: What are the dimensions of the PMSV scale?

Research Question 1b: Are these dimensions stable across sensation seeking levels?

Research Question 1c: Are these dimensions stable across antidrug PSAs for different substance abuse populations?

Though not directly applicable to the assessment of dimensionality of the PSMV scale, the other two research questions asked whether the dimensions of the PSMV are related to PSA processing measures and positive/negative reactions to the PSAs (Research Question 2) as well as whether those relationships differed for high- and low-sensation seekers (Research Question 3).

A total of 368 adolescents in Grades 9 through 12 watched three of six 30-second public service announcements aimed at preventing marijuana use. Each of the PSAs clearly used narratives as the basis for the message. More than one PSA was used for each group to increase external validity. Each participant rated the PSAs on the PMSV scale as well as other scales relevant to the substantive relationships queried by the second and third research questions. The PSMV scale was explored using and exploratory factor analysis followed by a confirmatory factor analysis. Criteria for the EFA included accepting factors with eigenvalues greater than 1 and rotated (using an oblique promax rotation) factor coefficients with at least a .60 primary loading, no secondary loading greater than .40, and a minimum of three items per factor. Criteria for the CFA goodness of fit included a nonsignificant chi-square, a CFI value above .90, and a root mean square error of approximation (RMSEA) value of less than .08.

Results of the EFA are reported in Table 11.1. The three emergent factors were emotional arousal, dramatic impact, and novelty. The three factors accounted for 61% of the total variance across the entire sample.

After observing the three factors in the EFA, a confirmatory factor analysis was run across four samples: high- and low-sensation seekers from the initial data set involving antimarijuana PSAs as well as high- and low-sensation seekers in a second data set where participants viewed anticocaine PSAs. The hypothesized measurement model placed appropriate items onto three correlated latent variables (factors). Appropriate fit was achieved for three of the samples, although to achieve acceptable fit, some error terms were unconstrained. The final fit statistics for each sample were as follows: marijuana low-sensation seekers, χ^2 (116, $N = 182$) = 194.49, $p < .001$, comparative fit index (CFI) = .94, RMSEA = .087; marijuana high-sensation seekers, χ^2 (112, $N = 186$) = 198.91, $p < .001$, CFI = .95, RMSEA = .065; cocaine high-sensation seekers, χ^2 (113, $N = 224$) = 227.48, $p < .001$, CFI = .96,

Table 11.1   Exploratory Factor Analysis With Oblique Rotation of the
               PSMV Scale

	Emotional Arousal	*Dramatic Impact*	*Novelty*
1. Unique/common	−.012	.121	*.829*
2. Powerful/weak impact	.074	−.002	*.820*
3. Didn't give/gave goose bumps	.098	*.696*	−.070
4. Novel/ordinary	.016	−.099	*.786*
5. Emotional/unemotional	*.632*	.138	.134
6. Boring/exciting	*.755*	−.015	.047
7. Strong/weak visuals	−.021	*.815*	−.012
8. Not creative/creative	*.760*	−.078	.016
9. Not graphic/graphic	.041	*.826*	.017
10. Arousing/not arousing	−.144	*.635*	.119
11. Unusual/usual	*.798*	.037	.059
12. Involving/uninvolving	*.752*	−.067	.092
13. Not intense/intense	.008	*.824*	.039
14. Weak/strong sound track	*.758*	−.004	−.039
15. Undramatic/dramatic	*.777*	.088	−.135
16. Stimulating/not stimulating	.123	*.702*	−.092
17. Strong/weak sound effects	*.734*	.038	−.017
Percentage of variance	38.4	14.9	7.3

NOTE: Italicized values in each column have primary loadings of at least .60 and no secondary
loadings of .40 or higher.

RMSEA = .068. For the cocaine low-sensation seekers, an acceptable fit was not achieved even after unconstraining error terms, χ^2 (111, N = 224) = 359.97, p < .001, CFI = .89, RMSEA = .101. Palmgreen and colleagues did not report factor loading coefficients for the various CFAs. Based on the results, they conclude that "the preponderance of evidence, therefore, indicates the hypothesized CFA dimensional structure was stable across different samples and PSA types."

REFERENCES

Park, H. S., Dailey, R., & Lemus, D. (2002). The use of exploratory factor analysis and principal components analysis in communication research. *Human Communication Research, 28,* 526–577.

Stevens, J. P. (2002). *Applied multivariate statistics for the social sciences* (4th ed.). Mahwah, NJ: Lawrence Erlbaum.

◈ Sample SPSS Printouts ◈

Maggie Quinlan and Scott Titsworth worked on a project exploring how students with various forms of disabilities experience classroom situations; in particular, how they experience various emotions related to interactions with teachers. To assist in exploring this topic, Maggie and Scott developed a scale assessing students' emotional experiences in classroom situations. Results of the exploratory factor analysis are reported below. The output provided contains the KMO and Bartlett's test, a table describing the number of factors extracted, a scree plot for visual inspection, and a rotated (using varimax) factor structure matrix.

KMO and Bartlett's Test

Kaiser-Meyer-Olkin Measure of Sampling Adequacy.		.924
Bartlett's Test of Sphericity	Approx. Chi-Square	4217.303
	df	120
	Sig.	.000

Total Variance Explained

Factor	Initial Eigenvalues			Extraction Sums of Squared Loadings			Rotation Sums of Squared Loadings		
	Total	% of Variance	Cumulative %	Total	% of Variance	Cumulative %	Total	% of Variance	Cumulative %
1	7.596	47.477	47.477	7.224	45.148	45.148	5.086	31.788	31.788
2	2.134	13.335	60.812	1.703	10.641	55.790	3.028	18.927	50.715
3	1.080	6.750	67.563	.792	4.953	60.742	1.604	10.028	60.742
4	.832	5.200	72.763						
5	.582	3.640	76.403						
6	.515	3.217	79.619						
7	.488	3.053	82.672						
8	.432	2.701	85.373						
9	.390	2.437	87.810						
10	.378	2.365	90.176						
11	.333	2.081	92.257						
12	.312	1.951	94.208						
13	.295	1.845	96.053						
14	.271	1.692	97.745						
15	.192	1.203	98.948						
16	.168	1.052	100.000						

Extraction Method: Principal Axis Factoring.

Scree Plot

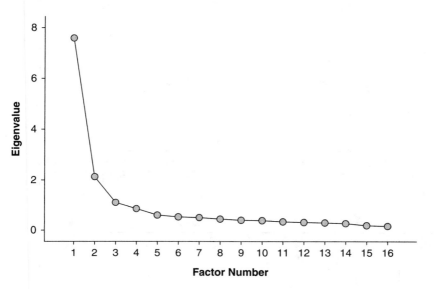

Rotated Factor Matrix[a]

	Factor		
	1	2	3
1. I can talk with my instructor about my personal problems.	.809	.009	.129
2. My instructor is willing to discuss my feelings and emotions about school.	.772	-.180	.162
3. I can count on my instructor when things go wrong with school issues.	.769	-.149	.219
4. I can count on my instructor when things go wrong in my personal life.	.748	.020	.126
5. My instructor is willing to help me make decisions about academic issues.	.681	-.222	.205
6. I CANNOT talk about personal problems with my instructor.	.678	-.341	.041
7. I get the emotional help and support I need from my instructor.	.675	-.245	.310
8. My instructor is NOT responsive to my concerns and feelings.	.625	-.492	.106
9. It is DIFFICULT to talk about school-related problems with my instructor.	-.551	.526	.009
10. Interacting with this instructor requires a lot of emotional energy.	-.087	.699	-.315
11. When talking to my instructor I have to conceal or fake my emotions.	-.433	.695	.026
12. Being in this class required a lot of emotional energy.	-.019	.593	-.294
13. I wish that I could better express my true feelings with my instructor.	-.014	.588	-.191
14. The emotions I display in class do not represent my true feelings.	-.438	.531	-.113
15. I would generally describe the emotions toward this class as positive.	.335	-.312	.756
16. I would generally describe the emotions I feel toward my instructor as positive.	.336	-.424	.735

Extraction Method: Principal Axis Factoring.

Rotation Method: Varimax with Kaiser Normalization.

a. Rotation converged in 7 iterations.

TWELVE

ADVANCED MODELING TECHNIQUES

—————•◦•—————

Communication researchers who study instructional communication often hypothesize connections between teacher communication behaviors and student learning outcomes. For example, one such prediction that has been replicated a number of times is that teachers' use of nonverbal immediacy causes students to have heightened affect toward a class. Many studies recognize but do not explicitly analyze the moderating effect that class size could have on this relationship. In other words, the teacher immediacy–affect relationship could change depending on the size of the class. To test this assumption, you could use path analysis to determine if class size moderates (i.e., enhances or suppresses) the teacher immediacy–affect relationship.

Well-developed social scientific theories often allow you to predict multiple causal relationships among variables. When testing sophisticated theories, you could perform several correlations and regressions to determine if your assumptions are correct; however, a more parsimonious approach is to test the overall model using advanced modeling procedures. While this chapter is intended only as an introduction to these techniques, we discuss underlying principles related to path analysis, structural equation modeling (SEM). We also briefly discuss other advanced modeling approaches such as hierarchical linear modeling and network analysis.

UNDERSTANDING ADVANCED MODELING

In the opening example, you read about the need to consider class size as a potential moderating variable in the relationship between teacher immediacy and student affective learning. Moderating variables affect the strength and/ or direction of a relationship between two other variables. Another type of advanced model includes mediating variables; mediating variables explain why there is a connection between two other variables (see Baron & Kenny, 1986). Figure 12.1 provides a visual illustration of moderating and mediating variables. As you can see, the top example shows how a statistical relationship between two variables can be mediated by another—if it were not for the fact that ice cream sales increased outdoor activity, there would be no connection. In the bottom example, you can see that the size of the relationship between teacher immediacy and student affect is dependent on the number of people in the class—this is a plausible example of a moderating relationship.

We introduce moderating and mediating variables to make the point that contemporary social scientific theory is generally oriented toward testing very

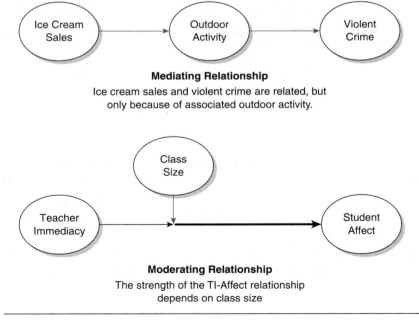

Mediating Relationship
Ice cream sales and violent crime are related, but
only because of associated outdoor activity.

Moderating Relationship
The strength of the TI-Affect relationship
depends on class size

Figure 12.1   Mediating and Moderating Variables

sophisticated models. Although the concepts of moderating and mediating variables are fairly straightforward, being able to test for them is not. Other statistical procedures we have discussed do not provide ideal or even suitable methods for identifying such variables. In addition to testing for moderating/ mediating variables, many theories are not so tidy as to include only one dependent variable. For example, interpersonal scholars increasingly orient research away from single-outcome variables such as "relationship satisfaction" and more toward multiple-process variables such as using verbally aggressive behaviors or strategically altering levels of self-disclosure. Because many of the models have a certain level of sophistication or complexity, more robust statistical procedures are required—for example, structural equation modeling or path analysis.

The commonality between path analysis and SEM lies in the fact that both are used to test theoretical models. In fact, both analyses can be thought of as essentially systemic (although individual parts of the analysis can be separately examined), which means that the overall hypothesized model is compared with the data to see whether it "fits" the data. As you will learn, path analysis is very similar to multiple regression in the sense that it tests how well a causal model predicts variance in an outcome variable. The main advantage of path analysis over multiple regression is that path analysis allows the inclusion of causal relationships among predictor variables—something multiple regression does not.

Although path analysis and SEM are very similar, there is an important difference. Whereas path analysis uses variables to test relationships, those variables are most typically composite variables generated from adding together survey items. You might recall our discussion of "artifacts" from Chapter 9 (e.g., unreliability) that unreliability can negatively affect the precision of statistical relationships; thus, in regressions, you have some error due to less than perfect reliability associated with the composite variables in your model. You cannot easily compensate for such error because the individual items comprising such variables are essentially hidden from the analysis. On the other hand, SEM allows individual survey items to be included as part of the structural model. Thus, any unreliability can be accounted for in the model. Because SEM allows more information to be available in the analysis, this technique can be very powerful in testing all theoretical assumptions underpinning a particular theory (e.g., assumptions about measurement, assumptions about relationships).

Path analysis and structural equation modeling are among the most advanced statistical procedures found in contemporary communication research. Although some aspects of these procedures are very straightforward and can be easily understood after a few introductory statements, planning, executing, and interpreting the results of a study using path analysis or SEM requires knowledge beyond the scope of this book. Consequently, this chapter is more of a primer to help you understand the procedure so that you can make informed decisions about further study.

DESCRIBING THE MODEL

At the heart of path analysis is the articulation and test of a theoretical model. By *theoretical model,* we mean a set of predicted relationships, accompanying explanations, and justifications. Suppose, for example, that we predict a model showing how verbally aggressive behaviors can cause a verbally aggressive response because it triggers negative affect or feelings. The image in Figure 12.2 shows how such a model would be depicted in a basic path analysis. Notice that the emphasis is less on independent and dependent variables and more on how multiple variables are simultaneously related as part of a theoretical system.

There are conventions followed when creating the path diagram to be tested. Typically, circles are used to represent unobserved variables (also referred to as "latent" variables), and boxes are used to represent observed variables (e.g., individual survey items). Straight lines are used to represent causal paths between variables. If the model includes correlated variables, a curved line with arrows on both ends is used to depict covariance. Each path has an associated path coefficient, which may or may not be significant (significant coefficients are typically "flagged" with an asterisk). Finally, most path models provide an estimate of variance accounted for by the model—that

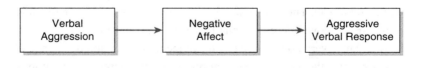

Figure 12.2   Path Analysis Diagram

value is typically placed above the "end" variable in the system (e.g., the aggressive response variable in Figure 12.2).

Path models are typically depicted in terms of causality because of some specified theoretical relationship. Consequently, the path model uses the underlying assumptions of the theory to visually represent the theoretical system of relationships, and accompanying text provides explanations and rationale for those relationships as well as the entire system. As you might expect, path analysis is used for well-developed theories and should be undertaken only when causal systems are well defined in terms of variables and connections between variables. Models tested in SEM expand basic path models by including not only hypothesized relationships between variables but also measurement models associated with each latent variable (see the previous chapter on factor analysis for a discussion of measurement models).

To further understand SEM, a brief review of terminology is warranted. First, all SEM models distinguish between *exogenous* and *endogenous* variables (in fact, this same terminology is commonly applied to basic path models as well). Exogenous variables are not caused by other variables in the structural model—they are more like independent variables. Endogenous variables, however, are influenced by other variables in the model and are more like dependent variables. Both types of variables can be directly observed or latent variables. Observed variables are just that—directly observed. Examples of observed variables include items on a survey, the number of times a teacher smiles, or the ratio of positive to negative comments given to an employee during a performance appraisal meeting. Latent variables are different from observed variables. First, latent variables are not directly observed. Second, we assess latent variables through observed variables that serve as prime indicators of the latent variable of interest. For example, we might use several survey questions (observed variables) as prime indicators of an unobserved latent variable.

With this terminology in mind, it is important to understand different types of structural equation models. In general, models tested through SEM can be classified into one of three types: observed variable, latent composite, and hybrid models (see Stephenson & Holbert, 2003). The first type of model, observed variables, includes only variables that are directly observed by the researcher—this is the basic path model we just described. For example, using single-item measures or tallies counting a specific behavior could be considered directly observed variables that could be part of a structural model. In addition, traditional path models using composite variables (but not the individual items) could be considered observed variable models. While these models are perhaps easier to design and test, they lack the ability to correct for measurement error and other artifacts; consequently, observed variable models should only be used when you have highly reliable scales or are using single-item measures.

The second type of model is referred to as latent composite. Unlike the observed variable model using composite variables, the latent composite model includes reliability information for the composite variable. Whereas composite variables in the observed model cannot correct for statistical artifacts (e.g., unreliability), latent composite models can acknowledge and account for random and systematic error associated with the measurement model. Thus, the latent composite model is advantageous over the observed model in most situations. Practically speaking, latent composite models require you to include information about reliability when specifying the model.

Finally, the hybrid model differs from the latent composite model in that it contains and tests complete versions of both the measurement and structural models. Whereas the latent composite model contains and corrects for an overall reliability estimate, the hybrid model includes information for each indicator (i.e., survey item) of the latent variable. Because comparatively more information is included in the hybrid model—the complete specification of both the measurement and structural models—this type of SEM analysis is comparatively more precise. In fact, Stephenson and Holbert (2003) conclude that the hybrid approach is advantageous in most circumstances. The lesson learned is that because the hybrid approach includes complete information about the measurement model, it is better able to account and correct for artifacts such as unreliability.

Finally, it is important to stress that regardless of what form of SEM is used, any model must be based on strong theory. Path analysis is sometimes called "arrow math" because the diagrams depict variables that are connected with arrows—the arrows show the exact causal relationships hypothesized by the theory. While one can test the individual connections (or path coefficients), the focus of path analysis is really on the overall model in terms of whether it is an accurate fit with the data. Moreover, SEM is notable in how it tests theory surrounding both the measurement model and the hypothesized structural model. Importantly, multiple structures will potentially fit any given set of data, and consequently, confirmation or consistency does not always provide proof that a theory is "true" or "accurate." If presented with a well-fitting path model (i.e., one that fits well with the data), one might conclude that the assumptions of the model are consistent with the data while recognizing that the theory is not "proven."

Engaged Research

Creating path models is a useful exercise for any project because it forces you to think about assumptions in the hypothesized model. Taking a variable such as civic engagement, how would you create a hypothesized model explaining connections between communication and civic engagement? What communication variables should be included in the model? What other variables might also be related to engagement?

UNDERSTANDING THE TEST

The test for a structural equation model is a bit different than other statistical tests. At other times in this book, you have learned about model testing. For example, in multiple regression, you test an overall model by examining the variance accounted for (adjusted R^2) and associated F statistic. Similarly, in ANOVA, you test whether independent variables cause (in the case of an experiment) predictable changes in a dependent variable. In both instances, you have a hypothesized set of relationships (i.e., a model) that you test. And, in both instances, you find support for your model by achieving statistical significance after analyzing appropriate significance tests (e.g., F tests, t tests, correlations) and appropriate effect size estimates. In essence, you find support for your hypothesized model when you attain significance.

In other procedures, you essentially test your hypothesized model against what you would expect to see by chance occurrence. If your significance tests achieve a certain level, you can conclude that chance was unlikely, which makes the hypothesized model more tenable. SEM is different because it is a test of tolerance. The chi-square measure normally used in SEM is not a test of whether random chance is unlikely; instead, the chi-square test is the degree to which the model departs from the data. So, in other tests, you are comparing your theory with what you would expect given random chance, whereas in SEM, you are directly comparing your theory with the data.

Normal significance testing seeks to find a significant outcome. A significant finding indicates that the null or random hypothesis can be rejected. SEM reverses that set of assumptions in the statistical test. For path analysis/ SEM, the chi-square should be *nonsignificant* to indicate a model that works. A significant chi-square indicates a significant departure from the model, and thus the model does not fit well. Conversely, a nonsignificant chi-square indicates that there is little error and that the hypothesized model fits well. This outcome is exactly the reverse of most statistical procedures where support for the hypothesis comes from a statistically significant outcome that rejects the null.

Because SEM traditionally employs the chi-square to test model fit, one word of caution is warranted. Larger sample sizes make it more difficult to accept a model. The chi-square is very sensitive to sample size, and consequently, a significant chi-square is commonplace in larger samples. What this means is that small sample size investigations that use causal modeling are more likely to find acceptable models because the level of permissible sampling error is greater. The chi-square test should not be abandoned, but you should understand that a significant chi-square does not mean that a model is poor if the sample size exceeds 100. Fortunately, researchers have a variety of options for assessing model fit (see Holbert & Stephenson, 2002). Based on the recommendations of Hu and Bentler (1999), goodness of fit can be assessed using the chi-square test for absolute fit as well as three incremental goodness-of-fit statistics: Tucker-Lewis index (TLI), root mean square error of approximation (RMSEA), and standardized root mean squared residual (SRMR). Adequate fit can be demonstrated if the model has a nonsignficant chi-square *or* meets the following targets for the incremental tests: TLI (.95 or greater), RMSEA (.06 or less), and SRMR (.09 or less). In situations where multiple models provide roughly similar statistical fit, models are analyzed for adequate explanatory power and parsimony to determine which model is best.

TWO METHODS OF ANALYSIS

Path analysis and SEM typically use one of two approaches: ordinary least squares and maximum likelihood estimation. We briefly describe both approaches here.

Ordinary Least Squares

The ordinary least squares (OLS) approach allows you to use correlation estimates and to assume that the degree of covariation represents the strength of association. In other words, the stronger the correlation, the stronger the association—this is no different from how we might interpret a simple correlation matrix. For a single path between two variables (e.g., $A \rightarrow B$) with no other route, the assumption is that the correlation of A and B (r_{AB}) is the same as the path from A to B (ρ_{AB}).

The relative simplicity of the OLS approach means that it can avoid some of the assumptions required by the maximum likelihood estimation approach and also allows you to control what corrections are employed on the correlations used in the analysis. For instance, OLS procedures generally do not require the assumptions of latent variables or correlated error terms. In addition, corrections such as restriction in range or attenuated measurement are done in a separate prior step before conducting the actual test of the model. The term used for this set of statistical procedures is often *two-stage ordinary least squares* or 2S-OLS. What this indicates is that model testing is done after adjustments are made to the associations and done prior to any model testing (this is very different from maximum likelihood estimation [MLE] methods). Because OLS methods permit model testing on uncorrected correlation matrices and give you control over what corrections are employed, any corrections or other assumptions must be made an explicit part of the model and are not assumed or operate as a default option.

OLS is the same basic procedure outlined for confirmatory factor analysis in Chapter 11 (and MLE can and is used in CFA as well). The reporting of a causal model using OLS requires an overall test of the model often referred to as Q and distributed as chi-square. The degrees of freedom is the number of unconstrained correlations.

The case of the hypothesized model simply has one variable A, predicting B, which in turn predicts C. A three-variable system generates three correlations. Two of the values are in the diagram, the link from A to B and from B to C. The indirect path (or path not in the diagram) is the relationship of A to C. In OLS, it turns out that in this diagram, the relationship of A to C should be equivalent to the multiplication of the paths ($AB * BC$).

This process creates a basis for comparison of the observed correlation in the matrix to the predicted correlation as a result of the diagram. This process is identical to the process used in confirmatory factor analysis (see Chapter 11, for example). The reporting of the model requires two elements: (a) overall test and (b) test of significance for each path coefficient. For an OLS, model the adequacy of the model. An adequate model will have an overall chi-square test that is nonsignificant (indicating that the model and the data are not significantly different).

Maximum Likelihood Estimation

MLE is a technique that finds a set of parameters to minimize the discrepancy between the observed covariance structure and the one best fitting the model. The process involves three sets of matrix equations: (a) relationships at the structural level, (b) relations of unobserved exogenous variables, and (c) relationships to unobserved exogenous dimensions (see Blalock, 1985, Chapters 13 and 14).

The process involves using these three equations and some iteration to find a system that minimizes the discrepancy between data and model. The iterative process in some ways functions similar to a principal components rotation in factor analysis but provides a means of generating a model that will fit the data. What the process does is adjust the various matrices to provide an outcome that minimizes discrepancy. When examining the output, there exist a variety of matrices, and those should be examined to make sure that none of the assumptions of the model are inconsistent with the adjustments. The researcher needs to make sure that all the output is not inconsistent with each element of the model. The reason for this is that the process of changing the diagrams can result in connections that are untenable according to the underlying theory. Remember, the purpose of this type of analysis is to find support for a well-justified theoretical model; consequently, any adjustments made to the model must be consistent with theory.

Choosing a Technique

Most computer packages (LISREL, AMOS) use a version of MLE as the default method for analysis. MLE provides for a better combination of options in the sense that both steps of the OLM approach occur simultaneously in MLE—the assumption is that fewer steps must be better. This is an advantage because the process is shorter and easier to manage than a process that requires multiple steps. The computer packages also provide for more flexibility in testing complex models.

Such flexibility, however, comes with a price. Since the method uses an iterative process, any error made early on (e.g., measurement, specification) can and does multiply throughout the entire model test. Such errors can prove difficult to identify and correct once in the system. What this means is that advantages gained through MLE require that the investigator test the assumption to minimize the various sources of error prior to using the technique.

The disadvantage is that it becomes difficult to assess the adjustments and the impact of those adjustments made in the default mode. Corrections (e.g., attenuation, restriction in range), while necessary, can provide for some differences in expected outcomes; when that is combined with the possibility of correlated error terms or other latent structures in operation, the difficulty of analyzing a printout becomes increased. Essentially, suppose a model does not work; analyzing the source of divergence and estimating what changes to the model would be necessary are more difficult in MLE procedures.

One advantage of OLS procedures is that the requirements for a model to fit are more demanding than the other technique, MLE. The usual rule is that an OLS solution will almost automatically work using the less restrictive requirements of MLE. However, many MLE solutions will not work in OLS. A lot of practitioners will work out a solution using OLS because the testing procedure is more parsimonious and the model easier to adjust. After getting an OLS solution that works, then MLE is applied. This approach is taken because many communication scholars, particularly the younger generation, are more familiar with MLE due to a heavy emphasis on using computer programs such as AMOS and EQS.

MLE has one clear and distinct advantage over OLS. When the measurement model is known, the comparison of fit between two well-defined theoretical models is easier and more parsimonious using MLE. In other words, MLE allows one to directly compare the variance accounted for by multiple models. Thus, if a research situation calls for you to test two competing models, the MLE approach may be a better option for such a direct comparison provided that you have clear measurement models specified.

Regardless of which approach you use, you should keep in mind the following. First, neither approach provides absolute proof of a theory. As stated previously, a good-fitting model could be joined by several other good-fitting models on any particular data set. Good model fit does not replace the need for replication, refinement, and careful consideration of alternatives. Second, super statistics should not replace sound theory. As with any statistical result, interpretation should be done with respect to the underlying theory as well as contextual knowledge. Finally, you should recognize that path analysis and structural equation modeling both assume linear relationships. If nonlinear structures are present in the data, the error associated with a model will be greater, and fit will be reduced.

OTHER ADVANCED MODELING APPROACHES

Although beyond the scope of this book, there are other advanced modeling techniques that deserve a brief introduction. First, multilevel modeling makes the assumption that people (or cases) can be nested into clusters that might or might not be hierarchical for additional discussion (see Slater, Snyder, & Hayes, 2006). For instance, if studying children, you might want to recognize that any effect at the individual level is influenced by clusters such as the child's family, community, and culture. Multilevel models allow you to analyze data at each level and take that into account. Thus, rather than simply focusing on students' perceptions, a multilevel model would take into consideration the fact that participants in a given study are influenced by broader clusters of variables. The advantage of this approach is that it provides a more realistic estimate of effects in regression (by not taking a lack of independence into consideration, the effects observed in traditional regressions could be overestimated) and allows you to explore substantive effects at the group level.

Second, social network analysis uses statistics to explore connective relationships between organizations, people, social networks, and so on. Scholars have studied networks within college classrooms, large corporations, government entities, and even virtual realities like Second Life (for a discussion of network analysis, see Rogers, 1987; Susskind, Schwartz, & Richards, 2005). The interesting thing about network analysis is that you can visually represent a "map" of a social network and use that map to theorize about the communication implications of the network. For instance, if some people are isolated from others in the network, what are the reasons and what are the implications? In addition, depending on what people need, do they establish different networks? For example, do college students have different networks for "social" and "academic" support? If so, what are the implications of having different networks? These are the types of questions that network analysis allows you to ask.

As is often the case, more specialized analyses require specialized software. Moreover, our brief introduction to SEM and other advanced modeling techniques is just that—an introduction. While you may develop a very basic understanding of the concepts and terminology surrounding these approaches to modeling, to use them effectively, you should take classes specifically devoted to the type of modeling you are interested in. Examining recent issues of communication journals can also help you understand the types of substantive questions driving use of these techniques.

SEM IN COMMUNICATION RESEARCH

Valkenburg, P. M., & Peter, J. (2007). Internet communication and its relation to well-being: Identifying some underlying mechanisms. *Media Psychology, 9,* 43–58.

Using measures of depression and loneliness as well as life satisfaction and positive/negative affect as indicators, several studies have explored the relationship between Internet use and well-being. Results of these studies are mixed with some showing positive relationships (e.g., higher levels of personal Internet use and Web surfing are associated with higher levels of depression) and others showing negative relationships (e.g., higher levels of e-mail use are associated with lower levels of depression). Similar inconsistencies were observed in studies examining relations between Internet use and loneliness and life satisfaction. Thus, studies attempting to connect Internet use and well-being result in a mixed bag of results.

Valkenburg and Peter suggest two possible reasons for inconsistent results in previous studies. First, earlier studies may have treated Internet use as a one-dimensional concept—they tend to use a weekly or daily log of all Internet use rather than disaggregating use by different types of activity. Valkenburg and Peter overcome this limitation by examining Internet communication, which is "the composite of the frequency, intensity, and rate with which the Internet is used for chat or instant messaging (IM)" (p. 44). A second potential explanation for previous inconsistency is that previous researchers did not specify why Internet use could be related to well-being. Whereas previous studies, through a lack of explanation, focus on a simple main effect of Internet use,

Valkenburg and Peter assume that an underlying theoretical model explains the connection—a model that involves more than simple main effects. Life satisfaction was used to assess well-being in the current study. Because depression is a particular clinical diagnosis, it was felt that life satisfaction was a better indicator of well-being in the nonclinical setting of the study. Moreover, adolescents were used because they tend to use the Internet for communication more than others, and they are also at a unique developmental stage where levels of self-esteem and well-being vary greatly.

Valkenburg and Peter hypothesized that Internet communication is positively related to closeness to friends (Hypothesis 1), which is also positively related to well-being (Hypothesis 2). They also hypothesize that a direct relationship between Internet communication and well-being will disappear when friendship is included as a mediator in the model (Hypothesis 3). Finally, they hypothesize that adolescents who often talk with strangers on the Internet will display lower levels of well-being than those who often talk with friends (Hypothesis 4) but that the potential connection between online communication with strangers and well-being will be stronger for lonely than for nonlonely adolescents (Hypothesis 5). A model of these hypotheses is depicted in Figure 12.3.

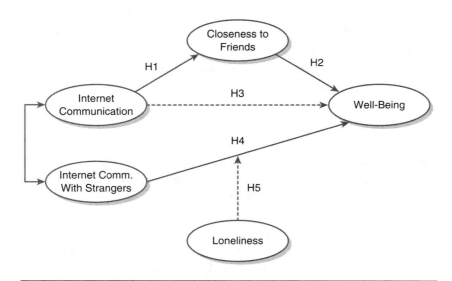

Figure 12.3   Hypothesized Model for Internet Communication and Well-Being

A total of 816 adolescents (10–17 years old) took part in the study. Internet communication was assessed by asking (a) "how many days this week you have used chat or IM," (b) "on the last day you were online how many times did you use chat or IM," and (c) "on the last day you were online how long did you use chat or IM?" Answers to those questions were used to create a composite variable. Previously used surveys were employed to assess adolescents' closeness to friends, well-being, and loneliness. In addition, two questions were used to assess the extent to which adolescents communicated with strangers. The data were analyzed using the computer program AMOS to simultaneously test the measurement model as well as hypothesized relationships between latent variables. Two fit measures were used to assess the model: a nonsignificant chi-square and an RMSEA of less than .05.

Structural equation models showed that Hypotheses 1 through 4 had support but that Hypothesis 5 did not. The model without the loneliness variable included fit the data well, χ^2 (23, $n = 687$) = 32.20, $p = .09$, RMSEA = −.02. The predicted paths, as shown in Figure 12.4, are all significant at $p < .001$. As you can see, well-being is predicted by an indirect relationship between Internet communication and well-being that is mediated by closeness to friends; well-being is also predicted by less Internet communication with strangers.

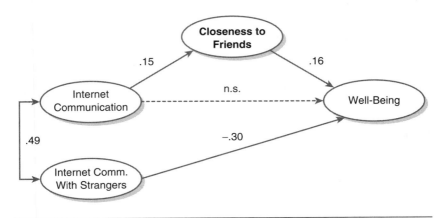

Figure 12.4   Structural Equation Model of Well-Being

REFERENCES

Baron, R. M., & Kenny, D. A. (1986). The moderator-mediator variable discussion in social psychological research: Conceptual, strategic, and statistical considerations. *Journal of Personality and Social Psychology, 51,* 1173–1182.

Blalock, H. M. (Ed.). (1985). *Causal models in the social sciences.* New York: Aldine.

Holbert, R. L., & Stephenson, M. T. (2002). Structural equation modeling in the communication sciences, 1995–2000. *Human Communication Research, 28,* 531–551.

Hu, L., & Bentler, P. M. (1999). Cutoff criteria for fit indexes in covariance structure analysis: Conventional criteria versus new alternatives. *Structural Equation Modeling, 6,* 1–55.

Rogers, E. M. (1987). Progress problems and prospects for network research: Investigating relationships in the age of electronic communication technologies. *Social Networks, 9,* 285–310.

Slater, M., Snyder, L., & Hayes, A. (2006). Thinking and modeling at multiple levels: The potential contribution of multilevel modeling to communication theory and research. *Human Communication Research, 32,* 375–384.

Stephenson, M. T., & Holbert, R. L. (2003). A Monte Carlo simulation of observed versus latent variable structural equation modeling techniques. *Communication Research, 30,* 332–354.

Susskind, A. M., Schwartz, D. F., & Richards, W. D. (2005). Evolution and diffusion of the Michigan State University tradition of organizational communication network research. *Communication Studies, 56,* 397–418.

THIRTEEN

META-ANALYSIS

---•◆•---

Patrick was asked to complete a literature review exploring the effects of violent programming on children. Convinced that he would discover definitive evidence suggesting that violent programming is detrimental, Patrick was shocked at the degree of inconsistency in the literature. Although most studies observed some sort of effect, the size of the effect varied greatly, and some studies found nothing at all. When writing his literature review, Patrick concluded that there is too much inconsistency from one study to the next to draw precise conclusions about the effects of violent programming.

You are probably familiar with the process of completing a literature review. Typically, you collect several articles, books, or other types of literature on a particular topic and then carefully construct a narrative summary of that literature. Such reviews meaningfully highlight topics that recur in the literature and are also potentially useful at pointing out trends in how theory is used as well as what areas have been excluded from analysis. This is precisely the process that Patrick went through. However, are narrative reviews effective at accurately summarizing results of quantitative findings? Of course, we rely on such reviews all the time, so the natural answer should be yes. But, as you might guess, the answer is more difficult than that.

Narrative reviews amount to something of a subjective voting method—they tally the number of studies that find significant results for a certain variable and compare that with the number of inconclusive or nonsignificant results. If the number of significant findings exceeds the number of nonsignificant findings, the author of the review typically concludes that a preponderance of evidence points to an effect. But what happens if several of the nonsignificant findings stemmed from studies with much larger sample sizes? Or, what if the effect sizes for the significant findings were very small for all but one of the studies with a larger sample size, which showed a large effect? Should the reviewer describe the effects as small or large or avoid the issue altogether? In reality, the voting method employed by narrative reviews tends to obscure conclusions because of the subjectivity involved in creating a story about research. As an alternative to the narrative review, another option is to conduct a meta-analysis of the literature.

Meta-analysis is a technique for quantitatively synthesizing results from existing literature or data (see Preiss & Allen, 2007). As mentioned previously, the narrative approach to summarizing literature has the potential to be both imprecise and misleading. Consequently, meta-analysis quantifies the results of previous studies in an attempt to (a) reduce Type II error, (b) correct statistical artifacts, (c) test possible moderator variables, and (d) evaluate theoretical arguments. Understanding the reasons for using meta-analysis provides a basis for understanding how a meta-analysis is completed and written up. Essentially, the process and outcome are the aggregation and presentation of existing statistical information.

The outcome of a significance test attempts to draw a conclusion about how likely the observed results from a sample are consistent with a "reality" found in the actual population. While we recognize that the term *reality* could be problematized (particularly by communication scholars), for now let's assume that there is an actual reality that is observable, quantifiable, and perhaps even predictable. There are two basic outcomes from a significance test: (a) The statistic is significant, or (b) the statistic is nonsignificant. The reality of a relationship is either that is exists or the relationship does not exist. That provides for four potential outcomes expressed in Figure 13.1. Notice in Figure 13.1 that there are two outcomes indicating correspondence—in these situations, the outcome of the empirical investigation and reality coincide. However, in the case of Type I error (saying there is a relationship when one does not actually exist) or Type II error (saying there is not a relationship when, in reality, there is one), there is a lack of correspondence, and therefore the results of the statistical test do not coincide with reality.

In both individual studies as well as in meta-analyses, you can take various corrective actions to try and reduce the likelihood of committing error or misrepresenting the magnitude of a statistical relationship. The correction of statistical artifacts becomes an effort to correct for the introduction of various sources of bias and error into the investigation. The problem with such sources of statistical deviation is that they do not occur uniformly across all investigations and would generate an average that is inaccurate. A summary of steps involved in performing a meta-analysis is provided in Table 13.1. The following section explains how such corrections are accomplished.

	Actual Relationship	
Test Outcome	Does Exist	Does Not Exist
Significant	Correct acceptance (correspondence)	Type I error
Not significant	Type II error	Correct rejection (correspondence)

Figure 13.1   Outcomes of a Statistical Test in Relation to Actual Relationship

Table 13.1   Steps in a Meta-Analysis

1. Carefully construct a database of all research relevant on a topic and select from that database articles meeting criteria that you specify for studies to include in your analysis (e.g., experiments comparing a particular treatment with a control group, studies using a particular dependent variable).

2. Analyze articles to determine sample size, effect size, and notable features that could emerge as moderating variables. Correct these values, as necessary, for any statistical artifacts such as attenuation due to unreliability (see Hunter & Schmidt, 1990).

3. Calculate an average effect, weighted by sample size, across all articles included in the analysis.

4. Test the average effect for homogeneity. If the effect is homogeneous, you are done and can report the overall effect.

5. If the effect is heterogeneous, you should code for and subdivide articles based on unique features to look for homogeneous subsets of effects—features that result in homogeneous effects are then identified as potential moderating variables.

MATHEMATICAL ARGUMENT FOR META-ANALYSIS

Understanding a meta-analysis involves understanding the underlying set of arguments about how meta-analysis functions in the context of statistical analysis. For example, when you have an empirical investigation to examine whether or not variable X is correlated with variable Y, the results are either viewed as significant (an association exists) or nonsignificant (no association exists). The key is the correspondence of outcome between what the investigation views and what in reality exists. A description of the possibilities is provided in Figure 13.1. Figure 13.1 has two outcomes that are considered correspondence: (a) The investigation concludes a relationship exists and in reality there is a relationship, and (b) the investigation concludes no relationship exists and in reality there is a relationship.

The problematic areas are the two outcomes that demonstrate no correspondence between the outcome of the investigation and reality (for additional discussion, see Lipsey & Wilson, 2001). One is labeled a false positive or Type I error. Type I error exists when the investigation demonstrates a significant relationship and there is in fact no relationship. An example of this would be a test that demonstrates that a drug provides a cure for cancer when the drug does not in fact cure cancer. The level of Type I error corresponds to the alpha error rate. For example, most significance tests are set at the probability of false finding at 5% ($p < .05$). This 5% is the rate of Type I error, so typically a person knows how much Type I error potential exists for any significant finding.

Type II error is a false negative. The results of the investigation indicate that no relationship exists when in fact there is a relationship. An example would be an investigation concluding that a tested drug does not cure cancer when in fact it does cure cancer. While many persons might not consider Type II error as serious as Type I error, the impact of Type II error has no less importance and should be considered and avoided.

Type II error is a combination of three factors: (a) level of Type I error, (b) size of the effect, and (c) size of sample. The theoretical maximum of Type II error is (1 – Type I error) or typically 95%. The other two considerations (size of effect and size of sample) work to reduce this maximum from this value.

The size of the effect is such that the larger the effect, the less the level of Type II error. Consider if you land on a planet and have no way to determine whether the air outside is poisonous or safe. We decide to toss one person out the airlock and watch. If the person goes outside and walks around with no ill effects, that does not mean the air is safe necessarily; the negative consequences may take some time to manifest. However, if the person goes outside and immediately gasps and falls down dead, most persons would conclude that the air outside is unsafe and not volunteer to be the second person outside. The reason for that is that the effects are immediate and observable, so a small sample size (one) is probably enough to conclude that the air is unsafe. But consider something that takes a long time to kill (like cigarette smoking); the effects are cumulative and difficult to demonstrate, and the level of Type II error (or false negatives) is higher.

The final consideration is the size of the sample. The larger the sample, the greater the probability that any effect will be statistically significant. This is because any sample statistic that has the size of the confidence interval becomes smaller as the sample size increases. The net result is that as sample size increases, the ability to detect any given effect increases. Virtually, any methods or statistical book advises persons collecting data to use larger sample sizes because the accuracy of the estimate for any statistical parameter increases with sample size.

A meta-analysis does not change the probability of Type I error or the size of the effect. The level of Type I error (usually 5%) is set by the community and not affected when a literature review is conducted. The size of the effect or relationship is what a scientist wishes to estimate and therefore should not be changed. The only part of Type II error that can be affected by an action of an investigator is the size of the sample. Meta-analysis does many things; the most central and important is to increase the size of the sample for the estimation of a parameter. By combining samples across many investigations, the average effect takes on the properties of the combined sample size, diminishing the confidence interval and increasing the accuracy of the estimate. What this should indicate is that meta-analysis reduces the primary problem of Type II error by increasing sample size, the only factor that can be addressed by the investigator.

But how often or likely is Type II error to occur? In other words, how much of a threat does a false negative represent to understanding the literature? Hedges (1987) estimates that with a Type I error rate of 5% and an average effect of .20 (this was across five areas of psychology) that relied on an average sample size of 80 (all three elements necessary to estimate Type II error), the Type II error rate would be 50%. Basically, if one had 100 studies, 50 would demonstrate a significant result and 50 would demonstrate a nonsignificant result. Hedges points out that the reliance on the significance test is as accurate as coin flipping to determine results. This outcome, more than any other probable outcome, provides a singularly important justification for meta-analysis.

THE PRACTICAL ARGUMENT FOR META-ANALYSIS

Many meta-analyses provide for some type of practical outcome through application. If one is examining the impact of a treatment on some source of anxiety, a finding that the treatment does or does not work to reduce anxiety provides for some practical advice. The goal of much of communication research considers some consequences or outcomes associated with a communication practice. Understanding the consequences of a particular communication practice can provide a basis for advice to avoid or use a particular communication strategy or technique. Through meta-analysis, you can provide a more accurate summary of what has been found in previous research so that communication practice can be enhanced.

STRUCTURE OF WRITING IN META-ANALYSIS

A meta-analysis provides a somewhat different writing challenge in comparison to traditional narrative reviews. The typical meta-analysis consists of four parts: (a) an argument or justification for conducting the review, (b) the methods used to conduct the summary, (c) presentation of results, and (d) the conclusions and/or discussion of the outcome of the results. Most general practices for writing of experimental/survey investigations probably should be followed, but the peculiarities or uniqueness of the process of meta-analysis creates for some interesting twists to traditional practices.

THE LITERATURE REVIEW

The writing for a justification for a meta-analysis becomes at times rather circular. How does one write a literature review to justify a literature review process? Generally, most writers can point to a controversy about the nature of the relationship due to contradictory or inconsistent findings. Often, previous narrative or nonquantitative literature reviews serve as the basis for justifying a quantitative or meta-analytic review.

The review should cover the underlying theoretical and methodological issues rather than simply summarize existing research. Often, commenting on the prototypical design, including sampling and measures, provides a context to understand the existing literature. When multiple types of designs exist, the review may explain and represent each of them. This part of the process provides the reader with a sense of how most of the data were collected. The challenge for the writer is providing enough detail about the designs so that the reader can understand what research is being summarized. When a meta-analysis contains more than 100 studies, a study-by-study review is both infeasible and often not very informative because the designs often rely on a common template.

METHODS FOR CONDUCTING THE META-ANALYSIS

The methods section for a meta-analysis usually consists of (a) description of the literature search methods, (b) coding of possible moderator or theoretical models, and (c) description of the statistical procedures used. While the writing rules follow the general expectations for any social science project, the particular content requirements do provide for some interesting variations.

The description of the literature search methods involves the time frame searched, an enumeration of the databases employed, and the key words used in the method of search. In some meta-analyses, certain methodological requirements may exclude potential data sets. In addition, the decision to consider nonpublished sources of information (convention papers, theses, dissertations, and other reports) becomes important. The rules for exclusion as well as inclusion for manuscripts should be articulated. Depending on the size of the literature, reasons for the exclusion of particular manuscripts may be detailed and/or provided in a footnote or available on request. In a large meta-analysis, there may be more than 100 manuscripts containing empirical data that were excluded for some particular reason.

Many times there will be features of the design (type or kind of measure, experimental or survey, etc.,), demographics of the sample, or other characteristics of the context of the investigation that may be believed to influence that particular relationship. In such circumstances, you will typically code (or categorize) specific manuscripts to test whether there are different results depending on those features. The methods section needs to explain the coding system in such a manner that another scholar could take the same manuscripts and be able to replicate the analysis. This section may or may not include various methods of estimating intercoder reliability (depending on the degree of judgment involved by the person in the analysis).

The final section of the methods should be a representation of the particular statistical analysis procedure employed. A variety of methods can be used and there may be some disagreement about the appropriateness of any particular procedure as applied to the task. What is most important is that you provide a detailed and complete explanation of each choice made in analyzing the data as well as justification for those choices. At the current time, there are a few statistical packages that provide for some of the processes or steps in a meta-analysis, but few packages begin to provide a comprehensive set of procedures that can handle all the steps of a meta-analysis from transformation, artifact correction, averaging, and then any more complex procedures. What this means is that the process of a meta-analysis requires a bit more explanation and reliance on primary reference material than most procedures. The single most comprehensive source for transformations and corrections, as well as the explanations for these, is Hunter and Schmidt's (2000) *Methods of Meta-Analysis*. Rosenthal, Rosinow, and Rubin's (2000) text also serves as an excellent resource for converting various reported effects to the basic correlation coefficient (r) for subsequent analysis.

RESULTS SECTION
REPORTING OF A META-ANALYSIS

This section of the paper simply reports results from the overall analysis. The relevant statistics are (a) average effect; (b) number of studies, often called k; (c) the overall combined sample size, or N; (d) a measure of variability of the sample of effects, usually expressed in standard deviation or variance; (e) an evaluation of the homogeneity of the effects, most often expressed as a chi-square statistic; and optionally, (f) some measure of the significance of the average effect. This format of reporting should be for all average effect sizes in the manuscript. Example calculations for average effect size, weighted by sample size, are provided in Table 13.2.

Table 13.2   Example of Meta-Analysis Calculations

	Observed Effect (A)	*Sample Size (B)*	*A * B*
Study 1	.10	200	20
Study 2	.20	400	80
Study 3	.30	200	60
Study 4	.40	400	160
Study 5	.50	200	100
Sum		1,400	420

$$r_{(Ave)} = \frac{\Sigma(Observed\ Effect * Sample\ Size)}{\Sigma\ (Sample\ Size)} = \frac{420}{1,400} = .30$$

Testing for homogeneity of variability is a test of whether the observed variability among the observed effects could be the result of random sampling error. Most homogeneity tests calculate the expected amount of variability and compare that with the observed variability (often reported as a chi-square statistic). There are many different versions of the homogeneity test, each with slightly different sets of assumptions and minor differences in formulation. You should consult a primary statistical book for basic formulas (e.g., Hunter & Schmidt, 1990; Lipsey & Wilson, 2001). Cooper and Hedges (1994) provide a good set of readings on some of the various controversies involved in any choice.

If the test is significant, that indicates that the level of variability is greater than one can attribute to sampling error, and the sample of effects is said to be heterogeneous. Heterogeneity indicates the possible and probable existence of some source of moderation. A nonsignificant test result indicates that the differences among the individuals effects can be attributed to sampling error, and the sample of effects is homogeneous.

After the overall analysis, the various tests of moderator and/or other theoretical systems occur. The results of a meta-analysis can be used and incorporated into other statistical forms such as a *t* test, ANOVA, multiple regression, or causal modeling. The use of these kind of analyses has specific adaptations from general forms, but the reporting rules and requirements follow the traditional expectations for the particular statistical analysis employed, and the chapters for those forms should be consulted.

There exist a number of statistical choices for post hoc or other more sophisticated procedures. You should articulate the methods and provide a citation to the appropriate reference material from which the formulas and procedures were developed. The problem is that when there is less agreement about procedures and few standardized statistical packages available, the process of documentation and explication for a procedure requires more effort than normal.

META-ANALYSIS IN COMMUNICATION RESEARCH

Novak, J. M., Markey, V., & Allen, M. (2007). Evaluating cognitive learning outcomes of service learning in higher education: A meta-analysis. *Communication Research Reports, 24,* 149–157.

Colleges and universities are increasingly developing robust methods to blend curriculum with community outreach. Although such programs take on different foci and labels at various institutions, most share a common method of attempting to blend community service activities within learning objectives. One such approach—one found in some degree at nearly every institution—is service learning. Service learning is a pedagogical strategy most commonly used by teachers in specific classes where students engage in community service activities relevant to the topic of the class. For example, students in a communication and technology class might engage in a project where they create a Web site for a community organization, or students in an interpersonal communication class might become "conversation partners" with children who speak English as a second language. The rationale for such activities is multifaceted; however, the basic premise is that students perform an important service to the community while simultaneously learning the value of community service as well as academic content appropriate for the course.

The pedagogical model of using service learning has expanded dramatically in higher education since the early 1990s. For obvious reasons, service learning has become a very popular pedagogical approach in communication departments throughout higher education. In 1995, a survey of 263 communication departments showed that 240 of them offered some sort of service learning opportunities for students (Sellnow & Oster, 1997). Given the rise in popularity of service learning within the discipline specifically and all of higher education more generally, evidence documenting the impact of service learning on student learning is important. The meta-analysis reported by Novak and colleagues addresses this question by asking the following:

Research Question 1: What impact on learning outcomes does the inclusion of service learning have on students?

The initial step in the meta-analysis was to locate articles examining the quantitative impact of service learning on cognitive learning outcomes. Using various electronic databases, including ERIC, Infotrac, and Proquest, as well as specialized collections such as the *Michigan Journal of Community Service Learning,* approximately 200 articles were obtained; the objective of this step was to generate a nearly comprehensive set of articles related to the key words *service learning, practical learning,* and *experiential learning.* Of the 200 articles examined, most did not meet the criteria necessary for the meta-analysis: For instance, many did not provide quantitative data, many did not provide a comparison of service learning programs to nonservice learning programs, and many did not report assessment outcomes for actual cognitive learning. After reviewing the approximately 200 articles, only 9 provided data sets appropriate for inclusion in the meta-analysis. Table 13.3 identifies the studies, sample size, effect size, and outcome measured.

After identifying Cohen's d for each study, the average effect was calculated to be, $d = .424$, $k = 9$, $N = 1,610$, $p < .05$. The positive effect indicates that students who participate in service learning activities perform better with respect to the outcomes examined than do students who do not participate in such activities. When examining the effects for homogeneity, it was determined that heterogeneity was present, $\chi^2 = 36.37$, $N = 1,610$, $p < .05$. Heterogeneity suggests the possibility of a moderator variable in the data. After examining the individual studies in the data set, one was identified as an outlier (the Tucker & McCarthy article). After removing the outlier, a homogeneous set of data was left, $\chi^2 = 7.56$, $N = 1,483$, $p > .05$; the reanalysis of the remaining 8 studies also suggested a significant positive effect, $d = .261$, $k = 8$, $N = 1,483$, $p < .05$. Without additional data, it was not possible to determine whether the

Table 13.3   Articles Included in Meta-Analysis

Study	Year	Effect	Sample	Outcome Measure
Cohen & Kinsey	1994	.545	88	Understanding
Kendrick	1996	.674	39	Understanding, application
Litake	2002	.121	60	Understanding
Mabry	1998	.409	144	Understanding
Markus, Howard, & King	1993	.571	89	Understanding
Moley et al.	2002	.161	541	Application
Osborne et al.	1998	.415	48	Understanding, application, reframing
Strange	2000	.204	474	Understanding
Tucker & McCarthy	2001	1.60	127	Application

outlier was simply an outlier (i.e., a random effect) or whether the outlier was initial evidence of some systematic, moderating variable.

Results of the study provide empirical evidence that academic service learning has a positive effect on students' cognitive learning in classes using that pedagogical approach. With an average effect size of $d = .42$, the binomial effect size display suggests that approximately 39.5% of students in a class using service learning would fall below the median, whereas in classes without service learning, approximately 60.5% of students would fall below the median. While the evidence in favor of service learning is apparent, the authors point out that no usable studies of service learning were available from communication journals; thus, additional evidence is needed before we can conclude that service learning is an effective approach within communication classes specifically.

REFERENCES

Cooper, H., & Hedges, L. (Eds.). (1994). *The handbook of research synthesis.* New York: Russell Sage Foundation.

Hedges, L. (1987). How hard is hard science, how soft is soft science? *American Psychologist, 42,* 443–455.

Hunter, J. E., & Schmidt, F. L. (1990). *Methods of meta-analysis: Correcting error and bias in research findings.* Newbury Park, CA: Sage.

Hunter, J. E., & Schmidt, F. L. (2002). *Methods of meta-analysis: Correcting error and bias in research findings* (2nd ed.). Thousand Oaks, CA: Sage.

Lipsey, M. W., & Wilson, D. B. (2001). *Practical meta-analysis.* Thousand Oaks, CA: Sage.

Preiss, R., & Allen, M. (2007). Understanding and using meta-analysis. In R. Preiss, B. Gayle, N. Burrell, M. Allen, & J. Bryant (Eds.), *Mass media effects research: Advances through meta-analysis* (pp. 15–30). Mahwah, NJ: Lawrence Erlbaum.

Rosenthal, R., Rosinow, R., & Rubin, D. (2000). *Contrasts and effect sizes in behavioral research: A correlational approach.* New York: Cambridge University Press.

Sellnow, T. L., & Oster, L. K. (1997, September). The frequency, form, and perceived benefits of service learning in speech communication departments. *Journal of the Association for Communication Administration,* pp. 190–197.

CRITICAL VALUES
FOR THE *t* STATISTIC

Y ou should identify the degrees of freedom for your test and locate the appropriate row. Using a standard significance level of .05, you can determine the critical value for *t* in the test you are running. If your *t* value exceeds the critical value, your test is significant. If the *df* for your test is between two values on this table (e.g., 35 *df*), you must extrapolate between the two critical values (e.g., 2.035 for 35 *df*). To find other values or to determine an exact probability level for a specific *t* statistic, consult an online calculator such as the one found at http://www.stat.tamu.edu/~west/applets/tdemo.html.

df	Two-Tailed Test $\alpha = .05$	One-Tailed Test $\alpha = .05$
5	2.571	2.015
6	2.447	1.943
7	2.365	1.985
8	2.306	1.860
9	2.262	1.833
10	2.228	1.812
11	2.201	1.796
12	2.179	1.782
13	2.160	1.771
14	2.145	1.761
15	2.131	1.753
16	2.120	1.746
17	2.110	1.740
18	2.101	1.734
19	2.093	1.729
20	2.086	1.725
21	2.080	1.721
22	2.074	1.717
23	2.069	1.714
24	2.064	1.711
25	2.060	1.708
26	2.056	1.706
27	2.052	1.703
28	2.048	1.701
29	2.045	1.699
30	2.042	1.697
40	2.021	1.684
50	2.009	1.676
60	2.000	1.671
80	1.990	1.664
100	1.984	1.660
120	1.980	1.658
∞	1.960	1.654

⊰ APPENDIX B ⊱

CRITICAL VALUES FOR
THE CHI-SQUARE STATISTIC

———•◆•———

U sing the *df* appropriate for your test, locate the critical value for the chi-square statistic below. If your observed value exceeds the critical value, your test is significant at the .05 level. For exact significance levels or to find a critical value for a test that does not have the exact *df* displayed in this table, consult an online calculator such as the one found at http://www .stat.tamu.edu/~west/applets/chisqdemo.html.

df	Chi-Square α =.05	df	Chi-Square α =.05	df	Chi-Square α =.05
1	3.84	31	44.99	61	80.23
2	5.99	32	46.19	62	81.38
3	7.82	33	47.40	63	82.53
4	9.49	34	48.60	64	83.68
5	11.07	35	49.80	65	84.82
6	12.59	36	51.00	66	85.97
7	14.07	37	52.19	67	87.11
8	15.51	38	53.38	68	88.25
9	16.92	39	54.57	69	89.39
10	18.31	40	55.76	70	90.53
11	19.68	41	56.94	71	91.67
12	21.03	42	58.12	72	92.81
13	22.36	43	59.30	73	93.95
14	23.69	44	60.48	74	95.08
15	25.00	45	61.66	75	96.22
16	26.30	46	62.83	76	97.35
17	27.59	47	64.00	77	98.49
18	28.87	48	65.17	78	99.62
19	30.14	49	66.34	79	100.75
20	31.41	50	67.51	80	101.88
21	32.67	51	68.67	81	103.01
22	33.92	52	69.83	82	104.14
23	35.17	53	70.99	83	105.27
24	36.42	54	72.15	84	106.40
25	37.65	55	73.31	85	107.52
26	38.89	56	74.47	86	108.65
27	40.11	57	75.62	87	109.77
28	41.34	58	76.78	88	110.90
29	42.56	59	77.93	89	112.02
30	43.77	60	79.08	90	113.15

CRITICAL VALUES FOR THE *F* STATISTIC

U sing the *df* for the denominator and *df* for the numerator, use the table below to identify the critical value for *F* in your test. If your *F* value exceeds the critical value, your test is significant at the .05 level. If the *df* for your test are not shown in this table, you can use an online calculator such as the one found at http://www.psychstat.missouristate.edu/introbook/fdist.htm.

df Denominator	df Numerator									
	1	2	3	4	5	6	7	8	9	10
2	18.51	19.00	19.16	19.25	19.30	19.33	19.35	19.37	19.38	19.40
3	10.13	9.55	9.28	9.12	9.01	8.94	8.89	8.85	8.81	8.79
4	7.71	6.94	6.59	6.39	6.26	6.16	6.09	6.04	6.00	5.96
5	6.61	5.79	5.41	5.19	5.05	4.95	4.88	4.82	4.77	4.74
6	5.99	5.14	4.76	4.53	4.39	4.28	4.21	4.15	4.10	4.06
7	5.59	4.74	4.35	4.12	3.97	3.87	3.79	3.73	3.68	3.64
8	5.32	4.46	4.07	3.84	3.69	3.58	3.50	3.44	3.39	3.35
9	5.12	4.26	3.86	3.63	3.48	3.37	3.29	3.23	3.18	3.14
10	4.96	4.10	3.71	3.48	3.33	3.22	3.14	3.07	3.02	2.98
11	4.84	3.98	3.59	3.36	3.20	3.09	3.01	2.95	2.90	2.85
12	4.75	3.89	3.49	3.26	3.11	3.00	2.91	2.85	2.80	2.75
13	7.67	3.81	3.41	3.18	3.03	2.92	2.83	2.77	2.71	2.67
14	4.60	3.74	3.34	3.11	2.96	2.85	2.76	2.70	2.65	2.60
15	4.54	3.68	3.29	3.06	2.90	2.79	2.71	2.64	2.59	2.54
16	4.49	3.63	3.24	3.01	2.85	2.74	2.66	2.59	2.54	2.49
17	4.45	3.59	3.2	2.96	2.81	2.70	2.61	2.55	2.49	2.45
18	4.41	3.55	3.16	2.93	2.77	2.66	2.58	2.51	2.46	2.41

19	4.38	3.52	3.13	2.90	2.74	2.63	2.54	2.48	2.42	3.38
20	4.35	3.49	3.10	2.87	2.71	2.60	2.51	2.45	2.39	2.35
21	4.32	3.47	3.07	2.84	2.68	2.57	2.49	2.42	2.37	2.32
22	4.30	3.44	3.05	2.82	2.66	2.55	2.46	2.40	2.34	2.30
23	4.28	3.42	3.03	2.80	2.64	2.53	2.44	2.37	2.32	2.27
24	4.26	3.40	3.01	2.78	2.62	2.51	2.42	2.36	2.30	2.25
25	4.24	3.39	2.99	2.76	2.60	2.49	2.40	2.34	2.28	2.24
26	4.23	3.37	2.98	2.74	2.59	2.47	2.39	2.32	2.27	2.22
27	4.21	3.35	2.96	2.73	2.57	2.46	2.37	2.31	2.25	2.20
28	4.20	3.34	2.95	2.71	2.56	2.45	2.36	2.29	2.24	2.19
29	4.18	3.33	2.93	2.70	2.55	2.43	2.35	2.28	2.22	2.18
30	4.17	3.32	2.92	2.69	2.53	2.42	2.33	2.27	2.21	2.16
40	4.08	3.23	2.84	2.61	2.45	2.34	2.25	2.18	2.12	2.08
50	4.03	3.18	2.79	2.56	2.40	2.29	2.20	2.13	2.07	2.03
60	4.00	3.15	2.76	2.53	2.37	2.25	2.17	2.10	2.04	1.99
70	3.98	3.13	2.74	2.50	2.35	2.23	2.14	2.07	2.02	1.97
80	3.96	3.11	2.72	2.49	2.33	2.21	2.13	2.06	2.00	1.95
90	3.95	3.10	2.71	2.47	2.32	2.20	2.11	2.04	1.99	1.94
100	3.94	3.09	2.70	2.46	2.31	2.19	2.10	2.03	1.97	1.93
110	3.93	3.08	2.69	2.45	2.30	2.18	2.09	2.02	1.97	1.92
120	3.92	3.07	2.68	2.45	2.29	2.18	2.09	2.02	1.96	1.91

CRITICAL VALUES FOR
THE r STATISTIC

———◆—◆—◆———

df	One-Tailed Test		Two-Tailed Test	
	.05	.01	.05	.10
1	.987	.999	.996	.999
2	.900	.980	.950	.990
3	.805	.934	.878	.958
4	.729	.882	.811	.917
5	.669	.832	.754	.874
6	.621	.788	.706	.834
7	.582	.749	.706	.798
8	.549	.715	.631	.764
9	.521	.685	.602	.735
10	.497	.658	.576	.708
11	.476	.634	.53	.684
12	.457	.612	.55	.661
13	.441	.592	.514	.641
14	.426	.574	.497	.623
15	.412	.558	.482	.606
16	.400	.542	.468	.590
17	.389	.529	.456	.575
18	.378	.515	.444	.561
19	.369	.503	.433	.549
20	.360	.492	.423	.537
21	.352	.482	.413	.526
22	.344	.472	.404	.515
23	.337	.3462	.396	.505
24	.330	.453	.388	.496
25	.323	.445	.381	.487
30	.296	.409	.349	.449
40	.257	.358	.304	.393
60	.211	.295	.250	.325
120	.150	.210	.178	.232
∞	.073	.103	.087	.114

INDEX

ABOUT THE AUTHORS

Mike Allen is Professor in the Department of Communication at the University of Wisconsin–Milwaukee. He received his PhD from Michigan State University, his MA from the University of Wyoming, and his BA from Lewis and Clark College. His primary research interest is in the area of social influence, in which he has more than 150 published works. The International Communication Association awarded him the John E. Hunter memorial award for lifetime achievement in communication research using meta-analysis. He is past editor of *Communication Studies* and current editor of *Communication Monographs.*

Scott Titsworth is an Associate Professor in the School of Communication Studies at Ohio University. Scott received his PhD from the University of Nebraska, his MA from Missouri State University, and his BFA from Emporia State University. His primary research interest is instructional communication, with a particular emphasis in connections between affect, emotion, learning, and classroom communication. He teaches a variety of graduate and under-graduate classes, including research methods, ANOVA, and regression; in 2008, he was awarded the title of "University Professor" for excellence in the classroom.

Stephen K. Hunt is an Associate Professor, Carnegie Foundation for the Advancement of Teaching Political Engagement Scholar, Co-Chair of ISU's American Democracy Project, and Associate Director of the School of Communication at Illinois State University. He received his PhD from Southern Illinois University at Carbondale, his MA from the University of

Northern Iowa, and his BFA from Emporia State University. He has published articles on several topics, including instructional communication, persuasion, and communication pedagogy. His major research interests include the pedagogy of political engagement, critical thinking, communication skill assessment, and training/mentoring graduate students. In 2008, he received the Stan and Sandy Rives Award for Excellence in Undergraduate Education as well as the University Teaching Award.